Praise for
The Guru Quest...

"The Guru   nination
of this f   son alike.
The bo   acredibly
importa   rehensive,
and suc   nal word
on the t   body on
a spiritu

                                             Spirituality

"Marian   ll-argued,
utterly   hat there
is. She   tty issues
withou   igh edges.
This bo   vell as for
anyone   ial master
is all ab

                                             Awakening

"Marian   etter than
any bo   and traps
of the   in authen-
ticating   nresolved
childh   book."

                                             hrough Sex

"Maria   u-disciple
relationship. Here Mariana balances her recognition of the depth and
sacredness of the relationship between a true teacher and a true disciple, with her recognition of the pitfalls that can arise when we seek
from another h   only come from

within. Writing from her direct experience with her own teachers, and drawing on the experience of others, she illuminates the mystery of the guru in a way that should be of benefit to many readers."

—Sally Kempton, author of *Meditation for the Love of It*

"The best disciple is one who is prepared. Mariana Caplan astutely and sensitively explains what this means. I strongly recommend *The Guru Question*."

—Georg Feuerstein, PhD, author of *The Encyclopedia of Yoga and Tantra*

"An honest, well-researched, and informative guide to this much misunderstood and yet important spiritual topic. A clear, insightful, and at times humorous look at the drama of the student-teacher relationship."

—Llewellyn Vaughan-Lee, Sufi teacher and author of
Sufism: The Transformation of the Heart

"The rising of spiritual aspirations in the West, where the values of 'having' have smothered those of 'being,' is a source of hope for the future of humankind. However, the interest in traditional teachings transmitted by masters to their disciples is developing in a context of confusion, misunderstanding, if not of scandals. And what was a promise of peace becomes a source of suffering. Many spiritual seekers think it is their right to meet a guru, and even an outstanding guru, without ever asking themselves: 'Who am I as a disciple to have such a claim?' Mariana Caplan explores the essential matter through her own experience and throws precious light on this theme. It pays homage to the truth, the truth being always greater than any illusions."

–Arnaud Desjardins, author of *Toward the Fullness of Life*

"Essential reading for those on the spiritual path, and for those who want to see effective spiritual paths developed in our culture."

–Charles Tart, author of *Waking Up*

THE GURU QUESTION

Also by Mariana Caplan

Information for all books can be found at realspirituality.com
and centerforworldspirituality.com

THE GURU QUESTION

The Perils and Rewards
of Choosing a Spiritual Teacher

Mariana Caplan, PhD

SOUNDS TRUE
BOULDER, COLORADO

Sounds True, Inc., Boulder, CO 80306

Published 2011

Cover design by Jennifer Miles
Cover image © Dougal Waters, The Image Bank
Book design by Karen Polaski

Printed in Canada

Library of Congress Cataloging-in-Publication Data

Caplan, Mariana, 1969-
  The guru question : the perils and rewards of choosing a spiritual teacher/
  mariana caplan.
      p. cm.
  Includes bibliographical references and index.
  ISBN 978-1-60407-073-6 (pbk.)
  1. Spiritual formation. 2. Self-realization—Religious aspects. I. Title.
  BL42.C37 2011
  207'.5—dc22

                              2010044808

ebook ISBN 978-1-60407-464-2

10 9 8 7 6 5 4 3 2 1

With greatest reverence,
I offer the fruits of this book in honor of my beloved teacher,
Lee Lozowick (November 18, 1943–November 16, 2010),
and to the loves of my life,
Marc Gafni and baby Zion Lee Caplan-Gafni

If you do not have the being of a disciple,
how can you hope to find a guru?
—ARNAUD DESJARDINS

Contents

FOREWORD

When an early version of Mariana Caplan's brilliant new book, *The Guru Question,* arrived in my inbox and I was asked to write a foreword, I spent quite a few days of wonder and delight with this book and its subject matter before putting pen to paper. This amazing book contains many lifetimes of concentrated wisdom and honesty and is a vivid narrative of an inspiring spiritual journey. It offers profound advice for seekers on the journey of self-transformation, and most important, this book burns with a devotion and love for the true guru born of unitive but also nondual realization. Traveling with Mariana on her adventures, and following her experiences and "points of discernment" concerning bad and good gurus, is an enlightening experience. (The author and I have never met personally, but I hope to be pardoned for use of her first name, having traveled with her in this book through her many trials and triumphs.)

Mariana's great journey of self-transformation and the deep relationship between teacher and student moves me to tell a brief story of my first encounter with my own "root guru" (or Lama).

When I first met this Mongolian lama, I didn't recognize him. I thought he was the butler of some big-shot guru because we met in the back room of a small, pink, New Jersey tract house that served as a monastery.

Arriving at the front gate after quite a search through a dusty suburb, I felt tremendous energy in the building and feared even to enter. My stomach was filled with butterflies; my legs wobbled. A small gentleman with short-cropped gray hair who wore a brown, kimono-like Tibetan *chuba,* entered the living room-cum-shrine room and asked my friend Chris and me our business. This modest man did not seem to be the source of the monastery's energy.

Chris and I were seated in a row of chairs; the gentleman sat on the other side of my friend and asked him what we wanted at his monastery. Chris had little to say, as he was mainly driving me from New York City. I, however, was on a guru quest that had already taken me through the Middle East to India and back. We'd heard of this Tibetan monastery in New Jersey, and Chris had a car. I was back in the States for a family event, and my full intention was to return to India to study with a Tibetan teacher.

Then the lama—Geshe Wangyal, to mention his name with respect—moved across the room to another row of chairs facing me. He seemed to expand in size, and then he asked me why I had come. To my amazement, I was utterly tongue-tied. Across the globe—in Greek monasteries, dervish *tekke,* mosques, and Hindu and Tibetan temples—I had explained my quest for enlightenment teachings in various languages and through gestures. Now, in this modest pink house, before this compact Mongolian lama who wore no lama's robe, I could say nothing.

Eventually I stammered that I was seeking higher consciousness and enlightenment. Laughing, he said, "That would be too difficult for either of us, since you were obviously unable to tread the path from New York to New Jersey on your own without getting into trouble. (I was dressed as an Asian *fakir* pilgrim with baggy Afghan pants and a sheepskin jacket. I had long hair, a scraggly beard, and a black patch covering my empty, left eye socket.) "I have a long way to go in that direction myself," he continued. "The path to enlightenment is far more difficult than the road to New Jersey!"

After dashing all my hopes for high teachings, he relented and pointed to the stack of Tibetan loose-leaf and cloth-bound texts neatly arranged next to the Buddha statue at the chapel end of the room. "Maybe you should try to learn the Tibetan language," he said. "Everything that has helped my life I learned in those books. Maybe you can find something in them about the 'higher self' if you learn to read them."

He asked me about my family, my studies, and why I was dressed so strangely (these were pre-hippie times). Then, the young lamas of the monastery brought in tea and a piece of Sara Lee blueberry pie. Just as Chris and I were about to leave, the Lama said, "I could help with your study of Tibetan in exchange for your giving these young lamas English lessons. Perhaps when you return from your travels in India."

As Chris and I walked across the lawn to the car, I turned to him and said, "I am going home, cutting my hair and beard, getting some regular clothes, and coming back here in two days. That man is my teacher!"

"Why on earth are you doing that?" Chris said. "You're soon leaving for India, aren't you? What about your job at the young lama's school over there in the mountains?"

"I will resign that job and stay here. The Geshe here is my real teacher. I can trust him totally."

"How can you know that?"

"Because he's just not there," came out of my mouth, I knew not why.

It took me years to understand what I had just said. I'm not even sure I fully understand now, forty-nine years later. "Out of the mouths of babes" surely applies. I had visited more than a dozen important and recognized gurus from four major religious traditions, spent time in their presence, and had wonderful experiences with most of them. Yet events at their centers seemed always to revolve around them. They were full of wisdom—some even full of light—all quite kind and hospitable, full of dignity, and surrounded by devoted followers. This little gentleman— the Mongolian (not even Tibetan!) geshe in the kimono—was calm, kind, peaceful, and matter of fact. There was a lot of energy around him, definitely, yet he did not present himself as its source. This made me feel a heightened sense of myself—an awareness of my own presence, with its worries and its concerns. Perhaps that's why I was tongue-tied at first. I felt I could trust him because he did not have any use for me, any agenda for me to execute. He completely declined the guru role. At the last minute, almost as an afterthought and to console me for my disappointment, he offered a limited way to engage in the exchange of language teaching, but only at my persisting. But his calm center had no agenda, no role for me to play. He was free to serve my needs, as it seemed to me.

As it turned out, the Lama was my root teacher of Buddha Dharma for the next twenty-one years until his death—although the actual time we spent together was not that long: a year and a half at the beginning, and then a few months, weeks, or visits here and there over the years. Throughout all that time, he never claimed to be my spiritual teacher, guru, or mentor, but preferred that I consider him a spiritual friend. He eventually introduced me to the elder teachers of His Holiness the Dalai Lama, who became important lamas for me, and His Holiness himself, who upon the death of the elder generation became for me a kind of quintessential concentrate of all of them.

I have served thousands of students as an academic teacher, and sometimes as a spiritual friend; over the years, many have asked me about finding themselves a guru or spiritual teacher, and I have always declined to name specific names. I gave them a rule of thumb: "When you meet a potential guru or mentor, if that person tells you that he or she has the answers you need—that you can get it all from them, sort of one-stop shopping—thank that person very politely, extricate yourself, and avoid him or her in the future. When a mentor freely teaches in response to serious request, but also encourages you to seek other teachers and teachings, then she or he may be safe to work with. But even then, observe that person's students or disciples. If they become more dependent the longer they have been with the teacher, that's a bad sign. If the teacher constantly pushes them to stand on their own two feet as much as possible, that's a good sign.

I tell this story as an offering to Mariana, who speaks so brilliantly of "aligning with a guru" and "conscious discipleship," and who offers many incisive "points of discernment" to enable seekers to decide whether they need to work with a guru, how to tell which guru is good for them, and how to develop the proper attitude toward the process. Her experience and insight are immensely valuable for the seeker—and whoever is not a seeker will not be likely to read this book, even though it also contains Mariana's remarkable personal saga, which she skillfully uses to illustrate her various concerns. She does this with knowledge and courage, since she is critically aware that the "guru" is nowadays a misunderstood concept and that the practice of "guru yoga" is much maligned by us self-styled, "individualistic" Americans. We are much more conformist and childishly authoritarian in personality than we like to think.

In the Buddhist tradition, perhaps more than in some others, the autonomy of the seeker, student, or disciple is stressed. Counter to the patriarchal patterns of Indian culture, Buddhism emphasizes that the spiritual teacher is more like a friend than a parent. In the early stages of study and practice, *kaly amitra* (or *geshe* in Tibetan) means "virtue friend" and defines the teacher role for exoteric practice in order to emphasize that the student must be responsible for her- or himself in the process of transformative study, practice, and realization.

However, in the advanced stages of such study and practice, when one enters the ocean of the Tantras, the usually esoteric depths of transformation, the rigid boundaries of self and other begin to be dissolved by the penetrating realization of critical wisdom, and universal compassion mandates the great adventure of transforming the unconscious, the body, as well as the mind. At that point, formal initiations are involved and the most profound kind of guru relationship becomes important. Then it is crucially important. To travel these profound and far-reaching paths, there is no question of proceeding without a fully qualified guru; the blessings and knowledge of such a guru are essential to enable the practitioner to gain real attainments quickly and easily—and there is also a great danger of being misled or abused by an unqualified pretender guru.

The lessons contained in this record of Mariana's odyssey, and the understandings she has gained along her way, are of immense spiritual and practical value. Mariana's pivotal discovery of her own root guru, Shree Lee Lozowick, and her "grand-guru," Shree Ramsuratkumar of Tiruvannamalai, reminds me very much of the tales of encounters between ancient Indian Great Adepts (*mahasiddha*). Though Mariana's tradition is the sublime nondual Vedanta of the Hindus, the implementations she recounts seem utterly Tantric under the surface, which is just as it should be, and "Hindu" and "Buddhist" have very little meaning at this level.

The relationship with a guru—a spiritual mentor, a master teacher—is the most important relationship in the life of a seeker of truth, as important or maybe even more important than one's relationship with mother and father. To enter seriously on an advanced path of spiritual transformation is to be "born again" in the very deepest sense, and the guru is the mother and father of that rebirth. Thus, in the Indo-Tibetan tradition it is said that the guru should examine the disciple for twelve years before accepting her or him as a spiritual child, and the disciple likewise should observe the guru for twelve years before choosing her or him as a guru. (One sometimes wonders how long-lived both of them would have to be!)

As I read along, I was glad that Mariana is so vividly aware of the difficulties in finding a good spiritual teacher. She writes, "The search for a spiritual teacher, as problematic as it is, is in many cases vital." So many pretenders to enlightenment are trapped in what the Zen tradition calls the "demon ghost cave": of thinking they themselves are "enlightened," hence beyond ethics. I also like how Mariana points out that those who are abused in bad guru-disciple relationships have their own responsibility for becoming victims; they are often caught by the abuser due to some unexamined neurosis arising from their own psychological imbalances, upbringing, and a loveless culture. She argues well, illustrating from her own escapades how basic psychological sanity is a precursor to a successful spiritual quest with the aid of a good guru.

In her own first meeting with her own root guru, Lee Lozowick, Mariana honestly recounts an incident that seems to contradict much of what she states earlier about the "good" teacher, caring, responsibility, integrity, and so on. She writes about her ego being "destroyed" by the powerful critique of the teacher. She tells how other students gather later on and tell her they thought the teacher was too harsh with her. They offer her their support. She declines because she somehow intuitively knows that he criticized her out of love and not out of a desire to dominate. I find her assurance believable, and I admire the teacher's candor and courage, but I worry about the incident in other cases, when "conscious discipleship" isn't at play, and so feel I must underline the fact that all the truly abusive teachers invariably justify their abusiveness by saying they are doing so in order to destroy the ego attachments of the abused disciple.

It is like the "crazy wisdom" idea, which Mariana also handles very well, pirouetting bravely and gracefully on some very slick thin ice. There certainly is such a thing in the tradition as the "crazy wisdom discipline" *(unmattavrata)*. We can see it in the behavior of some Zen masters and some of the Great Adepts of Tantric India, whether Buddhist or Hindu, or later Sufi or Sikh. But the adepts and masters rarely have full biographies. We can read in the records only the accounts of some singular moments of spiritual transmission that may have been highly unorthodox or that may have broken ethical rules and appear downright harmful, yet these methods worked wonders in liberating the disciples for whom they were intended.

When we occasionally have a fuller biography, as in the case of the great Tibetan yogi Milarepa, we see that these Adept Gurus are usually kind, easy-going, generous, and ethical. *Only as an exception,* in special circumstances, do they break the rules. If someone is invariably "crazy," then it is not exceptional, and then there is only the finest of lines between creative craziness and abusiveness. I doff my hat to Mariana for her sage advice about how to adopt a discerning awareness about whether a crazy-wisdom guru's use of sex, money, or intoxicants is helpful or harmful.

Following the book's main chapters, Mariana includes an extremely worthwhile epilogue. She dissects the process of assault on gurus who are perceived to have behaved badly, using the particular case of the false defamation of her own spiritual partner, in which jealousy and neurosis drives rival rabbis and former associates to team up to destroy the reputation of a worthy, devoted rabbi/guru. At first, I wondered if this discussion was necessary—whether it detracted from the rest of the marvelous work itself. But the tale, her analysis, and her cautionary points of discernment about how accusers and accused should handle themselves becomes fascinating and very worthwhile—an example of Mariana's own burning faithfulness and courageous honesty, holding nothing back.

After this breathtaking, instructive account, Mariana includes a set of interviews with thirteen great spiritual teachers, which shows the author's openness to disagreement and her continuing curiosity and investigative bent. These interviews create a sort of Greek chorus that rounds out her saga. These added treasures give the book a greater weight and value as a trusted advisor and companion—a kind of manual for the serious business of conscious discipleship.

Let me conclude by quoting one of my favorite paragraphs, in which Mariana discusses the Magnificent Teaching of Nonduality that underlies all the interpersonal and spiritual advice she so eloquently dispenses:

> *In many forms of psychological work, we project onto the therapist those qualities of our psyches that we have disavowed because our conditioning and wounding have limited our range of mental and emotional experience and expansion. As therapy progresses, healing occurs through*

reclaiming the disowned aspects of ourselves. The
student-teacher relationship works in a parallel manner,
albeit on a different level: we project onto the teacher
our highest Self, eventually (ideally) coming to embrace
this full possibility for ourselves. In the student-teacher
relationship, the teacher ideally is in essence that which
we project onto him or her as well as an ordinary human
being. In fact, we may only come to consciously perceive
such a vast possibility for ourselves by seeing it lived
through another.

———— ∞∞ ————

When a Tantric guru performs unexcelled yoga initiations, she or
he must be perceived as one with the divine form of enlightened
being to whom the disciple is being introduced. But the disciple
is not simply installed at the door of the mandala palace, gazing in
awe and devotion at the guru/deity in the center. The point of the
initiation is when the disciple is led into the center herself or himself, and her or his oneness with the chosen divinity *(iṣhṭadevatā)*
is opened as a possibility and celebrated as a reality, only veiled by
the unfolding time of the performing practice *(sādhana).*

Right after this revelation of the absolute nonduality that is
the heart of the guru, Mariana sings the key role of the disciple's
love for the all-too-human manifestation of the guru, balancing
the impersonal absoluteness of the guru as the indivisible Self
with the personal unique and even quirky human vessel. A wonderful reconciliation of dichotomies! Not that the dichotomy of
the nondual and the dual is laid to rest—rather it is anchored by
wisdom to securely kindle the fire of compassion and love, the
will for the freedom and happiness of the Beloved, who turns out
to be none other than all conscious beings.

Mariana expresses most passionately and beautifully this love for the guru and for his human presence in all beings.

I once believed that I would gain something from spiritual life, that enlightenment would be mine if I played my cards well. My teacher taught me that spiritual life is about giving instead of getting. I thought there was something in it for me, but in spite of myself I have learned that it is only about Love, and that Love is about God, and that relationship to God is about ceaseless praise of the One in the form of service to the many.

I need quote no more from Mariana Caplan's pearls of cool wisdom and gems of fiery commitment to the well-being of the sincere "conscious disciple." You yourself can now enjoy this fabulous feast of generous wisdom for the discerning intellect and honest love for the true heart.

Namo gurubhyo! Sarvamangalam!

— Robert A. F. Thurman, aka Upasaka Tenzin Dharmakirti
 Jey Tsong Khapa Professor of Indo-Tibetan Buddhist Studies,
 Columbia University
 President, Tibet House, U.S.

Ganden Dechen Ling
Woodstock, New York
March 5, 2011—New Year of the Iron Hare

ACKNOWLEDGMENTS

Just prior to the revised edition of this book going to press, my spiritual teacher of sixteen years, Lee Lozowick, left this world. I offer every acknowledgment, honor, and gratitude to him—for his value to my life and to countless lives on inner and external levels, for his profound spiritual gifts and example of impeccable integrity and lifelong loyalty, for his most deeply human companionship and guidance, and also as the source of all my books. For it was he who suggested to me, when I was the "ripe" age of twenty-six, that I write my first book. He then suggested I write another one, and another. From this single suggestion emerged my vocation as a writer, and a life of relationships with authors, teachers, spiritual practitioners, and readers that has nourished me throughout the years, and which I am able to feed back to my readers.

Yogi Ramsuratkumar, his guru, remains the most extraordinary, cosmically wild, God-mad, bleeding-hearted, love-filled, fully enlightened human being I have ever known, and he has graced me with his undeserved personal regard and affection long after he left this world in 2001. I am grateful to God to have had the opportunity in this life to encounter a human being who embodies the greatest spiritual possibility that I believe exists.

Many of the teachers, scholars, and senior practitioners I most respect in the field of contemporary spirituality supported me with my research by granting me extensive personal interviews. Two of these teachers, Vimala Thakar and George Leonard, have left this world since the publication of the first edition of this book, and I would like to honor and celebrate their lives through the publication of this new edition. Vimala Thakar, through a simple sentence she shared in her interview, deepened my faith in the Divine and my experience as a woman, and her example of enlightenment in the form of a woman remains engraved in my psyche. The others continue to thrive and gift the world with their teachings: Lama Caroline Palden Alioto, Father Bruno Barnhart, Arnaud Desjardins, Gilles Farcet, Georg Feuerstein, Robert Frager, Ram Dass, Daniel Morin, Charles Tart, Jai Uttal, Llewellyn Vaughan-Lee, and John Welwood. I am grateful to each of them for their generosity and commitment to this project.

My publisher, Sounds True, has given me the experience of a publishing company comprising a team of disciples of life who are intelligent, efficient, dedicated, and caring toward their authors. Lead by renegade Tami Simon, Haven Iverson, Sheridan McCarthy, Jaime Schwalb, Shelly Rosen, and all the others are a blazingly brilliant team to work with.

Nancy Lewis, my friend and personal editor, whom over the past sixteen years I have come to call my Writing Angel, has lovingly supported this book and all of my projects.

As always, my deepest acknowledgments go to my readers, who give me the reason to write.

INTRODUCTION
A Call to Conscious Discipleship of Life

In the Western world, we have not learned *how to learn* when it comes to knowledge of the soul. We are taught to use our minds to process large amounts of complex data in many fields, and we've achieved unprecedented advances in the material world and even in the arts. Yet we receive no instruction on how to educate the higher heart, higher emotions, higher mind—to refine the subtle systems necessary to perceiving those qualities that lie at a deeper dimension of our experience. We are not taught from a young age to nurture our spirit and cultivate our relationship to the inner life and a deeper dimension of experience. Beyond that, many have forgotten there is even something to remember. As the Kabbalistic teachers of old taught, "We have forgotten that we have forgotten."

Despite this lack of understanding, many of us find ourselves on a spiritual path in some formal, intentional way. I have also heard a master say that there is nobody who is not on a spiritual path, and this is also true, for in some real way, life itself is a spiritual path. Yet still, in many people this longing to understand—to open, to know, to transform—is a deep craving and longing of the soul. We want to maximize our lives and live to our fullest potential. Author Peter Baumann engaged deeply on the spiritual path after achieving a world of riches and success, and looked for the highest-quality life he could pursue. Whereas it is impossible to define exactly what a spiritual path is, many of us feel that we nonetheless dedicate large amounts of our lives to it, and prioritize it in our hearts.

Many people who involve themselves in spirituality do so, consciously or unconsciously, because they want to be happier. Or because they feel broken. All of us want to enjoy our lives and suffer less. We sense that something deeper is possible, something called transformation. There may be a deep wish within us to serve. We come to the path for different motivations, and yet once we begin to engage with practices and teachers, the teachers and practices themselves begin to awaken and inform us.

As we go along, many different questions arise within us, and oftentimes there is little guidance on how to meet these predicaments. There are very few books that teach us how to approach the path and what to consider at various junctures along the way. Nobody can walk the path for us, and yet we all benefit from pointers.

One of my mentors, sociologist and best-selling author Joseph Chilton Pearce, says that whenever he wants to learn about a subject, he writes a book on it and waits for the feedback, stories, critiques, and new data to emerge: "Then the real book begins," he writes. In the ten years since the publication of the first edition of this book, I have heard literally thousands of stories of student-teacher relationships, from the highly refined to the most grossly abusive, and, more commonly, many in between.

Originally this book on the gifts and complexities of aligning with a guru was my doctoral dissertation. I wrote this book to help sincere spiritual seekers and practitioners wrestle with the many challenging questions with respect to the spiritual teacher. Most among those who consider themselves as walking the spiritual path in a sincere way will come into contact with teachers in some form or another. We will have questions that arise, and challenges to wrestle with, even in the best of circumstances.

I am aware that in a culture that values independence and autonomy—one in which many of our authorities have failed to live up to their stature and have often acted hypocritically if not reprehensibly—the idea of the spiritual teacher is unpopular. Within the current climate of interest in spirituality, the teacher or guru is not favored and the disciple-teacher relationship is poorly understood. Even those who do contemplate working with a teacher have well-considered concerns and a measure of confusion about the prospect. And these are justified, given the complexity of the issue.

One of my primary responses to the many challenges spiritual authority presents is the principle and practice of *conscious discipleship:* a fully empowered, intelligent, discriminating studenthood in relationship to life and the path, whether we engage with spiritual authority intermittently, for extensive periods, as a way of life, or not at all. Conscious discipleship—the topic I will consider in depth in this book—is the connecting thread in the unfolding study of the great labyrinth of the student-teacher relationship in Western culture. The contents of this exploration come from teachers and students of numerous traditions—from religious scholars and scriptures. I will share and synthesize some of these discoveries here. My contribution to the study is also informed by my twenty-plus years of contact and personal involvement with just about every kind of guru, shmuru, tulku, sensei, sheik, shaman, rabbi, therapist, sage, mentor, non-teacher, healer, and Divine Mother you can imagine.

At the onset of my spiritual journey, my involvement with such authorities was that of a seeker desperately looking for anyone or anything that could help me find sanity, truth, and wholeness in a world that seemed utterly mad and heading for its own demise. In the years after I met my teacher, Lee Lozowick, my relationship with other teachers turned from one of a seeker to one of a researcher, not only in an academic context, but in the most personal sense of the term. As I grow up on the spiritual path, many of these teachers and scholars have now become my friends, colleagues, and collaborators. We have opened a dialogue often on these subjects and continue to explore new possibilities. We often dialogue on still-controversial topics in Western spirituality and continue to explore cutting-edge topics such as World Spirituality. Still, I remain in awe of wisdom and cultivate a deep respect for my teachers and the elders who have come before me.

The purpose of my ongoing study has always been twofold. First, I want to augment my understanding of my own transformational process—to deepen my transformational experience and to integrate that experience into my life. Second, I want to fulfill an internal commitment to do my small part in helping spiritual seekers in the West gain a spiritual education and cultivate discernment so their paths unfold with as much understanding, clarity, and efficiency as possible.

Understanding the complexity of the student-teacher relationship is important whether one has a teacher, wants one, or has been disillusioned by one and seeks deeper understanding. It is also important if one does not want a teacher at all but wants to understand the points of discernment relative to this important relationship. This book outlines the principle of conscious discipleship and offers multiple points about using spiritual discernment to decide whether and how to work with a spiritual teacher. It is designed to help the reader articulate into consciousness many of the questions and challenges one would encounter when engaging the spiritual path and the question of the teacher. Through my personal and professional research I have had the privilege of meeting and spending extended periods of time with many individuals whom I consider to be the world's greatest spiritual teachers, psychologists, yogis, healers, and religious leaders. Many of the quotes you will read here are from personal interviews and conversations with these individuals. My deep wish is that you benefit from these discussions and proceed on your spiritual journey with effectiveness, radiance, and minimal disappointment and disillusionment.

Chapters 1 through 11 describe the spiritual mishaps and extraordinary encounters I experienced on my search to find a teacher, and the accompanying inquiries and points of discernment that accompany the process of exploring, and perhaps finding, a spiritual teacher. In the latter part of the book, and continuing into the epilogue, I share developments and perceptions from my life experience since the publication of the first edition of this book and describe where my current work is taking me, as well as present a new and complex set of questions with which I was unexpectedly faced. We are endlessly developing, both individually and collectively, and as a writer my perspective shifts as I study, learn, change, and mature. I hope this book reflects my development. Finally, for those who are interested in further study, the appendix contains a series of interviews with well-known teachers and scholars of multiple traditions.

I hope you are able to enjoy the adventure of this book and laugh along with my mistakes (and your own) while simultaneously engaging in a deep inquiry regarding the perils and rewards of choosing a spiritual teacher; I also hope you gain a distilled ability to make choices with respect to this important subject. May we become refined as questioners, and humble with respect to needing answers, respecting that the spiritual path continues to unfold as long as our lives do. May your adventures, challenges, and breakthroughs be aided in some small way by my own. And together, may we live lives of increasing discernment, radiance, and wisdom on the spiritual path.

ENTERING THE
SPIRITUAL SUPERMARKET

If frequently enough, the question of the guru is
not properly considered, it is because the question
of the disciple is not properly considered.
—ARNAUD DESJARDINS

My story begins in a lifetime within this lifetime that seems so long ago, it is hard to believe it is the same life. I am in a remote desert village in the heart of Mexico, not yet twenty but imagining myself to be a blossoming goddess of significant maturity. I am the specially chosen apprentice of Hozi—a renowned Aztec shaman, mystic, and artist. I have come to Mexico as his invited guest to fulfill the first segment of the shared destiny he claims we have together, as fated by the gods.

On this night, I am feigning sleep on a makeshift cot that passes for a bed in Hozi's one-room cottage/art studio. The building has been donated to him by one of the mothers of his various children throughout the world, so he can afford to paint and teach. (These mothers, I later learn, have all been "specially chosen" apprentices, too.) I am lying on my stomach with a blanket covering my arm, which is tucked under my pillow. My fingers firmly grip a large stainless-steel knife I sneaked from the kitchen moments earlier as I returned from the outhouse.

My personal shaman is stoned and drunk in the loft, where he is creating life-sized, erotic paintings of gods, daemons, cosmic vaginas, massive multicolored phalluses, ethereal dimensions, sacred objects, and sublime interior landscapes. I am all too aware that there are only two telephones in the whole town, and I do not know where either of them is. I make a mental note to locate them the following day, assuming I make it through the night.

I contemplate various escape plans but am internally tormented by my thirst for the wisdom this shaman has promised—a thirst I'm nearly certain will not be quenched if I flee. For a moment, I rationalize sleeping with him willingly instead of fighting if he tries to attack—for the sake of the higher knowledge I wish to obtain—but my stomach curdles at the thought of his whiskey breath and smoke-saturated, bristly gray moustache.

I hear him breathing. Following each smoke-filled in-breath, the out-breath echoes with carnal lust for the naive, young wannabe shamaness in the bed below him. I listen to the rhythm of his breathing, praying to whatever Aztec gods exist that he will pass out from intoxication before his shamanic balls boil over. Instead, the breath deepens, and I hear in it a combination of lust, frustration, and a hunger for vengeance. I hold the knife firmly and resolve to do what is required to save my remaining innocence—and prepare to be attacked.

Fortunately, I make it to morning with my shamanic virginity still intact, and I last two more weeks in Mexico without being raped, having very intense and frightening experiences. It was the beginning of a long, winding, passionate journey toward spiritual discernment. In the end, this experience proved to yield many important lessons in spiritual discernment, but at the time I was a terrified and confused, albeit passionate, young woman.

The shaman's battlefield wasn't the first destination on my spiritual sojourn. It began long before that, in a family with a father whose own father did not know how to love him, because *his* father had not known how to love *him*. Thus my father could not help but bring some of that same fate to bear on his own children. In me, his youngest daughter, the wound this created led to my discontent with a world I saw as asleep, as drained of the living mystical possibilities of compassion, inner harmony, and selflessness. It began with a false interpretation of the Jewish religion—a transliteration that damaged my mind by instilling fear of God and damnation, even as it fertilized my heart with prayers and chants written in a language that engraved their perennial truth in the same heart and mind they confused. It began with a car accident that almost took my life but, through grace, left me instead with an acute awareness of the preciousness of existence. I learned that life must not be wasted, and we must be continuously devoted to the fulfillment of its highest possibility.

By the time I hit twenty, I was an overachieving hippie: a feminist activist who ran campus organizations that I told myself would save the world, or at least part of it. I had managed to travel half of that world in search of cultures that evidenced greater humanness than my own. I had undertaken a serious study of anthropology to justify my search on academic grounds and had already learned that no culture, love affair, beach paradise, or adventure translated into the inner freedom I already knew was the only thing worth living for.

So when Luna, a self-proclaimed Wiccan priestess and the elder sister of one of my college roommates, waltzed into the living room of our 1930s Victorian house in Ann Arbor, Michigan, I was ripe and ready. Luna led us through meditations and guided visualizations about the *inner self* and our life's "true purpose"—the first time I had ever heard those terms. Luna's simple visualizations blasted open my hungry psyche, and for the next seven years I was like the ugly duckling. I asked every yoga teacher, Tai Chi master, massage therapist, philosophy professor, guru, rabbi, and Native American wannabe shaman I met, "Are you my mother?" "Are you my father?"

I was new to the path amid a culture that did not provide an instruction manual for spiritual seekers. As the Sufis ask, "How do you find your way through the desert when there is no road?" What do you do, in Middle America, when circumstances conspire to make the rigid walls of your psyche crack open, revealing your soul's cry for truth? When this happened to me, I joined billions of other human beings—past, present, and future—in the shared questions: Where do I begin? Is there a religion or spirituality that will truly speak to me? Will I find it in a book? A teacher? A friend? A place? A martial art? An LSD trip? A pilgrimage to India? How do I know where and how to look? Am I really crazy, as everyone from my past believes, or could this intuition of something far beyond my limited perceptions truly exist . . . please?!

Start simple, I thought: study. I discovered Ann Arbor's only New Age bookstore and was confronted there with thousands of titles ranging from *Discovering the Child Within* to *Everyday Buddhism* to *The Way of the Shaman* to *Celestial Messages*. The sheer number of books only confused me more. I needed recommendations, but who could I ask? Who was spiritual? The people who worked at the bookstore? The long-haired hippies on campus? The women's studies professor who wore the Ghanaian fertility-goddess necklace? Did I even know anybody who was wise? In the end, I asked them all for recommendations and looked for repeats among their lists.

It also struck me as obvious that, beyond my reading, I would need some personal guidance, but once again, where to begin? What was a guru? Was that the same as a lama? How did that compare with a shaman? And what on earth did it mean when somebody professed to be a Divine Mother? Could *avatars*—human incarnations of God—really exist among us? Was everyone who called him- or herself a "spiritual teacher" really such a teacher? Was there a board of certification somewhere? Or was it true that every rock, child, lover, and tree was my teacher and I should avoid "intermediaries," as the more cosmic literature suggested? And if that were so, how could I truly trust that I was hearing the rock itself and not my hoped-for interpretation of its message? Would a ladybug *really* tell me if I was going astray? Little as I knew then, I knew enough about the nature of mind to want something more than a blade of grass for guidance. Thus I began my search for a spiritual teacher.

❦

When beginning a book such as this, it would be ideal if we could articulate with certainty and widespread agreement definitions for the terms *spiritual teacher, master, guru, guide,* and so forth. The problem is that it is impossible to do so. Objective distinctions cannot be made, and there will always be countless gray areas, exceptions, refined points of discernment, and ever-evolving understandings within each of us. Instead what I will do is offer an overview of the issues involved, suggest how I will be using the terms in this book, and encourage you to make further distinctions and refinements as your own understanding unfolds.

Relative and Absolute Authority

In his book *Toward a Psychology of Awakening*, John Welwood makes a distinction between relative and absolute authority.[1] *Relative authorities* are human like the rest of us but are perhaps steps ahead on the path, functioning as mentors or guides. *Absolute authorities* include the gurus and masters: seen either as incarnations of the divine, or powerful (if not flawless) vehicles of transmission for divine direction.

Yet even within the model of relative versus absolute author-ities, the function any given teacher serves in relationship to a given student depends largely upon how we relate to the teacher. Some people may consider a spiritual leader an inspiration and a guide, whereas others see that same person as a master—or even an incarnation of God. His Holiness the Dalai Lama, for example, is an inspiration and teacher to tens of thousands of people, but to his closest disciples he is a master, a representative of God Itself, the ultimate authority to be obeyed and wor-shipped. In many contemporary Buddhist traditions, students do not relate to the teacher formally from a devotional stance, and the teacher may refuse many of the outward expressions of adulation commonly bestowed upon formal spiritual author-ity; still, the teacher's inner circle of students will often confer uncompromising reverence, obedience, and discipleship. Simi-larly, there are great gurus who have the capacity to fulfill the formal function of master, but some aspirants relate to them as "guide" or "friend" according to their needs at that time in their spiritual development.

In my own case, for several months I practiced rigorously in the company of the disciples of a very famous guru. From the beginning, I had the unshakable sense that she wasn't *my* guru—although I would have liked her to be, as I was actively looking for a teacher. I was serious about my spiritual studies, too: serious enough to get up at 5 a.m., walk a mile across town in subzero temperatures in the dark Ann Arbor winter, sit in a room lit only by candles, and chant an hour-and-a-half-long Sanskrit prayer I couldn't understand, much less pronounce. The other students thought I was a disciple who "just didn't know it yet," but I knew I was not. I was in training for something and someone else whom I had not yet met. Therefore, my distance from and lack of devotion toward that guru was right for me given my circumstances at that time, and nobody else could have known that for me.

In the course of spiritual life we are also likely to encounter various relative spiritual authorities who are of genuine importance to us on our path. We may find ourselves attending meditation sessions or retreats with a particular teacher whom we respect and admire but do not wish to have as our principal teacher. Or we may practice under the guidance of a teacher's senior practitioner as we investigate that particular path. Relative spiritual authorities could include a spiritual friend or an Aikido teacher or conceivably even a wise therapist (but beware—many therapists who subtly assume this function do not live up to it!).

To learn from these relative authorities and receive what they have to offer, we must offer them a certain amount of respect and trust. This is no different from going into a yoga class—or even a calculus class—for the first time. If we go in to profess our knowledge and do what we want and what we think is best, not only will we irritate all the other students, but we will be too full of ourselves to be empty enough to receive anything.

The majority of traditional Judeo-Christian spiritual authorities such as rabbis, ministers, and priests tend to fall into the category of relative spiritual authorities. The nature of the religions they represent in no way suggests that such individuals are, or should be, fully realized beings, much less divine incarnations. Rather, they have undergone a set course of study that certifies them to represent the spiritual teachings and ethical laws of their respective traditions.

Although they know the rules of their religion and may have a deep regard for others, many such relative authorities do not express through their lives an understanding that elicits a natural response of reverence and trust among their congregants. We may grant them respect and deference, but we do not feel genuine confidence in their wisdom. All too frequently, many of us unconsciously and automatically form a belief structure about all spiritual authorities based on this traditional model, a model that is not always suitable to deep spiritual development.

One way to consider this issue of relative versus absolute authority is Ken Wilber's model of spiritual translation versus spiritual transformation. *Translation* refers to a horizontal process in which the contents of ego or personality are progressively uncovered, understood, and worked with in order to create a greater sense of well-being within the individual, and hopefully greater workability in one's life. *Transformation* is a vertical process in which the nature of ego itself is understood and undermined, and the individual shifts from an egoic identity to a universal identity. In *One Taste,* Wilber writes:

> *With typical* translation, *the self (or subject) is given a new way to think about the world (or objects); but with radical* transformation, *the self itself is inquired into, looked into, grabbed by its throat, and literally throttled to death. . . [Transformative spirituality] does not legitimate the world, it breaks the world; it does not console the world, it shatters it. And it does not render the self content, it renders it undone.*[2]

It is my belief that the most optimal relationship between teacher and student includes both translational and transformational elements, and translation without transformation is not enough to satisfy many spiritual aspirants.

Just as it is challenging to define the terms teacher, guru, spiritual guide, and so forth, the same is true in attempting to define the functions of terms like student and disciple. In some ways, this whole book is an attempt to articulate this—not in service of creating a definitive definition of the terms, but once again to assist the reader in cultivating piercing *discernment* with relationship to the complexities and subtleties of his or her inquiry. In this way, we are able to navigate our spiritual journeys more radiantly and effectively.

The following chapter will more deeply examine various types of spiritual authority, and the chapters after it will examine the nuances and discernments required to navigate a successful spiritual studenthood on the path of life. Meanwhile, if we were to make some broad brushstrokes of the terrain, we could say that terms like *guru* and *disciple* tend to refer more to an Indo-Tibetan approach to the spiritual path, and are found in Hindu and certain types of Buddhist practice. These types of student-teacher relationships, although operant under different titles, are also present in Sufi traditions and other non-Western approaches. There are obvious challenges with translating this into Western traditions and into a Western psychological model, yet many attempts have been made and continue to exist in the West with varying degrees of apparent success, even as we consider that to effectively evaluate a process of cultural translation may take hundreds of years.

What is clear is that we are in a vast cultural and evolutionary experiment. We can't deny that the usefulness of teachers and a teaching function, as well as the essential function of learning and studenthood and apprenticeship, has existed and will likely continue to exist throughout the expanses of time. The purpose of this book is to help all of us navigate this realm more effectively. As will become apparent throughout the book, becoming a great student is not only more essential than becoming a great teacher, but it's also true that the genuinely great teachers are, first and foremost, the greatest students on the path.

TYPES OF SPIRITUAL AUTHORITY

The forms in which spiritual authority emerge, the ways that we as human beings relate to such authorities, and the stages and seasons of relationship to spiritual authority are as numerous as human beings on the path. There is no right or wrong way to engage with such teachers—all the more so because in the Western world we are updating, recreating, and adapting many of these models. There are both successful and corrupt teachers in all of the categories considered later in this chapter. Still, through the cultivation of discernment in relationship to these challenging circumstances in our lives, we can increase the likelihood of effective and fulfilling relationships with our spiritual teachers. Furthermore, when we have been disillusioned by a spiritual teacher or community, we can process through, integrate, and benefit from our loss when we understand more clearly what we have been through.

In my experience over many years, particularly since the publication of the first edition of this book, I've tended to see three general outcomes among individuals who have spent several decades on the path and engaged deeply with one or more spiritual teachers: the first group is content with the path they have chosen, even if their understanding of what that path and the function of the teacher is has changed over time and even if there has been a certain amount of disillusionment; the second are those who have been disillusioned by a particular path or teacher, and in some deep way dismiss the student-teacher relationship and perhaps even the spiritual path itself; and the third are those who have been deeply disillusioned many times over, sometimes by the path or a particular teacher, but equally as often by their own psychology, blindness, and inevitable human failings within the process of trial and error, and yet they remain optimistic and ever open to the depths and challenges of spiritual life. They consider themselves to have made what author Marc Gafni calls "mistakes in the right direction."

In this chapter, let us consider some of the more common contemporary models of spiritual authority, and begin to look at their advantages and disadvantages. Using yet another misadventure of my own as a jumping-off point, we will then consider the role of the spiritual student and her complicity in the creation of these various dynamics as she wakes up to her own weaknesses and psychological blind spots and engages her own process of spiritual awakening.

Non-Teacher Teachers

An increasing number of teachers say they are not teachers. There are many reasons for taking this position. In many of the contemporary neo-Advaita-Vedanta nondual traditions, for example, the labels of "teacher" and "student" are often considered illusory distinctions within the nondual truth of oneness, and therefore obstacles to the nondual realization of oneness. This model suggests that the affirmation of the teacher outside of oneself often distracts the practitioner from the truth of the inner teacher or guru, and disempowers the student's self-awakening and the cultivation of trust in her own inner authority.

The point of discernment to be aware of in this circumstance is as follows: when two people are functioning as teacher and student in the Western world, there is an almost inevitable arising of psychological projections and power dynamics in spite of what a teacher does or does not call him or herself; and when the student-teacher relationship is not acknowledged or well structured, built-in structures to help both the student and teacher navigate the psychological complexities that arise for each of them often go lacking. For the purposes of this book, this type of teacher will be referred to as a "non-teacher teacher."

In contemporary times, one of the most renowned non-teacher teachers was the late J. Krishnamurti, an authority of tremendous power and capacity who introduced hundreds of thousands of Westerners to the Eastern nondual teachings. Declared a prophet and world savior in his youth—labels he felt were grave impediments in his authentic quest for liberation—Krishnamurti worked hard to extract himself from his early followers' projection of holiness. As Vimala Thakar, a revolutionary Advaita teacher and Krishnamurti's "non-successor," said:

> *Krishnamurti lived his life, and thousands came to be*
> *helped through his communication and the presence*
> *of his person. Krishnamurti communicated his own*
> *understanding. He shared it because that was his role. It*
> *helped many, but he did not help.*

The Inner Guru

Another type of authority is the "inner guru," a subject I dealt with extensively in *Halfway Up the Mountain*. To access with clarity and to be able to effectively rely upon the guidance of the inner teacher or guru is one of the great fruitions of a life of diligent spiritual practice. The mature student must ultimately learn to access and be guided by his or her own inner authority, whether he or she lives independently of, or in close relationship to, a living spiritual teacher.

Returning to John Welwood's distinction between relative and absolute spiritual authorities, the absolute spiritual authority or guru is ultimately a reflection of the true Self of the student (though many relative spiritual authorities are likely to serve this function only for periods of time), and therefore the inner guru, or teacher, is ultimately no different from the external guru or teacher. However, as discussed in Patañjali's *Yoga Sutras,* this truth is generally only realized and integrated through consistent, intensive engagement with spiritual practice over a long period of time.[1]

For many people, however, the inner guru is not an adequate substitute for relationship with an external teacher—at least during certain critical stages of the path. Similarly, rarely does the teacher who is not in the body and whom the student has never met serve as an alternative to a flesh-and-blood teacher. The external teacher serves several very specific functions of instruction and transmission that the inner guru, as most people understand it, cannot provide until one reaches a later stage of studenthood. The external guru awakens and supervises the training of the inner guru as it passes through the necessary and often arduous stages of metaphorical kindergarten, grade school, high school, college, graduate school, and so forth. We must be careful to not mistake our intellectual understanding of the inner guru for the very real human need for the external teacher.

Life as Guru

There are those who proclaim that everything in life—rocks, trees, animals, children, spouses and romantic partners, and all situations—is their teacher and guru. Ultimately, in the best-case scenario, this is certainly true. If we are either well practiced, inherently wise, or lucky, we stand to learn from everything we encounter. Yet to use the term *teacher,* or especially *guru,* in these circumstances necessitates the widest definition and interpretation of the word—resulting in confusion and even a diminution of the term itself. If this is our preferred approach, it might be more accurate to say that we have a rich relationship with life in which we intend to learn from all of life's aspects, or that this approach is what is available and congruent to our present experience.

As with every approach, there are notable exceptions. Author and teacher Arjuna Ardagh, for example, states with great conviction that his relationship with his wife serves as his guru, and from my experience of relating to him as a friend and colleague, I tend to agree with his assessment. However, his capacity to use "life as guru" has arisen through more than three decades of intensive discipleship under some of the world's great spiritual teachers, and a life of consistent and disciplined spiritual practice that has allowed him to access such circumstances as his "guru." Again, we must always be aware of subtle distinctions and know that there is no substitute for long-term practice.

Organic Authority versus Presumed Authority

A further distinction to be made regarding types of spiritual authority is between those whose authority is an organic expression of inner wisdom and those whose spiritual authority is largely, though often unconsciously, mixed with a strong degree of their own egoic ambition. If we closely examine many of today's most popular teachers, we will find that in many cases their popularity is less a function of their realization, and more a result of highly effective strategic marketing. According to Welwood, "True masters have access to an absolute, uncon- ditional source of authority—awakened being. . . . The genuine teacher is one who has realized the essential nature of human consciousness, usually through practicing a self-knowledge dis- cipline such as meditation for many years."[2] Many of today's most popular spiritual teachers, although possessing a certain degree of wisdom and knowledge, do not have a deep, abiding, and integrated spiritual realization.

Functioning from an organic and authentic expression of inner authority suggests that egoic motivations are no longer the source of one's actions; the authority of a more refined con- sciousness is then able to flow freely through that individual. When we recognize true authority, we cannot help but feel a sense of reverence in relationship to it. For it is *It*—God, Truth, Clarity—that we find ourselves in awe of, not the personality of its carrier, which may or may not be pleasing to us. The natural and appropriate response is to respect the human being who is the vehicle for this extraordinary authority; such an individual is worthy of acknowledgment. And, in most cases, over time and with little or no effort toward self-promotion, his or her authority is recognized. Would-be students will commonly approach such a person and ask for guidance because they are drawn to do so, not coerced or tantalized into doing so.

My teacher's master, the late Indian saint Yogi Ramsuratkumar, is an excellent example of organic authority. Throughout his life, he expressed no desire to be a spiritual master of any sort and shunned the role whenever possible. On the contrary, he lived as a beggar on the streets: he slept under a tree at the bus station or in a vacated building filled with scorpions and snakes, and let himself be considered a madman. Slowly people began to recognize his mastery and traveled far and wide to sit with him at the bus stand, help him carry the bags of trash and newspapers he collected, or follow him around the temples and hills of Tiruvannamalai, South India, where he liked to roam. Over the course of fifty years, such people persuaded him first to live in a Spartan room in the marketplace, then in a house, and in his final year, at an ashram they had spent two decades beseeching him to preside over.

We can contrast this example of organic authority with one of presumed authority that I encountered upon the publication of *Halfway Up the Mountain*. An author of a book on nonduality asked to meet me for lunch to "compare notes" on our various experiences in the field of contemporary spirituality. "I'm frustrated," he told me, "because I have become a teacher but nobody seems to recognize it, and I don't know how to get them to. Do you have any suggestions?"

"Tell me more," I said, fascinated by the manifestation of ego that sat before me, housed within a very sincere human being.

"Well," he continued, "I recently had an experience in which one of my closest friends cut off contact with me over this. He said he couldn't deal with me in my new function of spiritual teacher."

"What did you make of that?" I asked.

"It made me realize that once you become enlightened you will probably have to lose a lot of friends because who you are is too threatening to them. If they are not strong enough to perceive who you are, their ego will instead react with criticism. I wish I could help him to see more."

I told this man that no matter how many books I wrote or experiences I had, I would never consider assuming a teaching function unless it was explicitly asked of me from *without*, and not from *within*.

This story is real, and common. Several years ago, a middle-aged woman who had just divorced an abusive Presbyterian minister came to a seminar I was giving, with the intention of learning how to become a spiritual teacher. She thought herself wise, and wanted to learn how to go about collecting students. Her intention was sincere enough, but her appreciation of her own wisdom was highly inflated, and distorted besides. She was a woman heavily laden with aggression, unconscious thirst for power, and deeply repressed sexuality. I didn't have the heart to tell her directly that she was not in a place of spiritual maturity that was likely to attract even one good student. Instead I told her that if her destiny was indeed to be a teacher and if she focused on her own spiritual maturation, students would come to her naturally.

***

As the reader may have glimpsed in this short discussion of spiritual authority, its spectrum is vast and there are subtle distinctions on every level. Most individuals do not fall into any single category but span a range of developmental capacities. As Ken Wilber suggests, different developmental lines (spiritual, cognitive, emotional, sexual, and so forth) can unfold independently from one another, so a person can be highly evolved in some areas but not in others.[3] For example, a teacher may be highly developed in his capacity to view life from an impersonal perspective, and thus may be able to articulate spiritual teachings with qualities of objective clarity and transcendent awareness. This same person, however, may still have tremendous difficulties in the area of interpersonal intimacy resulting from disruptions in the bonding process that occurred in infancy.

More important than the developmental level of the teacher, however, are the student's purity of intention, his or her capacity for discernment, and the relational quality between them.

An infinite number of potential qualities of relationship exist between teacher and student. As we learn from intimate relationships, even a good student and a good teacher will not necessarily yield a powerful outcome without the correct chemistry. The whole domain of spiritual authority and discipleship is not only subjective, but intersubjective. It is fully relational.

———⚬⚬⚬———

My encounters with the Aztec shaman Hozi all those years ago—distressing though they were at the time—nicely illustrate how a dysfunctional student-teacher relationship can manifest. When I lay in bed clutching a knife in Hozi's studio, I was not the victim of a sleazy shaman's sexual advances; I was naive and driven by still-unconscious psychological forces.

At nineteen years old, as a Spanish-English translator for the Piscataway tribe (with whom I kept idealized company in the initial years of my spiritual quest, before Native American spirituality became trendy), I had my initial opportunity to become acquainted with Hozi. The tribe flew him in from Mexico to conduct a ceremony to invoke the spirit of a young native woman who had died unexpectedly and without proper time for closure. Hozi looked the part, straight out of a script. He was 100 percent Aztec—unlike the many Caucasian shamans wandering about claiming to be one-eighth or one-sixteenth Hopi on their step-grandmother's side. He had thick charcoal hair that fell to his waist and was adorned with clay beads, eagle feathers, arrowheads, and all the other accoutrements you would expect from a rock-star shaman. I felt a certain unease with him energetically, but I couldn't put my finger on it. I interpreted my critique of his slightly shady and unattractive physical characteristics—brown teeth and glazed eyes—as being due to my vanity instead of an indication that my intuitive feelings were accurate.

My family was skeptical, and not without reason. When Hozi came over to celebrate my birthday while my parents were out of town, I did not know he would burn large quantities of the purifying herb sage, saturating the newly upholstered living room with a scent that, to the untrained nose, smells exactly like marijuana. Imagine trying to explain *that* to your older brothers, who are also wrapped up in suburban, young adult life. When Hozi called upon the ancestors to bestow their blessings on me for my birthday by howling like a wolf and screaming in primal release, the neighbors called to make sure everything was all right. Thinking fast, I politely told them that I had taken an interest in theater and was practicing for an audition. What else was I to do in such a circumstance—ask the Aztec shaman to tone down his calling-in of the ancestors? I rationalized that the ancestors lived so far away that he had to yell to attract their attention.

When I told my parents that their nineteen-year-old daughter had been invited to Mexico to be personal apprentice to a famous Aztec artist-shaman, they—instead of being impressed (as all my "spiritually evolved" friends were)—wanted to know what he could possibly want with me. But then, my conservative family was skeptical of everything I did, and I felt insulted. At the time, I couldn't see in myself what I now recognize was an undeveloped capacity for discernment, the subject of my book *Eyes Wide Open*.

I remember sitting on the airplane to Mexico City, shaking and sweating. Was I crazy, or were they ("they" being the 99-plus percent of the population who wouldn't consider doing what I was doing for any price)? I will never forget intensely scribbling in my journal that, although it would probably be difficult, if I worked *really hard*—gave it my heart and soul for about two years—I would become enlightened. I would have mastery of the inner worlds. I would be a woman of power, a true Coyote Woman. Such was the content of my thinking.

Bear in mind that I had read the books of Carlos Castaneda—the man who brought shamanism to the attention of Westerners in a way no other had before. The books spilled over with his adventurous and romantic tales of running through the scorpion-ridden desert barefoot in the black of night, using only intuition to keep from being scratched by rocks or scraped by thorns. I respected Castaneda and appreciated how others revered him, and I desperately longed to receive such admiration myself. Unaware of just how strong this drive to receive external validation was, I unconsciously figured that if I could become that special, the ache inside from feeling unloved would finally dissipate.

Still, something was indisputably askew. My friend Libia, who self-identified as a witch, was one of Hozi's lovers. I worked hard to deny my knowledge of their sexual relationship, even when she asked me to bring him a large stuffed teddy bear. As I took it from her, I was confronted with the conflict between my mental image of myself—possessing the maturity of a woman of at least forty years—and reality. I was going to get off a jet in a tie-dyed skirt carrying a stuffed teddy bear, and I would be looking for a fifty-something, long-haired Aztec man with a feather headband and gourds hanging from his belt. The imagined scene gnawed at my gut.

And then I was in Mexico, and we were stopping off at his gallery to view his artwork, an odd blend of cosmic imagery and perversity. I told myself that Hozi's creativity arose from a level I simply didn't understand yet. We arrived at La Tierra de Maravillas, or "Wonderland"—the ethereal estate of his mystic-architect friend Guillermo—and were shown to "our" room, the master suite. A sterling-silver bowl filled with peyote buttons rested in the center of the bed, and I finally had enough sense to realize that either our hosts had the wrong picture or that *I* did—more likely the latter.

Once I realized the nature of the game Hozi expected me to play with him—sex in exchange for teachings—I faced the exacting task of avoiding intimate contact with him while keeping him just hopeful enough that he wouldn't give up and send me home without the teachings. Our days passed with my doing everything I could to avoid being mated with the shaman: I feigned sleep, stomach cramps, culture shock.

When Hozi had invited me to Mexico, he was all too aware that my yearning for God placed me in a position that was as suggestible as it was vulnerable. I was gullible and credulous—so intense was my desire for transcendence. He knew that his knowledge of Aztec shamanism stirred my interest, that the exotic gourds that hung from his belt intrigued me, and that his familiarity with hinted-at planes of existence whet my voracious, youthful appetite for inner and outer adventure. He knew that his compelling flattery could render me willing to overlook small inconsistencies. His only mis-estimation was that I would be willing to pay with sex for the mysteries he held.

No better was his shaman friend Guillermo, who one night gave us a ride home from a party high in the hills of Mexico City. Guillermo was already spirit-intoxicated—from tequila—well before we left for a party at still another shaman's house. He sped down the winding one-way roads with one hand on the wheel, the other clutching the bottle. There was a steep cliff just inches from the beat-up Mexican-style VW Bug we rode in, and I genuinely feared this would be the last ride of my life. Finally, terror overcame me to the degree that I didn't care how many shamans I was trying to impress. Tears streaming down my cheeks, I pleaded with Guillermo to slow down. He responded with a howling laugh and literally closed his eyes as he continued on his way. He mocked me because I did not trust the Great Spirit, and told me I had a long way to go to catch up on the inner planes if I was going to be worthy of keeping shamanic company.

You Get What You Ask For

You get what you ask for—consciously or unconsciously. This is both the bad news and the good news about the spiritual search. That was certainly my experience with Hozi. Of course it was unconscious, but nonetheless it was the first in a series of "mistakes in the right direction" that would provide important learning and integration for me later on. If you are pleased with what you have, it is less a stroke of good luck than it is a manifestation of what you have asked for, whether you're aware of the asking or not. If the path and its teachers have disappointed you, you may not have learned what to ask for and how to ask. This often-unwelcome philosophy suggests that if we end up with a screwball teacher who wants to take all our money, this either represents something unresolved within our psyche, or some karma that needs to be fulfilled,[4] regardless of the weaknesses in the teacher. The fact that we get what we ask for should come as good news, for it puts the ball back in our own court and reminds us that we can steadily inquire, discern, and develop our consciousness to a point where we will indeed know what to ask for.

There is a distinction, however, between the theory that you get what you ask for in a teacher and the common New Age slogan "You create your own reality." The egoic interpretation of "You create your own reality" encourages us to conjure scenarios of what the ego imagines would best adorn itself, and then to assume that if we play our cards right we should and will get exactly what we want on a silver platter. And if we don't get what we think we deserve, we're doing something wrong.

But it is not that simple. We create our reality from all that we are on all levels, conscious and unconscious. As Ram Dass suggested in a lecture after suffering a severe stroke, "being here now" includes being with all of what is here now at every level—psychological, ecological, conscious, unconscious, past, present, future. If we do not get what we think we're asking for, it doesn't mean that it's our fault and we're bad and we should crack the whip on our already wounded hearts and psyches. It simply means that in a given realm of our path we have not yet gained enough knowledge, wisdom, or healing to refine our capacity to attract what is ultimately in our own best interest. It is not about good or bad, only about learning to accurately assess where we are—and using our free will to empower ourselves to create change.

Knowing What You Want

The corollary to getting what we ask for is knowing what we want, particularly when we seek a spiritual teacher. Knowing what we want is not altogether simple since, as Abraham Maslow suggested in his hierarchy of needs, we have needs and desires on many levels. Whereas it is ultimately true that, as the Persian mystic Hafiz wrote, "there is no one on this earth who is not looking for God," we are each also looking for a lot of other things; some support our spiritual growth while others thwart it.

As the Russian mystic Gurdjieff suggested when he referred to "the battle of yes and no," conscious and unconscious factors swirl about in the psyche on the soul's ultimate journey to self-knowledge: desires both to preserve the ego and allow its annihilation, to be liberated and fulfill the death wish, to serve and hoard. Self-fulfillment and self-destruction continually enact inner warfare on the battlefield of the psyche. Our only chance for peace is to show up at the scene and negotiate.

When we know what we want—both our egoic desire and the deepest aspects of our selves—we are not surprised or let down when what we get does not look like what we *think* we asked for. When there is a discrepancy between what we ask for and what we get, and we do not succumb to the temptation of self-pity, we can take inventory of those areas where we remain blind or unconscious.

If only we could say honestly and without shame, "I want a teacher who will help me straighten out my life and make me suffer less, but who won't ask me to do strenuous practices." Or, "I want a teacher whom I can visit when I need a spiritual 'pick-me-up' but who doesn't require any commitment to the path she represents." Or, "I want a substitute Mommy/Daddy figure because I'm determined to get the love I never got as a child." Or, "I want to be with a teacher and spiritual community so I can feel like I belong somewhere." None of these motivations are a problem, and even if our search for a teacher is motivated by one or more of them, we may gain more benefit than we bargained for. But our unconscious and automatic ego-based tendency is to upgrade our more mundane or primal motivations into something of spiritual meaning and import. Since transformation only begins by knowing and starting from where we are—however much we might wish to be elsewhere—being honest regarding our own motivations is a powerful stance with which we place transformational possibilities back in the domain of self-responsibility.

Getting What We Need

Another way of relating and learning from the challenges of the student-teacher relationship from an empowered perspective is to assume that we get what we need. My teacher, Lee

Lozowick, once received a letter from Yogi Ramsuratkumar that read, "My Father in Heaven blesses Lee with everything he ~~wants~~ needs." Another term for this attitude is *faith*. Ram Dass said, "faith protects you," and I believe it protects us from believing that things should be other than they are. Great saints and practitioners of all traditions have made tremendous strides in their spiritual development by anchoring themselves in the faith that every thing and every circumstance that comes to them is precisely what they *need*. It can be argued that simply holding this belief (though it is not so easy to do), and accepting with gratitude what we are offered, bears an untold harvest of transformational possibility.

Returning to my personal story from this self-empowered perspective, the fact that I found myself in a dodgy situation with a horny shaman doesn't necessarily indicate that spiritual authority figures are dangerous individuals who take advantage of naive and helpless young female spiritual seekers, but more about where I was at that time. There were areas of my relationships to men and sexuality that were blind and unconscious, finding expression through my otherwise very genuine motivations for truth seeking. The situation into which I had put myself was also an indication that I was simply young and naive and in real need of a spiritual smack in the face so I could learn what did *not* work. Then, eventually, I would be able to help others learn spiritual discrimination from the fruits of my own experience.

We are all in the same boat in this regard. The ego mixes with our authentic aspiration and longing, leaving most of us with an inevitable and very human psychological maze to find our way through on our spiritual journey. It is not *bad* or *wrong* that this should be so. It is simply what is.

The Problem with Playing It Safe

I was raised with an insurance mentality. My parents regularly put small quantities of money in the bank for my retirement before I was in kindergarten. Door locks were always double- or triple-checked. The gas tank was refilled at three-quarters full, and the term "prenuptial agreement" was part of my vocabulary by age seven, even though there was no great money to protect. I've even had a gravestone reserved for me for many years! My family made decisions based upon a programmed plan about what a successful human life looked like. It is not that many of these things are not highly beneficial, but they also arise because we are afraid.

We are afraid because we know we are going to die and we do not understand our true identity. The reality of the inevitable annihilation of the body is present within every human being. We are trained to preserve the body, and this is a wonderful thing: human experience is utterly precious and represents a specific transformational possibility not available in the same way to any other life-form. A glitch in this fine plan, however, is the body-mind identification's belief that *it* is who *we* are, and that if *it* becomes threatened then we are going to die.

This fear represents a significant obstacle in our relationship to the spiritual teacher. This relationship is *not* safe, and is not supposed to be. It is, by its very nature, the ultimate dangerous relationship; it is designed to eradicate our current (unenlightened) sense of identification, which is exclusively attached to the body-mind. The spiritual master is employed for his capacity to dismantle, decompose, and annihilate the limited self-perception that keeps us suffering needlessly.

There was a movement in the nineties among a certain group of Zen Buddhists who wanted to make the student-teacher path more safe and secure. Their perspective was understandable. There had been a couple of major scandals—the temptation to abuse power even among learned teachers had become evident. Senior practitioners did not want sincere or potential students of Zen to lose faith in the tradition, so they worked out a code of ethics with which all teachers of Zen were expected to comply. But this approach severely limits the range of the teacher's behavior in relationship to the student—a range that may include behaviors that are as unconventional as they are indispensable to what the student needs in order to take the next step in his or her growth.

We are again benefited by defining for ourselves what we want and what we are asking for from the spiritual teacher, and continually revisiting and reevaluating our intention. The function of relative spiritual authority—particularly that of wise religious leaders—is to augment our wisdom without any excessive demands or risks. The function of a relative relationship to absolute authority is to be pulled in the direction of greater risk, with the option of ducking out through the back door at any moment. The function of absolute relationship to absolute authority is to tear apart the safety net and to toss us to the mercy of God's divine piranhas, whose function it is to eat up all false perception and leave only the bare bones of naked reality.

In other words, we get exactly what we pay for, in terms of what kind of teacher we attract and the quality of relationship we engage in with a teacher. This does not suggest we should squander our accumulated internal riches on the first shmuru who comes our way; only that when the right moment arrives, we must be willing to pay for the goods offered. In the words of Jeanne de Salzmann, a disciple of Gurdjieff, "You must pay dearly . . . pay a lot, and pay immediately, pay in advance. Pay with yourself. By sincere, conscientious, disinterested efforts. The more you are prepared to pay without economizing, without cheating, without any falsification, the more you will receive."[5]

I recently spoke at a conference abroad. A man stood up on his soapbox and aggressively argued the danger of the spiritual teacher for all the reasons we will consider in the following chapter.

"Have you ever had a teacher who has committed the atrocities you so eloquently speak of?" I asked him, searching for the source of his reactivity.

"No, I don't want one. I wouldn't hang out with those teachers. I see straight through them. I know myself far too well to fall for such con men."

"Exactly," I told him. "So why are you spending all your energy protesting dangerous teachers? Be the kind of disciple who will under no circumstances attract such a teacher and you have no reason to worry."

The late Swami Muktananda, disciple of Swami Nityananda of Ganeshpuri, comments on this issue:

> *Why do false Gurus exist? It is our own fault. We choose our Gurus just as we choose our politicians. The false Guru market is growing because the false disciple market is growing. Because of his blind selfishness, a false Guru drowns people, and because of his blind selfishness and wrong understanding, a false disciple gets trapped. A true disciple would never be trapped by a false Guru. False disciples want a Guru from whom they can attain something cheaply and easily. They want a Guru who can give them instant samadhi. They do not want a Guru who follows discipline and self-control; they want one who will participate in their own licentious lives. They want a Guru who is just like they are.*[6]

While sincere students of the path may at first attract myriad false teachers in their initial period of discernment training, over time, conscious students are highly unlikely to attract false teachers, by and large because such teachers will not be attractive to them. If we want somebody to reflect the beauty of our own ego and to gently urge us toward self-love, a good therapist or rabbi will do. If we want more, we have to be prepared to dig into the pockets of our soul and present the teacher with the currency of our willingness to give ourselves over to the process of transformation.

Spiritual life is dangerous. That is the point. It is reserved for the rare few who dare to step off the ten-thousand-foot cliff. To get the goods, you have to put your money on the table—all of it. The people who have succeeded in spiritual life—the great ones whom the uncompromising spiritual student longs to emulate— have risked *everything,* especially who they think they are.

Conscious discipleship, or studenthood, means taking intelligent risks with the help of our increasing discernment, and then taking responsibility for the outcome. The position of *conscious discipleship* is a powerful one, a possibility that undermines our sense of victimization by false gurus and empowers us as mature students of transformation and Truth.

"GURU" AS A FOUR-LETTER WORD
Criticisms of Spiritual Teachers, and the Nature of Spiritual Scandals

The very term "guru" has become so pejorative
that it really means "bad spiritual teacher."
—ROBERT FRAGER

Oftentimes the term *guru* brings up an automatic association with "danger" or "scandal." Therefore, before understanding how we recognize an authentic teacher, let us first look directly into the headlights of common criticisms of spiritual teachers, and how spiritual scandals arise.

As if my first shaman were not inappropriate enough, the next was no better, although it took me a while to realize it. Aleph was also an artist. His paintings were not of cosmic penises and snakes slithering up the vaginal openings of goddesses, but they did capture precisely the erotic aspect of an eggplant, a melon, a fence, a tomato. Or they carried the penetrating presence of a deer's eyes, a lion's footprint, the waiting dawn. When he invited me to El Salvador to study with him at his ranch, I was eager to apprentice to his knowledge, and the play of Eros between us was palpable:

I was ready to engage on all levels. But Aleph had left out one minor detail when he proposed that I move into his studio for an indefinite period of time, and I used more than one four-letter word to describe what I thought of him when I learned of his wife and three children.

I have spent time with gurus who are living proof that "guru" can be a four-letter word. Nobody has asked me to drink cyanide-laced Kool-Aid, but I have been offered plenty of other substances. And most of the other types of crimes of power and passion one hears about in relation to purported gurus have been perpetrated upon me and people I know. After seventeen years of experience on four continents and ten years of research in the field, I am both personally and professionally all too familiar with the shocking abuses of power that have been committed in the name of spirituality. Yet I cannot denounce spiritual teachers in general, any more than I can denounce all men simply because I have had some less-than-desirable lovers.

Of course, my adventures with Central American shamans were benign compared to the far greater horrors that have taken place when spiritual authority is abused; among the most notable of these in recent decades were Jonestown and Heaven's Gate. In both cases, a charismatic leader convinced his followers— through what could be labeled "magical thinking"—to commit suicide. Such phenomena reveal the presence of both abusive authoritarianism and blind submission. Our psyches' attraction to both of these qualities means that the same storyline repeatedly plays out across all cultures and in every era. And it will continue to do so.

Since Jonestown, thousands of spiritual groups and leaders have risen and fallen—a few exemplary; many benign, though weak; and a small percentage truly dangerous. When people point to Jonestown and comparable tragedies as proof that all spiritual teachers are suspect, I see what I call "the Jim Jones mentality" at work. This is not a solid argument.

Gurus Are Old-Fashioned

Many people who argue against hierarchy in the world of spirituality contend that the concept of the spiritual master as imported from Eastern traditions is old-fashioned or cannot be adapted to Western culture. They say that we in the West have evolved beyond such a dated system of authoritarian rule. Within spiritual circles in the United States, the argument can be summed up as follows: the gurus came West in the sixties; we believed in them; we gave them our money, lives, and souls, and they betrayed us with scandals involving money, sex, and power. We have passed through that immature phase and are now ready for the new: the great return to rugged spiritual individualism.

But isn't this a classic example of American thought? We burned through thousands of years of tradition as quickly as we are burning through all the rest of the world's natural resources. While we may be surpassing prior technological advances in human history, we hardly outshine our predecessors in terms of spiritual wisdom.

We in the West have been attempting the mass importation of foreign ideals into a culture that is not prepared to support them, and many think such ideals won't work here. But compare this to the Jews arriving in the desert land of what is now Israel and deciding to develop forests and fields and sources of water. Their vision did not manifest in ten or thirty or even a hundred years, but over millennia. To claim we have outgrown the ancient idea of the student-teacher relationship after only a few decades' experience with it is equivalent to the Israelis planting a thousand seeds and then quickly abandoning the land, complaining that because there are not yet forests, nothing will ever grow.

It seems to me less that we are failing, and more that we are learning—and just beginning to, at that! Transplanting spiritual traditions and practices from one culture to another is likely a job of several generations—a labor of love and patience in which we each fulfill the small part we are called upon to play. While we naturally evaluate the process as we go along, it is unwise to jump to quick conclusions about any aspect of it. The traditions we are trying to import require appreciation of their perennial wisdom and careful study of how the knowledge and wisdom they embody can best be integrated into a radically different land. In order to effectively transport Eastern traditions onto Western soil, we are each called upon to fulfill the function of "gnostic intermediaries": individuals who, according to Carl Jung, "personally incorporate the wisdom of a tradition and can then speak directly from their own experience and understanding into the language and concepts of the culture to which they wish to communicate."[1]

Why Spiritual Scandals Occur

> *If people think that a Guru is unnecessary, it is either because certain Gurus make themselves useless in people's eyes, or because people don't understand the Guru, and so misuse him and then consider him useless.*
> —SWAMI MUKTANANDA

To discuss why spiritual scandals arise, we must consider both the conscious and unconscious motivations that prompt teachers and students to become involved in them. Some psychological tendencies exist in what is truly a blind spot—a latent area of the psyche that is difficult to access because of intense early psychological conditioning. Many other motivations, however, remain unconscious; we choose to be blind toward them in order to gain or maintain certain advantages or comforts. In the words of the contemporary Jesuit master Anthony de Mello, "People don't really want to be cured. What they want is relief; a cure is painful."

For example, a spiritual teacher may convince himself that he is having sex with his disciple's attractive thirteen-year-old daughter in order to transfer special spiritual energies that will enhance her *kundalini* awakening. If he looked just slightly deeper, he might discover that he is simply attracted to her sexually. A married woman who is in love with her teacher might wish to seduce him, but she feels guilty about betraying her husband. So she tells herself that if she receives her teacher's spiritual energy through sex, she can use it to heal her strained marriage. The line between what we allow to be conscious and what remains unconscious, between integrity and the lack of it, can be hard to discern. As Zen master Jakusho Kwong Roshi said, "A crazy and a sage are pretty close."

Scandalous Teachers

It is rarely the case that a teacher consciously instigates a spiritual scandal, but when this does occur, the deeply troubled individual wishes to gain some advantage in the arenas of power, money, or sex by playing on other peoples' weaknesses. Badly wounded in childhood, usually by severe abuse or neglect, they feel that they have been cheated so much in life that they now have every right to take advantage of others. The far end of this continuum includes individuals like Adolf Hitler and Jim Jones, whose consciences appear to have been so twisted they perceived their abuses to be virtuous.

More relevant to us as spiritual students or potential students is the multitude of unconscious factors stemming from complex psychological tendencies that prompt teachers to use their positions of power to manipulate and coerce. Many charismatic leaders who abuse their positions have been badly abused in childhood— whether physically, emotionally, or sexually—and whereas these wounds may have resulted in catalyzing a deep transformation, or perhaps the ability to function as the "wounded healer," the unhealed wounds do emerge and often cause damage in the teachers' relationships with their students. In other cases, a family history of intellectual or artistic genius psychologically disposes leaders to an exaggerated sense of their own greatness.

Any given teacher's spiritual realization may be authentic and accurate on the level at which it has occurred, but there may be higher—or deeper—levels at which the individual is not realized. There may also be psychological realms in which the person is ill equipped to handle all the responsibilities that come with realization.

The interplay between psychology and spirituality is important, because while a balanced psychological makeup is not necessary to achieve high degrees of spiritual realization, significant psychological awareness is usually required to be able to function as a spiritual teacher. If one's knowledge of nonduality, for example, is reasonably stabilized but issues around sexuality are not, when students come to the teacher with strong erotic transference (a subject to be discussed in depth in subsequent chapters), the teacher may not have a sufficiently grounded psychological matrix to see the transference for what it is—or the strength to turn it back over to the student, as is appropriate.

This is what has occurred, and still occurs, when Eastern teachers—celibate monks in particular—come to the West to share the teachings of their respective traditions. Their cultural background and monastic training have in no way prepared them for the onslaught of explicit sexual energy they encounter in Western countries. They have spent years in celibate monasteries and been raised in cultures in which sexuality is notably more repressed than it is in the West. Often, they have unconsciously chosen the monastic life to escape the world rather than to be fully in relationship with it. Now they find themselves suddenly exoticized and eroticized by Western women who are culturally trained to seek power, knowledge, position, and recognition through their sexuality. Nothing in these monks' background has prepared them for the desires, temptations, and even perversions that may arise when they finally encounter these forces.

There is clearly nothing morally or even spiritually "wrong" with these surprising sexual feelings, but those who have taken vows of celibacy are in a difficult bind: their reputation and vows are at odds with their desire to know a different kind of freedom and pleasure. Scandals commonly take place when they attempt to sustain their status as celibate monks while at the same time engaging in sexual experimentation.

Difficulties often arise when someone who has "woken up" begins to gather a body of students—and then his or her realization fades. *Satoris,* or experiences of enlightenment, are not uncommon. They may last for a moment, a week, a couple of months, or even some years. One of the most striking examples is found in the life of the Chilean writer-sage Claudio Naranjo. Naranjo's initial experience of enlightenment lasted three years. When several months had passed after his initial awakening and it appeared to be a steady state, he allowed students, an organization, and a teaching system to arise around him as a vehicle to share what he had to offer. Then slowly—and at first imperceptibly—Naranjo's enlightenment began to fade. According to his own testimony, at first he fervently resisted recognizing what was happening. Finally his own greater honor won out, and he dismantled his organization and denounced his own authenticity as a spiritual master.[2] How few people would be willing to act with such integrity amid so much temptation for the ego! After three years of realization, with an ego fully educated in the subtleties of profound mystical experience and the "walk and talk" of enlightenment, it would be easy to maintain one's "greatness" in the eyes of others—and even in one's own.

More often than not, individuals who have experienced some degree of realization or awakening and have begun to teach will unconsciously use that realization as their link to power. They remain blind to the depths still hidden within them; these will not surface until they are willing to surrender what they know and accept what they do not know.

Scandalous Students

A scandalous student is someone who places him- or herself in a circumstance that is corrupt or is likely to become so, or who continues to remain in such a situation in order to extract unconscious payoffs. In almost all cases, the sincere student stays with a corrupt teacher because he or she has areas of blindness that the teacher feeds or reflects. The principle of mutual complicity—known colloquially as "It takes two to tango" and psychologically as "intersubjectivity"—suggests that both student and teacher participate in any instance of corruption. If the student is unwilling to support the teacher's corruption, the teacher has no one to corrupt. Similarly, many teachers have dormant tendencies toward psychological blindness that are awakened by the student's own parallel corruption or weakness. The student and teacher legitimately need each other to fulfill their respective student-teacher functions, but they also "need" each other to create a circumstance of scandalous behavior. The situation is entirely interrelational.

We usually gain some unconscious benefit from negative situations, even if it is only the comfort of what is familiar. And if we look deeply enough, long enough, and honestly enough, we will eventually discover the roots of our own complicit involvement in these situations.

Maintaining the role of victim to a spiritual teacher is thus a strategy of avoidance on the part of the scandalous student. At the deepest level of our experience, we understand that we are never victims of anything. At the same time, our false, egoic identity thrives on victimization. The ego gets to experience the delicious sensations of vengefulness, justification for its own weaknesses, the solace of others' sympathy, the safety of separating itself by making another person wrong and itself right, and the comfort of staying in its own familiar, cozy little box of false identity.

Conscious discipleship, on the other hand, involves a commitment to learning how to step outside the familiar and comfortable stance of perceiving oneself as the victim of the teacher—or of anyone or anything else.

The Question of Hierarchy

If you want to make friends in elite spiritual circles, telling people you have a spiritual teacher is not the way to do it. Walking into a party and telling someone you have a guru is like saying, "I'm a heroin addict." Dead silence.

"What's his name?" your listener may venture.

"Lee Lozowick."

"I've never heard of him," she replies, and it is as if her lack of knowledge about my teacher invalidates him. The continuing awkward silence in the room implies: *Oh, you're still adhering to that dinosaur model of patriarchal hierarchy. Don't worry—you'll grow out of it.*

One of the main arguments against the spiritual student-teacher relationship is that it's hierarchical, as if hierarchy itself is inherently unethical or objectively dangerous. In progressive circles, the rule is that hierarchy is out, egalitarianism is in; vertical relationships are out, horizontal ones are in; gurus are out, mentors and inner gurus are in; God is out, and either the goddess Gaia or science (depending upon your particular circle) are in; patriarchy is out, and matriarchy (in principle) is in.

The fact is, not only does culture past and present function according to hierarchical structures, but so do nature, the psyche, the process of spiritual unfolding, and the domains of the gods and goddesses. Whether we accept it as spiritually correct or not, hierarchy occurs on all evolutionary levels and in all domains. Ken Wilber prefers to use the term *holarchy* to describe this continuum of nested spheres in which "each senior level transcends and includes, or enfolds and embraces, its juniors."[3]

An amusing example of the organic creation of hierarchical structures can be found in the "rules of the road" in India. Ironically, cows sit at the top of the structure—both because they cannot be moved from the middle of the road and because in Hindu philosophy the cow is, at least theoretically, considered sacred. Next come trucks. They are massive, take up most of the road, emit copious toxic fumes that push everyone as far back as can be managed, and honk relentlessly, warning all others on the road that they are coming and will not change their course for any human or animal (except cows). Next are the cars. They belong to the rich, and in all but the largest cities are an indication of wealth and power—the nicer the car, the more prominent its position on the road. Next down are auto rickshaws—three-wheeled taxis run on motors. Down further are bicycle rickshaws, followed by bicycles, oxcarts, pedestrians, and then animals other than cows. Whereas from a politically correct standpoint such a structure is classist, elitist, and "Homo sapiens–centric," from a practical standpoint it simply works. When everyone understands the hierarchy, it provides a relatively workable structure amid the chaos of India's roads.

It strikes me as incongruous that whereas we generally accept (though perhaps not without complaining) that corporations are run hierarchically or that the United States government and the royal family of England are hierarchical structures, when it comes to spiritual mastery, the guru cannot be the guru. He must be a "spiritual friend," a "mentor," a "guide." He must be a "non-teacher teacher." Writers on spirituality who want their books to sell often take great pains to assure their readers that when they talk about their teachers they are not talking about gurus (as if this necessarily implies negative authority), but instead about egalitarian, non-authoritarian relationships between elder and younger peers.

I find this approach potentially problematic, for wearing the clothes and talking the talk of non-hierarchy excuses both leaders and followers from directly confronting the inevitable, ever-present dynamics of hierarchy. Egalitarianism is a worthy ideal, as well as a natural reaction to centuries of misused authoritarian power. But it has not proven itself successful in society, much less in the training grounds of the soul, which often require the teacher to fill the role of head trainer.

Perhaps the true source of our concern is that we realize *manipulative* and unconscious hierarchy is dangerous; *abusive* hierarchy is unethical; and *uninformed* hierarchy warrants caution. Our collective rebellion against spiritual hierarchy is perhaps an expression of fear: fear that we and our loved ones do not have the strength or clarity to navigate the hierarchy in a way that will help us and not hurt us. While many of us intuit the possibility of informed guidance from spiritual authority figures, we also know that most of them are shaped by the same forces we are.

I suggest it is the abuse and corruption of hierarchy that are problematic, not hierarchy itself.

When We Get Burned

I have met many individuals who have turned against the possibility of authentic spiritual authority because they have been disappointed by someone who was widely professed to be a world-class master or guru. When one such person's guru died, he turned his devotion to the guru's lineage holder—as his teacher had requested—only to find his new guru to be unworthy of his devotion. Thus he came to be suspicious of both. Another, famed for bringing his guru to the attention of the world, came to oppose spiritual authority when the guru told him he must break up with his male lover, or at least keep the relationship hidden, if he wanted to continue to publicly represent her message. One woman's guru convinced her that she was his divine counterpart; he then had a baby with her and proceeded to enact this drama with several other women in the group. Another woman was devastated when her guru insisted his disciples not have children, then later changed his view when she was beyond childbearing age. A young man traveled all the way to India to meet the man he was certain was his guru, only to find he could not visit with him because the man was in jail: he had murdered two dozen disciples.

In each of these instances, the student felt badly betrayed, and understandably so. Stories like these reveal how much responsibility a spiritual authority has, not only to his or her own students but to the reputation of all spiritual authorities. Although conscious discipleship requires 100 percent responsibility on the part of the student, the teacher is also 100 percent responsible. The difference is that a teacher's weaknesses and mistakes affect not only all who come into his or her sphere of influence but also the reputation of all spiritual authority.

Ultimately we cannot know the destiny of any given student, but the apparent tragedy of such errors and betrayals is that potentially exceptional disciples turn away from the student-teacher relationship, effectively "throwing out the baby with the bathwater." This is where the great questions, complexities, and karmic aspects of these challenging situations come flooding in: How did such mature and psychologically developed individuals find themselves in the hands of weak spiritual masters? Was it a karmic inevitability? Was it the result of some blind spot in the disciple? In the master? A mutually complicit need? Since the true disciple will continue to develop in spite of the teacher's weaknesses—even drawing upon her teacher's limitations to enhance her own understanding—we cannot even objectively conclude that such situations are tragedies at all.

Fortunately in many cases, students do not permanently turn away from the student-teacher relationship, although it may take many years to heal wounds and establish the possibility of trusting another. Individuals who have had these shattering experiences find themselves in a very tender bind. They have been touched by the teacher. They know the taste of that possibility and are continually reminded of it through its absence. Yet they remain conflicted about whether they want to risk so much again. Their lives may feel meaningless or empty without the presence of a master, yet they have become understandably doubtful about whether they can recover the trust and faith they once had.

Betrayal or disillusionment in the student-teacher relationship can be particularly devastating because it usually involves love—love that has not died *and* that the student cannot afford to maintain in this relationship. This love and its loss do not function according to the laws of reason but in accordance with their own mandates. When I meet people suffering in this way, my deep wish is that they will eventually discover a way to separate a bad experience with a particular spiritual teacher from the whole field of spiritual mastery. I also wish for them to understand that the love they experienced with their teacher was not unreal, but instead that the relationship was unhealthy. I wish that if it is their eventual destiny or highest possibility to again find themselves in the company of authentic spiritual mastery, they will be open enough to receive its offering.

What Is Scandalous?

Exactly what constitutes a scandal is a question that is as crucial as it is unanswerable. Aside from the most extreme instances, it is not as clear-cut a line as we might think. There are many contemporary examples of teachers whom some highly intelligent students and scholars consider to be indisputably scandalous; meanwhile, other equally worthy evaluators of spiritual authority consider these same individuals to be masters of rare capacity. In fact, most of the popular teachers of our time are met with a similar mix of adulation and demonization.

The problem with judging as scandalous the behavior of those considered masters is that we are judging *their* behavior from the perspective of *our* morality or degree of understanding. Ken Wilber describes this beautifully when he says, "It is not what a person says, but the level from which they say it, that determines the truth of a spiritual statement."[4] If I grew up with alcoholic parents and was significantly wounded by the symptoms of their disease, a teacher who drinks is likely to be completely unacceptable to me; I may take this behavior as a definitive sign that the teacher's mastery is less than complete. If, on the other hand, alcohol has never been an issue in my life, and I have a teacher who drinks a little bit—or even a lot—but demonstrates integrity and consistency over time, alcohol may be of only minor relevance to me. I may even find it a relief.

In the West, alcohol, tobacco, and other substances have been labeled as unspiritual and addictive, yet great masters throughout the ages have used them, at times for their work with students and at times for no apparent reason whatsoever. In many tantric traditions, alcohol, meat, and other intoxicants are employed as aids in processes of transformation and alchemy. Indigenous people of many cultures have used hallucinogenic plants for psychological and spiritual healing and growth. Some people consider this to be immoral; others find it natural and of no concern. Some people have no problem with a Native American chief using psychoactive plants but find it immoral when a Caucasian Advaita Vedantist uses them. Is using these substances neurotic? Divine? Both? Neither?

I do not side with any of these perspectives. I suggest only that our concepts of right and wrong, moral and immoral, sacred and profane are themselves worthy of ruthless scrutiny. Scandals are not determined in a court of spiritual martial law. It would be much easier for all of us if there were an objective source who could impartially dictate which teachers and groups were corrupt and which were not, but the subtleties of soul work can only be evaluated circumstance by circumstance, moment by moment, individual by individual.

Fool's Gold

Rumi said, "Fool's gold exists because there is real gold." While we may find ourselves outraged by spiritual scandals that appear in the media, the fact remains that there have been false teachers in every age and every culture. We might consider false prophets as decoys whose function is to deter the masses of less-determined seekers so that only those who are serious enough to pay the price for true mastery will discover it.

Sometimes I wonder why real gold can't be made available to all. Why do so many wannabe gurus peddle false metal? I have no concrete answer, but I do know that whether we like it or not, conscious union with God (or Truth, or Reality) does not come at a discount. Everyone is certainly *entitled* to real gold, but the rule of the game seems to be that it only comes to those who are willing to mine it.

Perhaps the work of learning to discover what a real master is—making the effort to understand and appreciate what the master represents and why such a function would exist—is an essential aspect of the path itself.

We can study the field of mastery and our own unconsciousness deeply enough that we are, at least intellectually, prepared to meet a genuine master. Or we can learn what genuine mastery is by meeting as many false masters as possible.

I chose the latter option, though for some it is less advisable: run-ins with false masters can jade you to the possibility of there being a true one. I often wonder what makes the difference between the person who discounts all masters because of a few false prophets and the one who just keeps looking, the latter figuring it to be the result of some weakness within himself—or a stroke of bad luck—that he hasn't yet found what he is looking for. In *Spiritual Choices,* John Welwood writes, "To discount all spiritual masters because of the behavior of charlatans or misguided teachers is as unprofitable as refusing to use money because there are counterfeit bills in circulation."[5]

After two fake shamans and a dozen other random healers, shmurus, and wannabe teachers, I had every justification to stop looking for a master altogether and instead worship the inner guru long before I was prepared to do so. But I had not given up, even on those who fell short. Each revealed a hidden void within me that drew me to that particular situation. By the time I reached India, as my story will later reveal, I was dubious about whether I could find a real master. I did not know if my true intention was strong enough to outweigh the gross unconscious forces that still dominated me, but I felt strong in what I had learned about false masters. And I figured if I played the lottery long enough—lifetimes if necessary—my number was bound to come up. Will we cease to believe diamonds exist simply because, so far, all we could afford were rhinestones?

4

THE IMPORTANCE OF A
SPIRITUAL TEACHER

*I still don't have much interest in Buddhism, in any
formal way. I bumped into a man in California who
impressed me. His name was Joshu Sazaki Roshi, and he
happened to be a Rinzai monk. I often say that if the man
I met had been say, a professor of physics in Heidelberg, I
would have learned German and studied physics.*
—LEONARD COHEN

A man cannot awaken by himself.
—P. D. OUSPENSKY

I never really questioned whether or not I needed a teacher.
Although I had the Buddha's dictate "Be a lamp unto thyself"
taped to my bathroom mirror, I knew I needed somebody
to teach me *how* to be a lamp before I would ever be able to light
my own way. I couldn't even seem to figure out how to get the
plug into the socket without getting shocked.

Ringo seemed like a decent choice. The circumstances of our
meeting had been anything but ordinary. I was camping out at a
traditional Native American Sun Dance hosted by the Piscataway
tribe in Maryland. Extending over a period of several days, the
ritual included intensive fasting, dancing, sweat lodges, prayer, and
bodily sacrifice on the part of the dancers. Hour by hour, through
cold rain and scorching sun, we stood beneath the sacred, circular
arbor of trees as the native brothers starved, chanted, and prayed

themselves into a visionary state. Once they attained this state, the chief pierced their chests with carved wooden pegs. Then ropes were attached to the pegs, and the men were hung from a sacred tree that transported their prayers to Father Sky until the pegs gave way and the men fell to the ground. A well-kept secret, the Sun Dance is a powerful indigenous rite still practiced in a few places in the Americas.

So there I was in the sacred arbor, not having eaten for three days, floating on indigenous magic energies and new ideas, eyes closed and lost in self-aggrandizing fantasies about becoming the girlfriend of one of the sexy native sun-dancers. I opened my eyes to an uncommon sight. The single Caucasian dancer came forward, and instead of having the wooden pegs put through his chest like the other dancers, he had the chief pierce his back, then attach the pegs to ropes that held a buffalo skull. The man whom I was later to know as Ringo dragged the skull around the arbor for more than an hour. Streams of blood dripped down his back, and sweat poured from his gray sideburns. Finally, the skin broke and Ringo collapsed to the ground, unconscious.

The event was so compelling and my empathy so strong that I formed a mysterious emotional attraction to this older man, whom I experienced not as a lover but as "grandfather." Later that night, as we all, exhausted, settled in around the sacred fire, I shared my feelings with Ringo. He responded with gratitude and delight, saying he had never had any children or grandchildren, and as he was getting older longed to pass on the fruits of five-plus decades of spiritual pilgrimage. During that span he had traveled as a wandering monk of no order, meeting and living with spiritual leaders and peace activists throughout the United States, Canada, Mexico, and Europe and serving up a message of interfaith peace and political activism. Ringo asked if I would like to join his pilgrimage and said if I did, he would introduce me to his friends and mentors: great Native American chiefs, Zen Buddhist monks and nuns, disciples of great gurus, Quaker and Amish leaders, and esoteric interfaith eccentrics such as himself.

Here was my chance! Finally I would meet many great masters, and surely among them I would find one who was rightfully mine. I corresponded with Ringo throughout my final months at university, once visiting him as he fasted for "forty days or until death" on the steps of the Capitol Building in Washington, DC, to protest the unjust jailing of Native American activist Leonard Peltier. Then four days before my college graduation, at which President George H. W. Bush was scheduled to speak (the only politically correct option was to boycott it—my poor parents!), Ringo picked me up in his '68 Ford van and we headed out to conquer the teacher circuit.

Thus began my Summer of Torment in the Van from Hell with my Grandfather from Hades. We met some impressive teachers, and some who were far less than impressive—the one I was traveling with being among the least inspiring of all. Ringo was one of these non-teacher teachers, the kind who, when somebody refers to him as a teacher, gives the person a knowing look of feigned modesty that implies: "The only Teacher is the Self. I am just a mirror." The problem with their non-teacherhood is that they feel free to abdicate any and all responsibility for mutually complicit projections to their "non-disciples."

Jun Sun, on the other hand, was a noble woman. Once a radical Japanese biker-chick now turned Buddhist, Jun Yasuda belonged to the Nipponzan Myohoji order of monks and nuns. They practiced peace through fasting, *long* walks (up to ten thousand miles!), chanting, and building magnificent monuments called *pagodas* that housed small bits of the actual Buddha's relics. Unlike non-teacher teachers, Jun Sun was a nun who served a teaching function only when others insisted upon learning from her. Still, she took full responsibility for her relationship with those who came to be near her and partake in her wisdom.

We stayed with Jun Sun while our van was immobilized at a local farm awaiting engine replacement by a schizophrenic friend of Ringo's who'd offered to do it for free. This took some time, and the weeks we spent with Jun Sun were unlike any others I had experienced. She defined discipline. We awoke at four each morning for mantra repetition in Japanese. We weren't required to get up, however; rather, *she* got up and chanted for an hour and a half while pounding a three-foot-high drum. And since the dorm-style open loft where we slept was in the temple-barn she used for this purpose, we had a choice: we could listen from the comfort of our toasty sleeping bags to somebody else gain the benefits of spiritual practice, or we could get up and join her.

Next we ate a scant breakfast of unsweetened porridge. Then we spent a twelve-hour day constructing a peace pagoda, with fifteen-minute breaks for lunch and rice crackers. At day's end, following a Japanese-style "bath" taken in a rusty oil can heated by a wood fire—which nearly left me with third-degree burns—there was another hour of chanting and then another meal. By eight at night, the rest of us were useless, and Jun Sun, the only one who could still function, cleaned the dishes, emptied the pots in the outhouses, and answered her correspondence by candlelight. In the same way as the Hassidic Jews "went to the rabbi to watch him tie his shoes," we subjected ourselves to Japanese temple torture watching Jun Sun work without complaint, relate to all people with fairness and concern, and serve her tradition unswervingly. It would be hard to find a disciple of the path with greater nobility.

Jun Sun convinced me that I was capable of completing a ten-thousand-mile, ten-month peace walk from Panama City, throughout Central America, to Washington, DC, to protest some important cause I can't remember but that seemed vital at the time. To think that I, former Jewish American Princess turned interfaith martyr protestor, could complete such a feat was so exhilarating that I committed to the project. I recall being *unable* to comprehend why my mother was so upset when I told her. Didn't she support *peace?* Other teachers that summer were less impressive, or at least their disciples were. In one instance, we visited a fancy ashram. When we approached the *guru seva* (service) desk to sign up for our daily service activity, the staff took one look at me and said I was not dressed well enough to work anywhere but the dish room. Later that summer, when I was "camping" in a car I had borrowed from a friend so I could get a twenty-four-hour reprieve from Ringo, the ashram police woke me at three in the morning and forced me to leave the two-thousand-car parking lot, even though morning meditation started one hour later.

At another ashram I befriended a cute, barefoot, orange-robed Hindu monk who gave me a banana and told me, "This is not a banana." He had me plenty confused until I learned that he had given me a gift of *prasad,* which contained a special blessing by the master.

The Quakers didn't lie, cheat, or steal; nor did the Amish. And aside from making the usual sexual advances toward young Western women, the Native Americans provided fascinating teachings.

Why Do We Need a Teacher?

Upon completing a three-year intensive course with Buddhist scholar and teacher Reggie Ray, students received Ray's final words of farewell: "If you don't meet a spiritual teacher and *go all the way with them,* you are wasting your life."

"Only in a time as confused as ours could one think that the teacher–student relationship—an archetypal and sacred form—exists as an option rather than as a necessary requirement, a station on the way," writes William Patrick Patterson in *Struggle of the Magicians.*[1]

Statements such as these may sound unusually strong, yet I believe that very few, if any, of us will be capable of navigating the full journey of the soul's unfolding without guidance during significant parts of our journey. Whether the teacher assumes the traditional authoritative role of guru or functions as a guide and mentor; whether teachers call themselves that at all; or whether the relationship lasts a few years or a lifetime, the student or disciple's unwavering commitment to that individual for as long as the teacher–student relationship lasts is a primary factor in the success of his or her spiritual unfolding.

There are several pragmatic reasons why a teacher's help is invaluable to one who dares strive toward the fulfillment of his or her highest human potential.

Mastery of Any Skill Requires Apprenticeship

People are willing to turn to master teachers in nearly every arena of life. From woodworking to philosophy to music, the individual who wishes to excel will seek out either a master or a specialist to apprentice to. Yet many people still believe that mastery of the human soul can be achieved alone. Rudolph Steiner disagrees:

> *In principle, of course, self-instruction is possible. Equally, every human being, provided he reaches a certain stage of clairvoyance, can discover spiritual truths for himself, but this would be a much more lengthy path. . . . The teacher is the friend, the counselor, one who has already*

lived through esoteric experiences and now helps the pupils to do so themselves. . . . It is simply a question of what is required for shortening the path to the highest truths.[2]

Returning to the consideration of hierarchy, it seems to me quite natural to place oneself in the position of junior to a senior if one hopes to achieve excellence in the area of the senior's mastery. Only in the spiritual student–teacher relationship does this present a problem for many people. This may be because the individual who submits his or her ego to a person whose function is to undermine that very ego is committing an intentional act of egoic suicide. It is easier to denounce the function of the true guru than face the fear that arises at this prospect.

Transmission

Light my lamp from your lamp, O Sadguru. . . . Remove the darkness covering my heart.
—JYOTA SE JYOTA

Transmission may be the most important function of the authentic teacher, especially if he or she serves as an absolute authority. Transmission is a rare and extraordinary process whereby the master's fire becomes ignited in the disciple. Transmission could be defined as the passing-on of living truth from one human being to another, such that the student receives an imprint or impression of that truth in his or her own bodily cellular structure. To a lesser extent, this is true even with a relative authority. Anything and everything the teacher does is secondary to this function. The Eastern teachings say that the guru is the tangent point to the Divine, likened to a vortex that can effectively receive and direct the powerful energies that are commonly referred to as Truth,

Enlightenment, or God. All human beings live in the Ocean of Mercy, drowning in grace, yet they are so immersed in it that they cannot perceive it. The student asks to borrow the teacher's eyes, to be taught how to see the essential Truth of our very nature. The teacher is only transmitting knowledge of the greater Self to the smaller self, but until we know that in and through every cell of our body, we are missing the opportunity to come into contact with who we really are at the deepest level.

Another way to consider transmission is as an awakening of grace within us. The seed of knowledge or truth lies dormant inside every individual, and the true teacher has the capacity to water that seed through the power of his or her own awakening. As that seed begins to grow on its own, the teacher's function becomes that of attentive gardener, offering feedback and guidance, and providing practices that will ensure the best conditions and nourishment.

Some traditions suggest that transmission occurs very early in the student-teacher relationship, at first sight or even upon first hearing the teacher's name. Teachers often first visit their students in dreams. It is said that spiritual teacher Da Free John, for example, had such detailed dreams and visions of his teacher, Swami Rudrananda (Rudy), before meeting him that he was moved to fly across the country. Guided solely by clues contained in his visions, he located the tiny antiques store Rudy owned in Manhattan. Some people's experience of transmission includes energetic phenomena, unprecedented insights, or unfamiliar bodily sensations; yet it is equally common not to experience such dramatic events. Neither the presence nor absence of such phenomena has any direct relationship to the depth or power of the transmission.

The principle of transparency is yet another means by which to consider the function of transmission. A teacher whose karmic and psychological tendencies have been purified and who has learned to disengage from the mechanism of the ego becomes *transparent* to energies of the Divine or Truth. When the disciple sees him- or herself in the reflection of this clean "mirror," his or her own obstructions become apparent.

Although transmission may well occur in the initial stages of discipleship, many commonly mistake this exchange for the end of the path. It is not. Instead, it is akin to a near-death experience: we are shown the light and the many paths leading to it, then return to our body, gifted with the opportunity to travel the arduous road to that light on our own two feet.

An Externalized Conscience

"The guru is none other than your very Self," it is said. We need the teacher because we do not yet know ourselves to be one and the same as the universal Self: the Self of all beings. Until we are consciously able to access that Self in a consistent way, the teacher serves as an externalized Self. We are drawn to the company and guidance of the teacher because he or she is the expression of the Self that represents the Truth in all things, including ourselves.

As a representative of the Self, the teacher instructs us in how we would live if we abided as the Self. If we allow ourselves to be ruthlessly honest, most of us know which of our words, actions, deeds, and relationships are in integrity and which are not—but it is difficult to be that honest, and sometimes hard to see so clearly. Thus we use the teacher as a stand-in for the unwavering conscience and integrity we find so difficult to maintain without guidance.

Eventually the externalized conscience becomes internalized, and the teacher—now as our own conscience—follows us every-where, is alive within us. At times this can be a real nuisance (acting from conscience all the time can be most inconvenient), but such clarity is the gift of gifts. The teacher in this form becomes our greatest ally, companion, and protection against our own internal corruption.

Feedback

The authentic teacher provides the student with a reliable source of feedback, both inner and outer. As the teacher is increasingly present in our own conscience, we are progressively better able to receive his or her guidance from a source within ourselves. Yet "the ego is hiding behind every corner," as Sufi master Irina Tweedie has said. Even strong practitioners, and teachers themselves, have blind spots and obstructions to clarity. Self-deception abounds in spiritual life as much, if not more, than in any other area of life, and long-term "do-it-yourself" seekers are often the ones most in need of external feedback.

During a recent lecture I gave, a man stood up and eloquently made the all-too-familiar argument that we are all enlightened. I agreed with him, then asked him if he was fully aware of that condition in himself at all times, not only through his intellect but in and through his body. He said he was. Yet as I listened to and watched him, I knew that whatever his definition of enlightenment was, I did not want to be near it. Later in the day we had a chance to talk, or rather *he* had a chance to launch into a narcissistic monologue about failures in his relationships and work life, general dissatisfaction, loneliness, and depression. Although hardships visit everybody—even those we call "enlightened"— his life in no way evidenced his self-proclaimed realization. He had conducted his spiritual life in isolation and had spent years intellectually "dharmacizing" away his own blindness.

The external teacher is a source of protection of the Self against the ego. Even for those who are many years into the path, the diehard's spiritual life consists of a continual fluctuation between egoic rule and abidance in the Self—what Gurdjieff described as "the battle of yes and no." The authentic teacher is consistently and solely on the side of the Self, and thus will reliably provide feedback regarding the individual's egoic tendencies toward self-deception.

A Tailor-Made Path

The true teacher can provide a tailor-made path for the student. This is particularly true when the teacher has a manageable number of students. The teacher sees clearly each student's strengths and limitations, and works to empower and reinforce the former and defuse the latter. Such guidance may express itself in an infinite number of ways. The teacher may assign specific projects (my teacher, for example, asked me to write my first book shortly after I came to live at his ashram). He or she may suggest that the student cohabitate or work with particular configurations of people—an exercise that can serve to teach love, to hold a mirror to the student's unpleasant tendencies, or to "infect" the student with the sensibilities of stronger practitioners. Or teachers may recommend specific meditation or contemplation exercises, or offer ideas about how to practice viewing a particular situation from a radically distinct perspective. The authentic teacher is like a business manager for the soul. He or she takes inventory, rearranges the stock, and makes suggestions that help the business of the Self run more effectively and efficiently.

For teachers who have thousands of students, such personal guidance is often not available. This presents a unique challenge for the dedicated student, for in such a situation, even while the student dutifully sings the teacher's praises and does prescribed practices, it is easy to "hide out" from the ego. It is similarly challenging to work with teachers who do not talk or do not give linear instructions. Strong students will be able to discover what the teacher wants from them even under such conditions, but weak ones may labor under false assumptions and misinterpreted directions.

A Useful Construct

Once while I was living in India, I was sitting in the *darshan* (literally, "sighting of the master") of a great saint, and in an instant I realized the nature of the guru game. There he was, up in front, playing the role of exalted saint; beside him were his attendants playing their role as ascetic renunciates who serve the saint; and here we were, playing our role as students and disciples. And it was all perfect. It was obvious that there was not an iota of difference between us—not really—yet each role was a necessary part of the whole. I was struck by a corollary in the human body: the heart is necessary to the functioning of the mind, which is necessary to the functioning of the hand. None of these separate physical systems is greater or lesser; all are beautifully interwoven into a unit of perfect functioning. The construct of the student-teacher relationship operates precisely according to this principle.

In the teachings of Advaita Vedanta, so often misinterpreted and watered down in the West, the nondual reality is that there is essentially no separation between "me" and "you," and therefore there can ultimately be no teacher and no student. However, since most of us do not abide in that realization, the student-teacher relationship becomes a useful construct to engage in as we move closer to this realization. In other words, we consciously choose to play the role of student in relationship to one who consciously chooses to play the role of teacher; ultimately, we realize there is no such thing as student or teacher.

Though a unique personality in individual form, the spiritual teacher, especially the guru, is none other than the true Self of the disciple—for there is only one Self. The difference is that the guru knows this while the disciple does not. The disciple perceives this Self in the guru and intuits it to be true in him or her, but remains stuck in the illusion of separation. This is the result of the seemingly endless baggage of karma and psychological conditioning that has left the student with a view of him- or herself and the world that is based almost entirely upon projected and subjective belief systems. And what better way to reveal this underlying drama than to engage in a relationship that reflects the individual's Self and the separation from that Self at the same time, exposing and magnifying every obstacle blocking the realization of that union?

The trick to "winning" this game of guru and disciple is that it must be fully engaged in order to work. In fact, it works optimally when the players immerse themselves so fully in it that they forget they are playing a game. A World Cup competitor doesn't go on the pitch telling himself that if at halftime his team isn't winning, he will forfeit the game. An Olympic gymnast doesn't decide in the middle of a triple back flip that she cannot follow through because she doesn't trust the coach who assured her she can. Similarly, the student-teacher relationship does not find its fulfillment when the student has one foot out the door, knowing that he or she will leave as soon as the going gets tough.

Speculation or intellectual arguments for or against the guru-principle cannot touch the experience of the played game, any more than philosophies of love can create a good marriage. The student-teacher construct is a serious game in which each player, fully committed to his or her function on the "team," practices in relationship to the whole with the shared aim of winning, while knowing that it is ultimately a game. The difference is that in this game, the desired outcome is one of total loss of egoic identification—in which everything is gained.

The Guru versus the Guru Function

> *Westerners, who are educated to be individualists, have difficulty in grasping the concept that the guru is not so much a person as a function. Of course, the guru function depends for its performance on a human being, and therefore it always occurs in the context of a particular personality. This is what is the most confusing to Western students, who tend to get caught up in externals.*
> —GEORG FEUERSTEIN

For the Western mind, making a distinction between the guru or teacher and what he or she represents is one of the most fertile grounds for misunderstanding. In *The Nine Stages of Spiritual Apprenticeship,* Greg Bogart writes: "In the Indian yogic traditions . . . the guru-principle is identified with the power to bestow grace. Thus, the guru is one through whom the concealed power and splendor of Shiva, the Supreme Light, is revealed and unfolded within a human being."[3]

Yet the external teacher is a person, replete with all of the physical, mental, and psychic functioning that is inherent in human nature. He or she has a personality—largely conditioned—which we may or may not like. It is wonderful if we happen to appreciate, or even adore, the person who is the teacher, for it is liable to make our experience of spiritual practice—our *sadhana*—much more enjoyable. But it is not a requirement that our personality resonate with the teacher's. What we need to look at is whether or not the teacher's personality impedes the work of dismantling the stronghold of our ego and empowering our Self—the teacher's true function.

The individual who assumes a guru function will not necessarily be a flawless role model, and is unlikely to fulfill the role of good parent, psychologist, personal confidant, or friend. If these functions should arise, they are simply icing on the cake—icing that can become a significant impediment to the student when its appealing flavor causes her to forget she came for the cake!

The situation contains a paradox: although the guru function is entirely distinct from the person and personality of the guru, it is at the same time intricately related to it. The function always exists, but it manifests in connection with the guru's physical person. Because it takes the form of a human being, it will not only include that person's personality but will, under optimal circumstances, utilize that very personality—with all its quirks, eccentricities, and even psychological conditioning—as the vehicle for transmitting its teaching. Because of this, there will be times when it requires sharp discernment to distinguish between when the guru function is making use of the teacher's quirks, eccentricities, and psychological conditioning, and when the teacher is just having a very human moment that has nothing to do with his or her teaching function.

Years after all the shamans and shmurus were mere memories, I found myself riding in the back seat of a car on the way to Denver with my teacher, Lee, and another of his students, who were in the front. I had not seen Lee in several months, and I found his physical presence was eliciting waves of tenderness within my body. Silent expressions of gratitude and praise for the universal, formless master arose spontaneously as I lightly chatted with him about this and that: who had married whom at the ashram, who had split up, where Lee had traveled, what I was writing about. The paradox of the guru versus the guru-principle was mind-bogglingly obvious in that moment. What on earth did the surge of feeling arising within me have to do with the guy sitting in the front seat? How could his simple presence melt my heart like hot lava dissolving glaciers formed from icy fear and cumulated sorrow?

Now where does an individual raised in a culture of Western scientism file *that* experience? The ego's filing system only allows for measurable categories, defined by a beginning and an end. The file cabinet of the Mystery is reserved for what can be perceived only by that which operates outside egoic logic, and this is why most logical arguments against the guru cannot be refuted. Lines of reasoning are convincing when argued in the domain of logic, yet on the non-egoic level they are irrelevant. Transpersonal psychology refers to this phenomenon as "state specific" knowledge, and Ken Wilber refers to the "three eyes"—the eye of the flesh, the eye of the mind, and the eye of the spirit—to describe the various levels or channels of perception through which it is possible to perceive any given experience. Both the guru and the guru function can be intellectually addressed through observable experience (the eye of the flesh) and the intellect (the eye of the mind), but can only be *understood* through the eye of the spirit.

The guru function is, in essence, impersonal. It is not *about* the personality of the student or the teacher. This is a particularly difficult reality for the student to wrap his or her mind around when the felt experience of the relationship between student and teacher is the most deeply personal bond of love and reverence he or she has ever known. Yet the impersonal nature of this bond is precisely why it produces a quality of feeling and a possibility of exchange rarely found elsewhere in the human experience. It is nothing other than God loving God, Truth loving Truth. In the words of Daniel Moran, "Absolute intimacy is absolutely impersonal."

When one appreciates the true nature of the guru function, commonly heard statements such as "The guru model is outdated" or "I don't believe in gurus" become patently absurd. The guru as the guru function cannot be falsified or outdated. It simply *is*. It is a function existing within the universe that is at times embodied by a particular human being, known as the teacher or the guru. *The Guru Gita* says:

> *The guru-principle moves and moves not. It is far as well as near. It is inside everything as well as outside everything.*[4]

The timeless function of transmission—which is what we should *really* be considering when we talk about the teacher—cannot be outdated. Instead of denouncing the concept and dismissing the possibility of its functioning in our lives, we can focus our attention on embodying our discipleship in such a way that it elicits the true guru function from even a would-be guru.

The ability to facilitate in another human being the soul's becoming is the greatest of skills, and the one who carries it out is worthy of humble reverence.

Ego and Annihilation

Lying deep at the bottom of even the most justified and intelligent arguments against the spiritual teacher is an all-encompassing terror of ego annihilation. So terrified is the ego of dying to its exclusive identification with who we are, and so clever are its ways, that more often than not, this fear camouflages itself in the guise of a bulletproof dharmic intellect whose classically favored target is the spiritual teacher. For the authentic teacher is ego's archenemy.

———— ⟨⟩ ————

My spiritual "grandfather" Ringo was a professional spiritual vagabond. For decades, he settled down only occasionally for a few weeks or a rare few months at a time. He served whomever he was visiting. He spread information from group to group, and even between faiths. He protested, fasted, provided manual labor, or did whatever else the people he visited needed. He was acquainted with many of the great spiritual leaders of our time, but knew none of them well. He toasted many, but bowed to none. The similarities between us blinded me from the limitations of our shared lifestyle. While it can be fruitful to receive this type of spiritual pollination, teacher-hopping and path-hopping are rarely ideal for optimal spiritual development. This is because the self-preserving egoic dynamic is rarely exposed when an individual is not in a consistent and ongoing relationship with others.

On the outside Ringo was indeed saintly, and it was this righteous exterior, and the benefits people enjoyed from his persona, which buffered him from receiving the feedback he needed to build a saintly interior. Behind closed doors, however—in this case, the doors of our beaten-up van and the confines of our unconventional "relationship"—he was somebody else. He was ego's slave rather than its master.

As the months went by in our endlessly breaking-down vehicle, Ringo often woke me in the middle of the night, needing to process some interaction that had occurred between us the previous day. It took months for me to figure out that in spite of an overt agreement to have a strictly platonic relationship, in his fantasy we were lovers and he was the victim of unrequited love. It took several more years—until long after I had left his company—for me to admit that in spite of our overt agreement, I had unconsciously sought to elicit that response from him. It was a selfish way to seek validation from a projected father figure; and it was more selfish yet to then frustrate that same father figure as an act of revenge for not providing that validation.

In a classic construct of mutual complicity (which I had no understanding of at the time), I was doing more than my part to sustain the dynamic. A conventional argument against spiritual authority would contend that Ringo was the person in the position of power. It was *his* responsibility, not mine, to hold integrity for both of us. But as fine as that philosophy might look on paper, it didn't work in practice. We were two egos cleverly disguised—one under the cloak of humble teacher, unseen and unappreciated in his genius by his foremost disciple; the other donned in the garment of star disciple, idealized and criticized alike by a psychologically confused master. Both of us were suffering victims, our egos having a glorious homecoming as long-forgotten childhood dynamics replayed themselves in the spiritual arena, providing the warped comfort of familiarity that only ego can fully cherish.

Ego is a function that arises as a condition of incarnation. Its primary purpose is to ensure the survival of the human organism. Its programming begins sometime after conception; within the first years of the child's life, it forms a set of core belief systems about who it is, what life is like, and what to expect from its incarnation as a body. Ego constructs series upon series of conceptual boxes in order to organize and manage the life of its host in an otherwise chaotic world.

Difficulties arise when the ego identifies itself with the body, which is what ego is designed to do, prior to intensive spiritual work. Since its function is survival, it then proceeds to base all activity, thoughts, and actions upon what will ensure the survival of the particular home (body) it inhabits. In so doing, it separates itself from everyone else and, in a subtle and unconscious way, begins to perceive the world as an adversary best conquered through control, ownership, and manipulation. Ironically, however, its only real adversary is itself.

When what existed prior to ego awakens within an individual, he or she often experiences a tremendous shift in inner perception. Something long dormant begins to yearn to know and be known. Thus begins the spiritual search. Sometimes one is fully conscious of the process; at other times it takes place entirely beneath the surface. In the latter case, people often say, "In retrospect, I realize I was always searching for God/Truth but didn't have the language to describe it."

When all elements are in their rightful place, in accordance with mysterious timing in the Universe, the meeting with the teacher occurs. It is as if the longing of the soul finally prevails over the heaviness of the ego—even if only for a short while. The teacher comes on the scene to respond to the call that has been held in the soul's throat until now.

However, because the teacher is simultaneously the benefactor and nemesis of the ego, the relationship with the teacher will always include elements of push-pull, love-hate. For the teacher does not love the student's exterior or personality, but the soul itself, which has been crying to be set free since its birth or even earlier. It knows that only a true teacher, and what he or she represents, can free it. Though the would-be student has been starving for the appearance of the teacher, that very presence represents the greatest egoic threat he or she has ever faced. This is the student's great bind.

The teacher's job description is to conquer egoic identification while knowing very well that at the crucial junctures of its defeat, the student will view him or her with scrutiny, doubt, criticism, and mistrust. From the student's ego's perspective, the teacher is trying to kill the student. Yet when a crack appears in the protective walls of ego and, through the vehicle of the teacher, something of God or Truth seeps in, the student experiences an unparalleled quality of love. Thus the drama of life with the teacher is one of alternating longing and resistance, love and war, emptiness and fulfillment. It is the only way it can be, a perspective important to maintain during more difficult periods.

"The Ramana Maharshi Argument"

"The Ramana Maharshi Argument," as I have playfully come to refer to this rather serious phenomenon of ego, is the argument that surely we can reach the highest fulfillment of spiritual realization without a teacher's help because Ramana Maharshi—perhaps the most revered Indian saint of the twentieth century—appears to have done it alone. I have heard this reasoning well over a hundred times, both in India and in the West. To say that we can do it because Ramana Maharshi did it is like saying that we can become President of the United States because Barack Obama did it. Of course it is *conceivable:* essentially, there are no greater or lesser human beings on this planet. But how realistic is it?

Furthermore, it is questionable whether Ramana Maharshi actually did achieve realization alone. He maintained that the great Mount Arunachala in Tiruvannamalai, India, was his guru. It is certainly an uncommon experience for a mountain to be a guru, but the point is that Ramana's existence was singular in every way. He underwent an exceptionally rare experience in which he—all but accidentally—fell into a profound realization that endured, found his guru in a mountain, and went on to deepen his realization in ways that only one in millions, if not not billions, can do.

The Ramana Maharshi argument is yet another of ego's cleverly disguised pleas for autonomy. Armed with the shield of spiritual *dharma,* ego nobly recites to itself scriptural justifications for its own position. Versions of the Ramana Maharshi argument are many. The "Advaita Shuffle," a term coined by Andrew Cohen, is the phenomenon in which the teachings of Advaita Vedanta, or nonduality, are co-opted to relieve the seeker of self-responsibility, spiritual practice, and the need to exhibit human integrity within duality. Other people use the Buddha's "Be a lamp unto thyself";

still others use the classic inner-guru argument to support ego's insistence upon autonomy. In the spiritual game, ego can and will attempt to co-opt anything and everything to maintain its own advantage and dominance. The reason we employ a teacher is to even the playing field.

As a former resident of Ramana's native Tiruvannamalai, I find that the Ramana Maharshi argument brings back wistful memories. Living there, however, was downright irritating. There we all were at the cowshed tea shop, everybody walking around blissed out, gesturing with a subtle nod of the head toward the large hill where Ramana spent many decades living in caves.

"It's the mountain," they'd say, as if we all shared a magic key to bliss. "It's the mountain."

And then, more often than not, they would offer listeners—unsolicited—their profound understanding of the Self: that the Self and the Mountain are One; that Ramana and the Mountain are One; and therefore, by implication, They and the Mountain and Ramana are One. That was well enough, save that in spite of everybody's Oneness, not a single person could convey what either Ramana or the magic mountain were able to communicate.

Prakash was a man whom I came to meet later in my search, but I will speak of him here, as he was such a striking illustration of this principle. Of Dutch descent, Prakash had lived in the village of Tiruvannamalai for more than fifty years. He'd come to India in his early twenties in search of God. Having lived through unspeakable horrors in concentration camps as a child, Prakash had suffered severe trauma from which he never recovered. When he set off looking for God, he went with the unconscious desire to be relieved of his inner torment. He was born with the IQ of a genius, took a great interest in Hindu philosophy, and within a decade had knowledge of Hindu and Sanskrit scriptures unparalleled by any other Western individuals I have met, save one.

Prakash revealed his unwavering dedication to awakening through a daily discipline that would cause most people to recoil if they even *heard* of it. I spent many months living in one of the cottages in the compound Prakash had inherited from a great Vedanta scholar who'd respected Prakash's genius, and I occasionally joined him for parts of his daily schedule. It included approximately four hours of meditation, three hours of worship, three to four hours of study, and a three-hour circumambulation of sacred Mount Arunachala—barefoot—in both desert heat and rain.

But Prakash practiced in a vacuum. He had no living teacher, not even a mentor. Having been so brutally betrayed by people in positions of authority in his childhood, he was unable to give his trust to another. The abuses he'd endured had resulted in such complex psychological defense structures that only a teacher of supremely skillful means would have had the mastery required to penetrate those barricades and let something of God or Truth in. Prakash was a prisoner of his own fortress, and in keeping everything else out, he also excluded his longed-for God. I am not suggesting here that every human being in every walk of life should have a spiritual teacher, but Prakash is an example of someone in great need of one. His single (conscious) intention was to know God, yet he was unable to open to the realization of his own Oneness without a teacher's help.

Prakash's story is a moving one. I often felt heartbroken watching this old man practice his painstaking disciplines day after day. He was aware of growing into old age without achieving his goal, and I knew that the odds of its fulfillment were slim. He had never availed himself of a source of external feedback; instead, believing he possessed superior knowledge, he had created a fortress of intellect to which no one could gain access. His distrust of other human beings made him impervious even to the softly spoken suggestions of friends such as myself.

Years later, I learned that Prakash had suffered a severe stroke. Who knows? Perhaps this was the final gift of grace that shattered his intellectual brilliance and allowed the brilliance of God to reign within him.

The spiritual teacher is not necessary if one does not aspire to fulfill one's highest human potential in God or Truth. But if this is your goal, I must recommend conscious discipleship in relationship with a deep and sincere openness to spiritual guidance. In the words of the late Robert Ennis from a personal interview:

> *The chances of someone awakening without a teacher are like the chances of getting pregnant without a partner. The spiritual teacher is the partner that is necessary for spiritual birth. Not too many immaculate conceptions happen.*

Having attempted many years of spiritual life without a teacher and spent many more as a spiritual vagabond, and having received the benefits of working with an authentic teacher, I cannot imagine why one would dare to cross the shark-infested waters of the ego without a boatman. Still, if you have not experienced an authentic teacher—or have had encounters with teachers who could not keep the boat afloat or tossed you overboard to fend for yourself—it is wholly understandable that you would be skeptical about finding a trustworthy teacher. But I remain convinced that true disciples in search of an authentic teacher will eventually find their way to the one they seek.

———— ∞ ————

As we have seen in these initial chapters, the search for a spiritual teacher is as problematic as it is, in many cases, vital. The solution lies in cultivating those qualities in ourselves as students that will attract an authentic teacher into our lives if that is our karmic destiny, while prompting both our own and our teacher's growth.

5

Basic Psychological Sanity

We have to face what psychologists call the shadow. Not
knowledge of the ultimate Self, but of one's own self—of
one's contradictions and unconsciousness. We cannot avoid
that, but we will go through that with much more success
if our aim is not only to feel better, but to find God.
—Arnaud Desjardins

Given the pervasive nature of commonplace psycho-
pathology among Western spiritualists, it is fair to
say that Ringo and I were both fairly insane from
a psychological perspective. The primary difference was that he
had already been through fifty years of psychological training
and spiritual austerities and was still insane, whereas I had only
pledged two. If ever there was a situation so stressful as to bring
to the surface the broadest spectrum of unconscious neuroses in
the shortest period of time, we were in it. Not only was I cooped
up in a van for three months with a lusty pseudo-grandfather
who wanted my body even while he insisted he was serving the
evolution of my soul, I was once again unconsciously using some
imagined spiritual benefactor to try to augment a very low level
of self-esteem. And to top it all off, the damned van wouldn't

drive fifty miles without losing the tailpipe, snapping the fan belt, leaking transmission fluids, overheating, or contracting some previously unheard-of van virus.

So more than half the time we had allotted to meeting the country's leading spiritual figures was instead spent befriending auto mechanics in garages across America. The van's favorite time to break seemed to be Saturday evenings at about seven o'clock, just in time to be stuck in the garage parking lot until the new workweek began. I distracted myself with whatever educational possibilities the local strip mall had to offer—taking resigned interest in picture-framing, doughnut-frying, commercial photo-processing, and generic haircuts—while desperately waiting for the auto-repair shop to open on Monday morning. Meanwhile, Ringo would accuse me (accurately) of avoiding intimacy and turning away from a spiritually conscious relationship with him. Desperate for company other than the man who was prompting me to engage the most twisted thoughts I had ever entertained, I spent hours watching the mechanics with feigned fascination, extracting a dose of pathetic self-esteem from their lecherous attentions.

When we ran out of *my* money (Ringo didn't carry any because he trusted the universe to provide for us), we would canvass the local neighborhoods, knocking on doors and asking people if they needed their trees trimmed at a rate no one but beggars would offer. If they agreed, I would stand anxiously below as my spiritual grandfather with a weak heart tied spikes to his shoes and a chainsaw to his belt, and then used ropes to scale tall trees and trim the branches. I collected the debris.

I knew I had descended completely from the upper world when I found myself in a shopping-mall bathroom taking a sponge bath with brown paper towels and washing my hair in the sink with hand soap. As I squatted under the automatic hand dryer, a woman with two bleached-blonde braids and a Bud Light half-shirt revealing stretch marks and a beer belly walked in. A half-smile of pity bordering on compassion crossed her face, as she saw in me the reflection of her own sense of being lost and confused.

"I'd never myself have thought to use one of those things as a hair dryer—pretty clever," she said in an attempt to console me.

"It's amazing what you think up when you need it."

"You got kids?"

"No."

"Why doesn't your husband buy you a hair dryer?"

"Don't have one."

"Don't have a husband or don't have a hair dryer?"

"Neither."

"Where are you from?"

"Michigan, most recently."

"Where are you headed?"

"New England."

"You live up there?"

"No."

"Where *do* you live?"

"Nowhere at the moment."

"I really feel sorry for you, kid. Wish I could take you home with me, but I'm on the road myself. I'll keep you in my prayers." I knew she meant it.

Ringo maintained that the van was manifesting the psychological difficulties between us. In retrospect, perhaps he was right, but by that point I was so nauseated by his ongoing litany of New Age psychobabble—thoroughly unverified by his behavior—that each cosmic comment was an assault to my fragile psychological armor.

"If the van is so expressive of our dynamic," I finally told him, "why don't we just spend our remaining savings, fix it up for good, and finally get AAA coverage? Then every time our screwed-up psychological dynamic empties the gas tank in the middle of the night on a desert highway because you've insisted *faith* will take us as far as we need to go, I won't be stuck with an eighty-dollar towing bill because you don't have any money or insurance—because you don't want to 'buy into the system.'"

Ringo informed me I was being verbally abusive.

Three maddening months later, we pulled up to the entrance of Monument Valley Navajo Tribal Park. We had already been through two engines (one rebuilt by our schizophrenic friend), four fan belts, two new carburetors, two timing belts, one radiator, and nine new tires, and we had run out of gas a sum total of eleven times. This tally says nothing of the emotional breakdown and damage accrued. Yet one singular factor was distinct that evening, and it would provide the human grace to allow me to finally write a new ending to a script I had endlessly replayed throughout my thus far twenty-two years.

In the camping area while Ringo was at the registration office, I encountered what looked like the four dazzling Dutch nymphs we had seen before at the Sun Dance at Big Mountain Navajo land, in Arizona. The vision of those young women—so much like myself but with the brightness of innocence as yet untainted—is still the closest I have come to seeing angels in my life. No more than three minutes after we exchanged names, I invited them to camp with us. Apparently seeing the desperation in my pleading eyes, they quickly agreed. I told them to jump in the back of the van and we would sneak them into the campground for free.

When Ringo came back, I introduced him to the young women and informed him they were going to camp with us.

"You what?!" he raged. "You told them they could come in *my* van without asking *me?*" Then he treated me to his standard rant about how I put everything else before him, how I was always inviting people to hang out with us because I didn't want to be alone with him, how I was using him for his spiritual knowledge, what an ungrateful bitch I was, and what a spoiled spiritual whore I had become.

But this time it was different. The resident angels lent me their vision. In an instant, I saw clearly. And how much I saw! In that poignant moment of my young-woman's life, I understood the undeniable relationship between my psychological childhood dynamic with my father and how it had recycled itself into every other subsequent relationship with men—shamans, professors, boyfriends, and gurus included. In a flash, I saw that my supposed Godlife had been cleverly and unconsciously constructed entirely around the avoidance of my childhood wounds. And this had caused my unconscious to recreate them in endless repetition with every spiritual teacher I met. In one exacting vision, I knew the course of my future had irrevocably changed.

At the campsite we ran into two Native American men who had also been at the Sun Dance: a muscular, tattooed ex-con who had just been released from prison and had gone to the dance as an "initiation" back into the world; and an elder chief who, through his work in prisons, had escorted him there. They were headed to Oakland, California, and since my whole future had been cancelled in a moment and had yet to be replaced with anything else, I begged for a ride.

The evening came, and the ex-con and the angels and the spiritual grandfather headed out into the valley to drum and chant. The temptation to feel lost and betrayed evaporated in the hot wind, which carried snippets of their song to the campsite. There, I slowly moved my life's possessions—four boxes of clothing and one of books—to the backseat of my new companions' twice-wrecked Edsel.

Internally, I placed myself on an indefinite hiatus from travel until I successfully completed a course of therapy. I hoped this would reveal to me what I had been running from all my life under the guise of wild spiritual escapades. For I knew then beyond a shadow of a doubt that I would not meet the awaited teacher until I had gotten a basic grip on my own aberrant relationship to authority figures.

I slept outside on the ground in the center of a circle made up of the bodies of my precious Scandinavian angels and breathtaking rock formations. The smoke of Ringo's fuming complaints about me seeped from his van, only to be absorbed by the vastness of the valley and the clarity of my resolve. Well before daybreak, as we sped up I-5 toward Oakland, I was lounging in the back seat of the car of my new Native American friends, listening to them practice Hopi healing chants.

I was distinctly aware that if I fell off the face of the earth then, nobody would have known where I was, and it would have been weeks before anybody knew for certain I had disappeared.

What Is Psychological Sanity?

My studenthood with Ringo failed because neither of us had the psychological matrix necessary to absorb the toxicity in the relationship. The concept of psychological sanity, as used here, suggests that we have some basic handle on our mommy-daddy issues. Between teacher and student (with the teacher ideally holding the greater part), there needs to be enough combined psychological sanity to keep both on track, moving toward their shared aim.

The issue of what constitutes psychological sanity in a *student* is somewhat straightforward: it means the student knows her own psychological dynamic well enough, and has done enough healing within herself, that she does not impede her capacity to receive help. It means she does not freak out every time the teacher speaks or does not speak to her, and that she has some capacity to sustain tension, live in relationship with others, and receive spiritual teachings without spending every spare moment absorbed in emotional crisis. It does not mean, however, that she is free from neurosis. Nobody is. And even if the student is not sufficiently prepared to engage in a relationship with the teacher now, this by no means suggests he or she will be unable to do so in the future after more psychological preparation.

Psychological sanity on the part of the *teacher,* on the other hand, is significantly more difficult to evaluate. The teacher should have his issues around Mommy, Daddy, money, sex, power, and intimacy settled enough so his blindness in any of these areas does not poison his relationship with students.

When a teacher is balanced in these areas, we would expect her to be financially generous, to maintain honesty and integrity in the realm of intimacy, to be emotionally available to students, and not to misuse her position of power to exploit others even in the subtlest of ways. Still, the job of the authentic teacher is to undermine egoic identification in her students, and doing so may require employing means that do not *appear* to reflect psychological soundness. In other words, once the teacher has come to terms with her own psychological makeup, she may still choose to *act* in ways that do not fit conventionally moralistic ideas of how a teacher should behave. Equally true, of course, is that the teacher may not act in accordance with widely held ideas of psychological sanity because she in fact lacks sanity. Also possible is a teacher whose psychological sanity is questionable but nonetheless provides tremendous service to humanity.

The fulfillment of the student-teacher relationship requires the basic psychological health of each party, but the relationship rarely begins with such health. The reality is that most

students—and a number of teachers—do not begin the relationship entirely sane. The difference between student and teacher
here is that the teacher's responsibility implies that his or her psychological structure will be steady enough so it does not interfere ·
with his or her capacity to serve the student; the responsibility of
the student, in contrast, includes the willingness to actively strive
toward psychological wholeness.

The essential factor is that at least at the beginning, the student is likely to be carrying around significant psychological
baggage, and he or she should not expect the relationship with
the teacher to *feel* the way it ultimately will once that baggage
is unpacked, washed, and pressed. If a suitable education in the
art of discipleship were available within our Western culture, the
student would enter the relationship fully aware that whatever
unfinished business remained lodged in the recesses of his or
her psyche would almost certainly immediately find its way into
the relationship with the teacher. As I suggested in the previous
chapter, the student-teacher dynamic is designed to evoke the
unseen so that it can be made conscious, purified, and no longer
a barrier to the student's full expression of his or her own divinity.

An authentic relationship between teacher and student is one
of *work on Self.* It is not designed to appease psychological weaknesses, but to expose them. Yet even when a student knows this
in principle, when his or her hidden psychological agendas arise,
one of two outcomes are likely:

1. Because the student's agenda is completely unconscious,
    the student can perceive the teacher's behavior as unfair,
    unethical, biased, or even demented.

2. The student may intellectually perceive that his or
    her response to the teacher is the result of his or her

own psychological weakness, but because the teacher's presence cuts so close to the bone, the student may still feel hurt, victimized, or enraged—this even as the student's mind comprehends the teacher's rationale.

A common example of the first principle is that the student sees the teacher as a good father/good mother figure and longs to receive the parenting that went missing in childhood. When the teacher does not provide this, the student is likely to feel jealous, unappreciated, angry, and/or resentful, interpreting the teacher's actions as a personal denial of the student's needs and desires.

The second principle—involving feelings of victimization even in the face of overwhelming conscious evidence to the contrary—provides an invaluable opportunity to engage in self-observation. I will give you an example. Once when I was translating a seminar into Spanish for my teacher, he told a story about me that was not only inaccurate, it made me look like an idiot—and I was the one who had to translate the message! I knew enough to appreciate that he knew *exactly* what he was doing, but it did little to save my squirming ego's face. This experience was appropriate for me at the time, but remember that such tactics can be used or misused by the teacher; for this reason it is imperative that the student cultivate discernment.

Psychological Projection

The issues of psychological projection, transference, and countertransference—terms frequently used in a therapeutic context—are fundamental considerations in the student-teacher relationship. Stated simply, projection and transference are the processes by which the student habitually transfers to or projects upon the teacher both positive and negative dynamics, expectations, and core belief systems that were formed long ago: in utero, at birth, and in childhood. Although these ideas and feelings are not inherent in the present situation or circumstances, the student's projections serve either to recreate the situation that originally caused such feelings in the present circumstance, or to convince him- or herself that this is what is happening. *Countertransference,* in this context, occurs when the teacher responds to transference and projections as if they were true of his or her own person, rather than seeing them for what they are. Countertransference is also used to describe the phenomena of projections and transference on the part of the teacher toward his or her students (e.g., the need to be liked, honored, respected, or seen as sexually attractive).

In the initial stages of the student-teacher relationship, transference is natural—and even sometimes useful. Just as an infant projects qualities of godliness onto the parent in order to feel safe and make sense of an otherwise chaotic and mysterious world, and just as lovers often pass through an initial "honeymoon period" that allows them to bond and form a deep connection that can endure future hardships, the spiritual "infant" may idealize the teacher in the natural course of bonding. This, too, creates some semblance of "safety" as the student enters this second birth into the great unknown world of the Mystery.

Charles Tart suggests:

> *A little bit of projection, if it inspires you to actually do something real and you can later drop the projection, can work out all right. We're a culture that's desperate for spirituality. So we are going to do all sorts of projections. We are going to take somebody from Tibet who's a cook and make him into a guru because he's from Tibet and he looks exotic. If that actually gets us started moving, that's fine. As long as we develop discrimination later, and work*

*on our loss of contact with reality—our projections—it's
not all bad.*

That projections, transference, and countertransference exist is not
a problem. What we do or don't do about them can become problematic. In a private interview, John Welwood described a common
scenario of such projections within spiritual communities:

*Spiritual communities can become a kind of substitute
family, where the teacher is regarded as the good parent,
while the students are striving to be good boys or good
girls, by toeing the party line, trying to please the teacher-
as-parent, or driving themselves to climb the ladder of
spiritual success.*

An idealizing transference is often necessary in order to initially
bond the student to the teacher, but it is essential that it be broken
eventually so the student can appreciate who the teacher really
is and take responsibility for a more mature expression of spiritual practice. (In psychological terms, this process is referred to as
"individuation.") As a mother weans her infant from the breast and
a robin casts her babies from the nest, a skillful teacher knows how
to break the student's transference at just the right time: neither
too early—interfering with the necessary process of bonding—
nor too late, inhibiting the student's process of maturation.

The breaking of transference sometimes occurs slowly and
subtly, through small gestures, comments, or a shift in the quality
of the teacher's attention. More often than not, simple expressions
of humanness on the part of the one who has been bestowed
with godliness break the transference. But if these subtle gestures
are not enough and the student persists, the teacher will break it
in a more dramatic fashion, perhaps acting in ways that are anti-
thetical to what the student expects.

A false teacher, on the other hand, does not consciously break the student's positive transference; instead, the teacher (usually unconsciously) affirms the student's fantasy, which then becomes dismantled when she matures and is able to see who the teacher really is. Behaviors she overlooked before are revealed when the rose-tinted glasses are removed.

Charles Tart believes that most spiritual teachers do not understand transference:

> *The real question about transference is, "How does a teacher work with it so that the student can see what it is, stop recreating it, and enter into a more mature relationship?" But I think very few spiritual teachers really understand much about transference at all.*

Tart writes of a time when he was invited to give a lecture on consciousness to five thousand people at a seminar on human potential. Each time he opened his mouth to say something, people interrupted him with applause. He started to feel very high, thinking, "Wow! I'm really saying wise things here!" Fortunately, he knew enough to challenge his own spiritual pride and acknowledged to himself that it was probably a good lecture, but not *that* good. Only later did he find out that such applause was a technique the group used to build self-esteem. Tart goes on to say that had he not been able to "stalk" himself in that way, he would have inevitably begun to think, "Oh, these are such wonderful people. I want to work with them," and would have chosen to get involved in their organization.

Given the dynamics of countertransference, it is not difficult to understand how even a mature teacher can enjoy the devotion and adoration of his or her students—too much at times. The crucial issue at this point is whether or not teachers are willing and able to be conscious of their own responses, neither acting out based on those responses nor taking advantage of students' projections in any way. A large percentage of scandals arise when a teacher gets carried away by students' positive transference and misuses it to his or her own self-serving, egoic advantage.

The classic example of this is the student who projects an erotic transference onto the teacher. This originates with the student's own desire for power, position, or to be loved or saved, and the teacher takes the transference *personally* and acts accordingly. Ram Dass (Richard Alpert) told me that spiritual groupies used to approach him after talks, begging for a button from his shirt or even a piece of hair. To be willing to look at what is still dark in oneself in the face of that much projected light is a tremendous challenge; it is one to which someone who calls him- or herself a teacher should be capable of rising.

In an authentic student-teacher relationship, the inevitable projection and transference can become our most valuable resources for learning about ourselves. Heinz Kohut's self psychology intentionally engages the inevitable arising of transference onto the psychotherapist as a tool for clients to understand the ways in which they are still dominated by childhood belief systems. Similarly, the psychotherapist uses the arising of countertransference both as an indication of the ways clients are projecting and to glean ever more insight into his or her own psychological dynamics.

The spiritual teacher who is aware of the dynamic of psychological projection is unlikely to work as a therapist will, since the function of such a teacher is entirely distinct from that of a therapist. The spiritual teacher will educate and support conscious disciples to use their own projections and transference as a means toward gaining greater self-knowledge. Students do this by engaging in ruthless self-honesty as they observe with sharp and penetrating detail their relationship to their teacher. Similarly, the circumstance of countertransference provides willing teachers with an exceptional opportunity to see what areas of psychological purification remain incomplete within them—in spite of whatever degree of realization they have attained.

Marion Woodman suggests that the mark of human maturity is the ability to withdraw projections. This sounds like it should be simple to do—it is obvious that the teacher is not Mommy or Daddy. But the sobering and uneasy truth of the matter is that most people live and die completely unaware that they are unremittingly transferring their forgotten past onto the present, dwelling in a certain degree of confusion and suffering because they are unable to withdraw projections they are not even aware they have. Conscious discipleship involves learning to be alert to these inevitable dynamics as they arise so they inform the student, rather than take away from his or her ongoing maturation as a spiritual practitioner.

Working with Psychological Issues

Sometimes it is necessary for the student to engage in some form of therapeutic work *before* working with a teacher, sometimes *while* working with a teacher, and at other times *within the context of the relationship* with a teacher.

If and when a serious spiritual student decides to seek the help of a therapist, it is important to find one who understands—or at the very least respects—the context of the student-teacher relationship and spiritual life in general. Otherwise, the therapist is likely to pathologize the student's relationship to the teacher as neurotic or over-idealizing, or reduce it to a certain earlier stage of psychological development. Such a therapist is likely to believe that when the client/student comes to terms with early childhood issues in relationship to his or her parents, the client will outgrow the need for the teacher. If students who are struggling in relation to their spiritual teachers seek help from such therapists, they are likely to become very confused. This is because similar dynamics are likely to be at work in relationship to both teacher and therapist.

On the other hand, if the timing is right and the therapist is educated in and respectful of teacher-student principles, the therapeutic environment may be an appropriate place for the student to deal with certain psychological dynamics. The student can work out authority issues with the therapist rather than getting entangled more than is necessary in such psychological processes with the teacher. Shifting this therapeutic burden onto the student-teacher relationship interferes with the student's ability to receive the teacher's transmission and demands that the teacher place undue attention on psychological issues.

There may be specific times within the student-teacher relationship when psychological work is more or less appropriate. For example, when one begins work with a teacher, there occurs a natural and almost unavoidable cycle of projection, idealization, and disillusionment. Sometimes it is best to allow this psychological projection to build a certain amount of safety and trust in the relationship with the teacher, before dismantling these projections.

———— ∞ ————

Fulfilling a student-teacher relationship requires basic psychological sanity, yet sometimes necessary healing occurs only through addressing the issues that arise as the relationship with the teacher deepens over time. Even someone who has completed years of successful psychotherapy and then enters into a relationship with a spiritual teacher may be surprised to discover dynamics arising that she thought herself free of. Working through those dynamics allows the student to fulfill his or her relationship with the teacher. It also prepares the student for a fuller relationship with the Divine, and with the infinite human expressions of that Divinity.

CONSCIOUS RELATIONSHIP
TO POWER DYNAMICS

*Over the table there may be smiles and handshakes. But
beneath the table there is the conscious demand of the
teacher that the student see himself for what he is, and
is not. . . . The student's wish for, or better, assumption
of, an "equal" position relative to the teacher is in
fact a psychological strategy to prevent his seeing.*
—WILLIAM PATRICK PATTERSON

There is no sin, there is only childishness.
—ARNAUD DESJARDINS

After having been burned many times by glaringly
unconscious relationships to power dynamics, I
decided to play it safe. I took to practicing Theravada
Buddhism, alternately under the guidance of a "nice Jewish boy"
American mentor and an eighty-year-old German practitioner.
On the one hand, neither of my Buddhist teachers demanded
practices such as absolute trust, spiritual "monogamy," sacrifice, or
anything else that would indicate a "dangerous" discipleship; on
the other hand, they required so little that I could have come in
and told them I was going to kill myself and they probably would
have asked me to simply observe that thought and return to my
breath. I was bored. In fact, many years later after I published
my book *Halfway Up the Mountain,* my former Buddhist teacher
called me at the ashram where I was living to congratulate me on

the book. "Hello," he said on the other end of the phone. "My name is _____."

"I know," I told him. "I was your student for three years." He hadn't noticed nor even registered my name among his many students, until I had written a book!

So though my spiritual practice was completely safe for my ego, with not even a tinge of a distorted hierarchical relationship to power, there wasn't much trace of any type of useful relationship. I was in a shared conundrum with thousands of other spiritual aspirants: how, in a world full of fraudulent teachers, does one decide whether it is worth even trying to find a good one?

The lateral student-teacher relationship is a contradictory notion. Conscious relationship to power dynamics suggests that we neither avoid equalizing them nor try to. Instead, the task is to become aware of the multitude of subtle levels of complexity that are involved in such a relationship—particularly in regard to our own hidden, unconscious agendas, fears, and biases—and learn to make increasingly conscious and mature choices within it.

Returning to the issue of hierarchical relationships discussed in chapter 3, the principle of hierarchy, or "holarchy," as Ken Wilber prefers to call it, is inherent in all things. Hierarchy is a neutral reality—neither good nor bad, right nor wrong—that has gained a bad reputation because of people's own unconsciousness in relationship to it.

At first glance, the construct of the student-teacher relationship appears to imply an essential inequality. This viewpoint represents a misunderstanding of the guru-principle, which is one of ultimate (as opposed to relative) equality. Many people talk about notions of equality and lateral relationships while continuing to project unconscious, subjective dynamics of "power over" or "power under" onto each relationship in their lives. They engage in a continuous dance of subjective relationship, expectations, competition, and psychological games, thus engaging the very power dynamics they imagine themselves to be avoiding by steering clear of spiritual authority.

Although it may not *appear* to do so at first glance, the guru-principle is designed to bring about the realization that the Self of the student is no different from the Self of the teacher. As I've noted, the only difference is that the guru knows this and the disciple does not. In other words, student and teacher are precisely equal in essence, but are in different stages of embodying this realization. The construct of apparent higher and lower is engaged precisely in order for the student to awaken to—within the cells of his or her body, and not only as a concept in mind—the principle of nonduality: that everyone and everything are the same. Equal, indivisible, whole. Apparent inequality is engaged only in order to realize unequivocal equality.

As I mentioned in chapter 4, the student-teacher relationship is a construct designed to fulfill a very specific purpose. It is a game between equals in which one plays the part of teacher and the other the role of student so that both can "win." The student wins liberation—or surrender, depending upon the aim of the given tradition—and the teacher wins through fulfilling a need to serve that awakening or surrender.

Furthermore, as I will discuss in subsequent chapters, often the greatest gurus and teachers are simultaneously students and disciples, and in fact, they identify with their studenthood at an essential level. The issue is not at all one of equality, only of function. For example, my own teacher is simultaneously master and disciple. In relationship to his students, he is teacher; in relationship to his teacher, he is student. The same is true of his own master: on one level he was a great saint, on another a speck of dust upon which *his* master walked—and the same was true of *his* master . . . No individual in the equation holds any objective position of authority, but each serves his or her function in the given hierarchical structure, which ideally works to promote love, service, and awakening.

Understanding Our Unconscious Relationship to Power Dynamics

Our template for relationship to spiritual authority originates from three primary sources: our parents, our cultural/political leaders, and our religious models. Our relationship to our parents is primary among the three, but all are interconnected, as each originates from and intersects with aspects of the other two. When we look closely at the sources of our conditioned beliefs about authority, we will find that our models are often weak, if not highly dysfunctional.

Psychological Authority Figures

The most significant influence determining our relationship to all future authority figures in our lives, including spiritual teachers, is that of our parents. This influence is passed on through both the modeling of authority our parents exemplified and our early childhood relationship to them. This influence is as obvious as it is overlooked. Children will learn to relate to future spiritual authorities in whatever manner they learned to relate to their parents. Given the ever-increasing instances of emotional, physical, and sexual abuse, neglect, and overall lack of healthy parenting even in the case of well-meaning parents, it is no wonder we are often consciously or unconsciously suspicious of spiritual authorities.

The helpless infant perceives Daddy and Mommy as God and Goddess. Serving as representatives of the life-giving force, and functioning as ultimate protectors, the parents are unconsciously endowed with ultimate spiritual authority, a role at which they are destined to fail. The particular degree and quality of that failure will influence all of the child's future relationships to spiritual authority. In conscious parenting, where parental faults are acknowledged and included within the relationship, the child may come to believe that although not all spiritual authorities are respectable, he or she possesses the intuitive ability to discern those who are trustworthy from those who are not. In unconscious parenting, even well-intentioned parents leave the child skeptical as to whether or not spiritual authorities are trustworthy. Abusive parenting, at the far extreme—whether the abuse is overt, emotional, or even in the form of neglect—leaves the child with challenging imprints regarding all forms of authority, though it's possible to overcome these imprints.

I would like to be clear that I am not blaming problematic aspects of spiritual authority on individual parents—for who are parents but grown children conditioned by their own parents? The human ego is a mechanism upon which impressions are imprinted and through which categories are formed, distinctions created, and human survival skills enacted. Even the best of parents will make "mistakes" that result in the child's lack of objectivity in relationship to future authorities. It is an unavoidable aspect of human development that, if made conscious, serves as a foundation for further spiritual development.

Clearly, those who call themselves "teachers" are the product of the same conditioning we all are. Many would-be students are skeptical whether an individual born into a comparably challenging psychic and psychological climate can adequately fulfill an authentic teaching function. They may also question whether they wish to subject themselves to repeating and working through their own childhood dynamics in the hope of discovering something different and better, an outcome well documented in contemporary spirituality.

Would-be teachers should be equally aware of the influence of their own childhood conditioning, which is always present alongside whatever degree of spiritual realization they have attained. If they do not acknowledge and explore this in an ongoing fashion and to a significant degree, chances are good that unconscious power dynamics will arise.

An example of this can be found in one of the many self-proclaimed spiritual teachers I have met. He told me he began teaching because his teacher had instructed him that the right time to become a spiritual teacher is when you feel you need to. This struck me as faulty, if not preposterous, thinking. There are many reasons one might "feel" the need to become a spiritual teacher: among them narcissism, an inflated sense of one's own realization, a desire to feel special, reaction to an unconscious feeling of powerlessness, and the desire to be loved and adored. Because I worked as a psychotherapist for many years, it was obvious to me that this man was clearly not viewing himself objectively and was suffering a kind of humbly guised grandiosity common among would-be messiahs.

A seemingly disproportionate percentage of strong spiritual students and spiritual teachers have experienced notably difficult childhood dynamics. I have observed that, in many cases, traumatic suffering in early childhood itself forces the human being to begin to "awaken" to various degrees—whether it be through dissociating into mystical domains, becoming hyper-alert and attentive to subtle energetic movements (a skill cultivated for the purposes of self-protection), or feeling a strong desire to emerge from the suffering present within his or her family of origin. Ironically, the very individuals who have had challenging relationships to authority in childhood are those most likely to look to spiritual teachers for help, occasionally even becoming spiritual teachers themselves. This in itself is not a problem, only a reminder that we should not assume we have a conscious relationship to power dynamics simply because we find ourselves either in the role of spiritual teacher or serious spiritual aspirant.

As if the situation weren't complex enough, investigation into the lives of the most ardent critics of spiritual authority reveals that, in many cases, these individuals were conditioned in childhood to rebel against it. Such individuals often believe their position against spiritual authority arose through personal reflection and contemplation, but it is more commonly the result of belief systems created in their early years. Perhaps the position arose when a parent taught them never to trust strangers; or when their religion forbade them to worship individuals or icons; or in the moment of disillusionment following the inevitable realization that Daddy and Mommy were not God and Goddess. In such moments, children may vow to guard themselves against future betrayal by anyone who claims any function that hints of externalized power. What appears to be a conscious and mature choice to denounce spiritual authority is more often a cleverly and intelligently disguised unconscious reaction against all external influences.

Authentic spiritual teachers are not meant to be parental substitutes, but this expectation commonly needs to be *unlearned* as we dismantle our projections within the context of the student-teacher relationship. As we mature throughout the course of our lives—ideally outgrowing the conditioned, narrow perspective on power dynamics gained during childhood—we are less likely to experience difficulty in relationship to spiritual authority. Our conditioning no longer forces either a childish relationship to authority or an unconscious rebellion against it. It is at this point that the possibility of conscious discipleship—either in relationship to a formal teacher or even to life itself—becomes a living possibility.

Cultural Authority Figures

Another influential source of conditioned relationship to spiritual authority occurs in the sphere of culture, most notably via our political leaders and the structure of the dominant political model. This extends to individuals and groups such as teachers, doctors, lawmakers, and military figures. In each of these cases and in most countries, regardless of whether they claim to be democratic, socialist, or communist, the model is largely authoritarian and patriarchal—and usually corrupt.

Our cultural models of authority are not ideal role models. They often—overtly or covertly—betray the trust once promised or implied. The virtually unbroken chain of political scandals in all countries leaves us with an implicit understanding that even those individuals endowed with the greatest positions of political power are not trustworthy, and will ultimately choose to serve their own aims rather than those of the people they represent. While it is true that many leaders in positions of power are authentic, the commonality of corruption sustains an environment of constant suspicion. We have little reference for benign or genuine authority.

Delving further into the matter, we discover that the student-teacher relationship runs in direct contradiction to political structures such as communism and democracy. The United States, for example, was settled by Europeans who left their country to escape spiritual and religious suppression. They fled their monarchs and religious authorities to develop a new country based upon the ideals (if not always the realities) of freedom of expression, individual rights, equality, and democracy—a system that directly opposes giving too much power to any single authoritative source. Government was made democratic precisely because the settlers had experienced abuses of authority and repression.

Furthermore, cultural models based on "rugged individualism" are diametrically opposed to the aims of the mystical traditions, which teach that there is no separate self and that the dualistic perception of the individual—whether rugged or compliant—is in fact a false assumption. Other Western countries may run according to models that provide a slightly stronger foundation for the precedent of the student-teacher relationship, but few prepare their citizens to entertain possibilities such as conscious, informed relationship to spiritual authority for the purpose of the soul's evolution.

We can contrast this model with many places in the East that have had an array of leaders who simultaneously served both spiritual and political leadership functions. These countries were founded not upon individualism, but upon service to the collective and to God. The extent to which corruption was generally absent from these systems of authority reflected the degree to which citizens were provided with a cultural foundation of confidence in spiritual authority. Unfortunately, such confidence has been largely lost as a result of both spiritual and political corruption. A parallel in the West may be the lineage of popes who, at least in recent times, have not inspired the trust or allegiance of the masses.

When we review the precedents for cultural models of authority in the Western world, we come to appreciate the fact that, aside from a few indigenous traditions, the West has lacked a larger context for genuine mysticism. Instead, we are taught that it is part and parcel of life that those granted the power to lead a nation will betray us. When this is the case, how would we expect otherwise from spiritual authorities, much less masters and gurus? Yet, while there is no cultural precedent for trusting would-be spiritual teachers, we forsake our own deeper possibilities in our unconscious adherence to the assumption that all spiritual authorities will betray us.

Religious Authority Figures

The problem of authority is the most fundamental
problem that the Christian Church ever faces.
                                        —J. I. PACKER

We have often been disappointed by our religious authority figures. Most individuals raised in Judeo-Christian religions never
feel able to trust, revere, and have a powerful spiritual relationship
with the religious leaders of their churches and temples. More
often the relationship—if there is one—is neutral; at other times it
feels deeply hypocritical to our young and hungry spiritual hearts.

The few Jewish and Christian mystics I have been exposed to
in my adult life (after many years of searching for powerful mystical authorities in all traditions), offer sorely needed role models
of beneficial and benevolent spiritual authority figures: people
such as my partner Marc Gafni, who brought Judaism to life for
me, and Father Bede Griffiths in India, who was a deeply awakened man whose perception of truth crossed religious boundaries.
They are the exception in a time in which terms like "recovering Catholic" and "Bu-Jew" (Buddhist-Jew) have become
catchphrases. Unquestionably, there are a number of mainstream
spiritual authority figures who naturally elicit qualities of respect
and honor, but there remain few who have the capacity to serve
the function of spiritual master or teacher, who can effectively
guide the aspirant toward the Godlife they long for.

More commonly, our models of spiritual authority have been
anything from uninspiring to substandard. This is because, while
their titles suggest wisdom, their function more closely resembles
"sustainer of religion" than that of the true mystic. They serve
as community or religious leaders—creating and maintaining an
environment in which people can congregate, socialize, sustain

their religious conditioning, and take comfort in familiar rituals. They have not trained to be, nor do they profess to be, mystics. Yet the absence of genuine mystics leaves us void of a template for authentic spiritual guidance.

Furthermore, our conditioned relationship to spiritual authority is one of obligatory respect, good manners, and life-less agreement (or silent disagreement): a model paralleling the typical unconscious child-parent dynamic. Thus it is fully under-standable that if we don't deconstruct our conditioned attitudes toward spiritual authority, we will feel wary about the possibility of finding spiritual satisfaction within a student-teacher relation-ship, either within the Judeo-Christian model or outside of it.

In fact, it is precisely because many of our mainstream spiri-tual authorities do not and cannot offer us guidance in esoteric and transformative practices that so many people have turned toward Eastern spiritual traditions, which offer both authentic teachings and practical instruction for the realization of those teachings. There is significant debate as to whether it is right for people to turn away from their original religions in search of esoteric teachings when those original traditions provide esoteric teachings if the right access can be found. My opinion is that the specific tradition through which people find wholeness is less important than the fact they find it. If we are able to heal the wounds of the spirit that have been wrought by our religious upbringing, we may alleviate the need to disavow our roots. We can then make a conscious and mature choice between returning to our own spiritual tradition and looking elsewhere.

Spiritual Childishness versus Spiritual Maturity

A conscious relationship to power dynamics naturally arises as we make the transition from spiritual childishness into spiritual adolescence and finally approach spiritual maturity. This process is a striking parallel to what occurs between parent and child.

Young children are at the mercy of their parents' power. Aware only of a sharp power differential, they do whatever they imagine will draw the parents' love, protection, and regard. Children do not have a conscious relationship to their parents' power until much later in life—if they ever achieve it. Similarly, students new to the path are unaware of the unconscious power dynamics at play in the student-teacher relationship, and enact a range of behaviors they imagine will garner the teacher's love. All such behaviors, of course, are cleverly cloaked in the clothing of spiritual dharma.

"Spiritual puberty" often consists of a rebellion, separation, and subsequent "individuation" in relationship to the spiritual teacher. Much as teenagers suddenly see faults in their parents as they develop their own beliefs and attitudes, students suddenly begin to see how they have given their power away, finding all kinds of faults in the very teachers they once idealized. Many people remain stuck in this developmental phase, refusing to make the transition into spiritual maturity.

However, in the same way children eventually become parents and realize the difficulties their own parents endured—and come to appreciate their parents' wisdom—spiritual maturity or adulthood offers the possibility to relate to the teacher's spiritual knowledge and inherent authority from the perspective of a conscious relationship between adults.

Childish Teachers

There are also childish spiritual teachers. Though they may be sincere in their intent and even authentic in their realizations, they remain at the mercy of still-unintegrated areas of psychological development.

"Guruji" was a classic example of such an individual. I met him during my first week in India. Like so many teachers I had encountered before and have since (only now, I don't usually take them seriously), Guruji felt that we had "found" each other as master and disciple. Rather than accept the fact that he was basically the first person I met during that particular trip, and that I was so desperate for human companionship and spiritual guidance that I would have talked to just about anybody who gave me the time of day, Guruji had convinced himself that a mystical, karmic bond had brought us together. Within a week he had pushed a Hindu *mantra* on me. Such a mantra is a formalization of the relationship between master and disciple—only in this case it was forced rather than requested. In spite of his sincerity, Guruji was a baby teacher, not even an adolescent. Yet I was willing to give him a chance until the following event occurred.

Guruji was the self-proclaimed lineage holder of one of these popular gurus who have so many tens of thousands of disciples that they cannot keep track of who claims to have received their blessing to teach. In this particular lineage, there are several documented instances of *vibhuti,* or sacred ash, manifesting itself "from thin air" when invoked by the intensity of disciples' aspiration and prayers. I did not even know if I believed in such a thing, while at the same time my ego leapt at the possibility of becoming such a special disciple. Thus, when after a few weeks of practicing under Guruji's instruction for twelve hours a day (beginning at 3:00 a.m.)—a program consisting of *pranayama* breathwork, meditation, chanting, mantra repetition, and so forth—I discovered a fine grayish-white substance on my bedcover, my attention and curiosity were aroused. Still suspicious of the plausibility of the phenomenon, I said nothing for days. I just noticed when it appeared, always looking for possible reasons and justifications for it.

When I finally told Guruji about what had been happening, he was ecstatic. He told me to collect the substance and bring it to him. We placed it on the altar, spoke about it, and smeared it on our foreheads. He boasted to all about it, me, and himself as my teacher.

Guruji was *too* excited, and I could not help but notice how good he seemed to be feeling about *himself*—rather than about God—as a result of this phenomenon. While my egoic pride basked in its newly affirmed specialness, seeing it reflected in Guruji's own feelings of specialness left me suspicious. In fact, the pomp and circumstance grew to such grand proportions that one afternoon I cynically returned from Guruji's temple, asked the housekeeper for the flimsy Indian broom, climbed up on my bed, and began to vigorously sweep the newly painted ceiling. Lo and behold, vibhuti rained upon me.

It made me laugh. Hard. But I was the only one. When I casually mentioned my discovery to Guruji the next morning, he did not find it so funny, instead suffering acute embarrassment. Of course his ego was embarrassed. Mine was, too. But I was more interested in seeing what he would do in the next moment. At first, he tried to convince both of us that even though the paint had fallen, the vibhuti was real, as well. When I suggested—as politely as I could—that he was deluded, he accused me of not having the sense to distinguish between cheap Indian paint and sacred ash. What I had sensed the moment he had pushed the sacred mantra on me became undeniably evident: our month-long affair of forced guru-disciple relationship had come to a close. When I told him as much, he unsurprisingly became very angry and told me I wasn't ready for what he had to offer.

In the same way spiritual students must progress through the necessary developmental stages, a spiritual "awakening" in an individual does not automatically imply that person's readiness to move into a stage of mature adult mastery. Though each situation clearly engenders a distinct process of unfolding, it can generally be observed that most teachers, even upon awakening, find themselves in a kind of spiritual "kindergarten" in terms of their function as a teacher. The awakening itself is not immature, since by nature it is timeless, but there remains a significant learning curve for teachers in which their own human development continues and there is an organic process of learning how to transmit effectively what they have to offer. Furthermore, awakening does not imply a mature and conscious relationship to power dynamics, for such dynamics lie in the realm of psychology, not realization. Teachers' awareness of this distinction will help them protect their students from the teachers' own influence, as well as guard the teachers from allowing their own growth process to stagnate. For this reason, it is ideal for spiritual teachers to have a network of friendships with other teachers, at least some of whom have been in the "business" longer than they have, to engage a source of feedback and/or mentorship as they learn the ropes of their new profession.

Self-Responsibility

Ultimately, both teacher and student must take responsibility for their respective roles if an optimal reciprocal relationship is to occur.

Teachers' obligation to take responsibility for their function is, or should be, a given. To assume the function of spiritual teacher is to take into one's own hands the responsibility for guiding the student's soul to its greatest possible destiny. It is also to assume the whole of the student's karma, a liability so enormous many self-proclaimed teachers dare not even entertain it in their conscious awareness.[1] Although teachers must take full responsibility not only for themselves but for all of their students, a great many do not—some because of unconsciousness and blindness, others because the temptations of power and fame overpower their consciences. When teachers fall short of taking full responsibility for themselves and their function, they do more than fail to provide for their students; they damage the collective reputation of teachers everywhere, thus raising general suspicion regarding the possibility that authentic teachers even exist.

Though it is obvious teachers must take responsibility for themselves, less apparent is the necessity for meticulous accountability on the part of students or disciples. Western translations of Eastern texts, when not recontextualized into the new culture, often serve to exacerbate this. For example, the scriptures might say, "The guru assumes the disciple's enlightenment." The individual who wants to abdicate self-responsibility might interpret this teaching to mean that all one must do is follow and love the teacher, and everything will be taken care of. An interpretation that embraces self-responsibility would be to instead assume the following: from an ultimate perspective, there is an invisible bond of transmission that provides a deep source of help to the disciple; still, it remains in the student's best interest to respect that fact by becoming someone whose psychological and spiritual maturity serve as living examples of the enlightenment the teacher is believed to assume.

My dear friend author Rick Lewis says that even though the master takes care of 99 percent of the transformational process and the disciple 1 percent, the disciple's 1 percent includes everything he or she knows and requires 100 percent of his or her efforts. In other words, the immensity of the teacher's responsibility to the student does not absolve the student from full responsibility for his or her own role. Both are fully responsible, only in different ways.

The student's responsibility includes committing to be ever vigilant in seeing and facing the myriad ways in which he childishly relinquishes responsibility for his own spiritual development; he must also foster a mature relationship to his teacher. And he must recognize the unhealthy ways in which he gives his power away to the teacher—often unasked for—only to blame the teacher later for taking the very thing he offered.

Many people criticize the student-teacher model of relationship, particularly the formal guru-disciple model, by suggesting that the structure itself undermines the need for the disciple to take full responsibility for him- or herself. Contrary to such beliefs, to fulfill the guru-disciple relationship with integrity requires far more self-responsibility than that required by "ordinary" life, or even by religious life. The tremendous gift of transmission that true disciples receive through their relationship with the authentic guru includes the obligation to serve all of life, including themselves, the teacher, and all other sentient beings.

———— ⬦⬦⬦ ————

Spiritual maturity lies in understanding and healing our own relationship to power dynamics so that we are no longer compelled to avoid or denounce power. If we should then eventually come to the path of conscious discipleship to a spiritual teacher, we will be more fully prepared to undertake it from the perspective of a mature adult choosing to engage with a source of help.

Chapter 7 considers the possibility of a relationship of mutual surrender between teacher and student that can result in a bond of mutual trust and profoundly satisfying love.

MUTUAL TRUST AND SURRENDER

Everywhere I go people ask me this question: "Baba, when does a person receive the grace of the Guru?" And I always say, "Only when the disciple bestows his grace on the Guru can the Guru bestow his on the disciple. If the disciple does not bestow his favor, how can the Guru give his blessing?"
—SWAMI MUKTANANDA

Alone in India on a one-way ticket, having dumped my wannabe Guruji and with nothing to hold on to save a vow to learn what my heart was by attempting to follow it, I found myself at a crossroads. I hadn't arrived at this juncture easily, to say the least.

———— ❧ ————

After I left the warped security of Ringo's van in Monument Valley and before my Indian sojourn, the intervening years I spent in California were fruitful on specific psychological and developmental levels while still void of fulfillment on others. Through training to be a psychotherapist and engaging my own course of depth psychotherapy, I had found and named the psychological daemons that had been pulling back on the reins of my spiritual life. I had graduated from a "spiritual grandfather's" broken-down van to a problem-free new Honda Civic. I dated worthy men. I had a career, friends, and even some *joie de vivre*. Yet although I had everything I professed to want, it wasn't enough. So what was it that I so dearly wanted? And how should I go about pursuing this invisible and unidentifiable something that was the only thing I lived for?

It was with these questions burning in my gut that I began to work with two skillful neo-shamans, Ahmed and Ariela, partaking of large quantities of "sacrament," as they called it. With the aid of bowlfuls of bitter brown mushrooms and one or two snow-white capsules, I excavated the contents of my mind further than I had been able to before. Many an afternoon I lay blindfolded in my sleeping bag on the floor of my shamans' "journeying room" as they sent sounds of sirens, symphonies, and everything in between from their stereo speakers through my ear canals and into my psyche, guiding me into chambers previously unknown to my conscious mind.

In spite of my general skepticism of such practices (excepting when done by the rare practitioners who use them with uncommon precision),[1] it was through one of these "journeys" that I had my first experience of the principle of surrender. I had been immersed in a study of the Persian mystical poets in graduate school, and as my body lay motionless within the sleeping bag, my mind traveled far within, to realms and worlds I had believed were only mythical and symbolic. As I voraciously took in the cosmic smorgasbord before me, sampling from the feast of Mother Earth, *devas,* gods, and angels, the words of Rumi suddenly beckoned me, telling me that even when I found myself in the domains of the gods I should let go of that, too, "for even angels have mortal bodies." I listened to his call, letting go further into experiences of oneness, emptiness, and finally approaching the realm of the Creator.

I realized in a practical manner that no matter how appealing or horrifying the vision before me might be, I needed to let it go. In so doing, my identity increased exponentially until I could see nowhere further to go, nothing more to let go of. In this way I received an internal template for what modern mystic E. J. Gold calls "the joy of sacrifice": the universal law that dictates that everything is "food" for something else; everything serves something else. That what we receive in the left hand we must then give from the right—indefinitely. That there is no bottom, top, or end.

I had a post-journey integration session with Ariela the following week. I told her that although I had every *thing* I had said I wanted in life, I felt bound by three tons of iron chains wrapped around my still-unfelt heart. She challenged me to give up everything I had found as an investment in the as-yet unrevealed.

I thought she was crazy but knew she was right. Within two weeks, I had given away everything I owned save the few possessions that would fit into my hatchback, which I parked in a friend's garage for an indefinite period of time. Then I purchased a one-way ticket to that fabled landmass in the East that marked the destiny of so many pilgrims like myself. I was determined to learn *something* about this heart I was told I had. I'd been given a sneak preview of the ancient door to surrender, and now I was left with the task of walking through it on my own two feet.

Trust and Surrender

The process and practice of trust and surrender between student and teacher is one viable and proven method to prepare the individual to trust in God and life and surrender to what is. This trust does not come all at once and is often learned within the context of the student-teacher relationship. Buddhist nun and teacher Pema Chödrön describes this process in relationship to her own teacher:

> *Long after I became his student, and long after I began*
> vajrayana *practice—long after practitioners usually take*
> *the formal* samaya *vow with their teacher—I finally*
> *knew without any doubt that I could trust him with my*
> *life; no matter what he said or did, he was my link with*
> *sacred world. Without him I wouldn't have a clue as to*
> *what that meant. It simply evolved that as I followed*
> *his teachings and woke up further, I finally realized his*
> *limitless kindness and experienced the vastness of his*
> *mind. At that point, the only place I wanted to be was in*
> *the jaws of the crocodile.*[2]

Whereas trust in life and surrender to it are undoubtedly the most satisfying ways to live, most people live from a context of fundamental mistrust in life and so attempt to manipulate and control all things. Few manage to grow up in the Western world with their senses of belonging and being loved intact.

Our mistrust occurs on two primary and inseparable levels: the Western psychological paradigm is generally mistrusting as a result of the emotional, cultural, and religious wounding prevalent in the culture; and the egoic mechanism, by its very nature, insists upon its separation from everything that is God, that is free, that is unknowable, that is the only trustworthy source there is. In the words of Lee Lozowick, "Reality is groundlessness, and the only thing we can trust is groundlessness." The ego lobbies to justify its lack of trust through a self-sabotaging mechanism that continually projects behaviors and beliefs that reflect back its conviction that life really is how the conditioned mind believes it to be. Meanwhile, the soul reaches out to the Universe and begs to be shown that our conditioning is wrong and the Universe/God can be trusted.

As the representative of the true Self, the authentic teacher will ideally reflect back to the student the ultimate condition of trust and love. Yet to the distrusting egoic structure, even the teacher's genuinely authentic behaviors and interventions will be regarded with suspicion. The student comes to the teacher to be shown that Love is true, that God is true—but continually defends him- or herself against that realization.

This essential dilemma of the true disciple is simply an external expression of the internal war between the ego and the soul—Gurdjieff's "battle between yes and no"—that wages continually within each individual. When the "yes" becomes strong enough, the student begins to attract the teacher, but the "no," or denying force, is not easily defeated.

Testing

For most of us, trust is earned rather than given. Teachers of integrity throughout the ages have encouraged their students to test them until they are fully satisfied that the teacher is trustworthy. But we must also remember that the teacher has an equal right to test the student. In the culture of privilege that pervades the West, it is common for would-be students to feel that they are automatically entitled to be the student of a given teacher simply because they wish to be. Arnaud Desjardins says:

> We take for granted that a guru is going to look after us and care for us, just because that's what we want. Westerners believe wanting to "have a guru" is all we have to do to be entitled to it. . . . According to me, the guru must have time to guide me, to know me intimately, to give me private interviews. But what right do I have to demand that? Why on earth should a man who—through his

own efforts and those of his master, through his personal
karma and a whole set of circumstances—has solved his
fundamental problems and reached liberation, why should
such a man take particular care of me? Who am I, that
destiny should grant me such unbelievable privilege.[3]

The teacher has every right to test the student. The true teacher
may create challenges—either conscious or unconscious—for the
student so that both parties can see clearly the disciple's intention. The teacher knows what true spiritual life will demand
and can gauge the student's degree of preparedness for the task.
When the teacher either rejects or delays the would-be student's
involvement, he or she is almost always doing so in the student's
best interest. The teacher knows that too much immersion too
quickly, or involvement at the wrong time, may overwhelm the
student, perhaps even causing a strong reaction that would propel
the student away from the spiritual life for years to come. This
latter consequence has occurred frequently under the guidance
of teachers who catalyze strong energetic forces, such as kundalini,
but lack the discernment to know how much energy their students can handle. Sometimes a few years of additional preparation
may be exactly what the student needs in order to engage spiritual life with a maturity that will be far more productive in the
long run; at other times, the teacher intuitively senses that the
student could be better served by a different teacher.

When Trust Fails

Sometimes our trust is betrayed, our surrender undermined. The
more the years pass, the more stories I hear of great breaches
in trust. This can happen for any number of reasons. It could
simply be random—plain "bad luck" with no hidden meanings

and nothing to analyze. The reasons could be spiritual naiveté and lack of discrimination, or there could be a karmic debt that needs to be paid.

But the most common cause of our imagined betrayals by the teacher and by life in general stems from still-active core belief systems created in childhood: an egoic programming that, until fully undermined, will repeat itself again and again throughout our lives in relationship to *everything*—our parents, children, intimate partners, spiritual teachers, and even our perception of God.

A long-term spiritual practitioner recently shared this poignant example. Conceived by "accident," this woman as a child was severely neglected by her mother (who was neglected by her mother, who in turn was neglected by *her* mother . . .). She bonded closely with her father—who was neglected by his wife—in the form of a "surrogate wife." She grew up feeling betrayed by God (a common core belief for those who were unloved, or not loved well, by their parents), unworthy, and afraid of love. At the same time, her wounds propelled her into a deep quest for wholeness and provoked a great thirst for that which lies beneath all falsity.

Her spiritual life unfolded in a series of events that recapitulated her childhood relationship to her parents. She had an affair with her first meditation teacher, who at the time she met him was married to someone else but who eventually left his wife to marry her. Then he left her for another woman, suing her for custody of their daughter. Next she became involved with another married man at the ashram where she was studying, remaining his "mistress" for years until he ended their relationship to strengthen his bond with his wife. She became disillusioned with her teacher, who was accused of sex scandals, and then engaged in study under several other male spiritual teachers, each of whom she ended up feeling disappointed with. She gave up on all teachers and all lovers, unconsciously concluding that the circumstances of her life confirmed the fact that she was unlovable, and that both spiritual teachers and men in general were untrustworthy.

Until a course of therapy began to undermine this woman's false belief in her essential unlovability, she continually fell in love with unavailable men whose loyalties lay elsewhere. And she found teachers who could not provide for her because of their own lack of spiritual, emotional, and sexual integration, thus continually proving her convictions of her unworthiness and God's betrayal.

We are fortunate when we come to see all of life as a projection of our own making. Our discipleship with God or Truth works itself out through a process of increasingly refined projections and circumstances that are entirely of our own making at the same time as they are also true in life. How we learn to deal with the seeming betrayals of trust and surrender has everything to do with whether they become confirmation of our own deep cynicism or challenging lessons in discrimination, trust, and fortitude. This is easy to say and much harder to do, but the only options are either to give in to imagined betrayal or to open ourselves once again, perhaps this time more discriminately.

Conscious discipleship involves offering discriminating trust to the spiritual teacher. We may take as long as we need before we are willing to give our trust, but until we do so we will not reap the rewards of our efforts. We wish we could get trust on credit and receive an advance on our promised payment, but it never works that way with the teacher.

Although the conscious disciple will ultimately be served through his own trust, developing the capacity for trust may take a long time. One client I worked with had left his teacher of a decade more than fifteen years before, after concluding that the teacher and his community had misused his surrender, and that he had "given his power away" in a circumstance when he should have been strengthening it. When he finally met a new teacher who he respected, he still feared that this would "happen to him" again. Together we considered the possibility that his twenty-five years of preparation had readied him to become a conscious disciple, able to offer himself to the teacher—if he so chose—as a man of maturity, power, and direction, and not as a childish student seeking psychological reassurance from a projected mystical father. His own naiveté had taken him on an extended journey, though it's one he has learned from.

Although none of us would wish this process to take as long as it commonly does, when we see it in the context of the lifetimes of the soul, we realize that if we can learn such an important lesson in just a few decades, we can consider ourselves most fortunate.

The Teacher's Surrender

The processes of trust and surrender are equally applicable to the teacher, only in a different way. In terms of trust, the teacher cannot rightfully expect the disciple to be trustworthy in the realms of clarity of perception, impeccability of practice, or capacity to surrender fully in the initial stages of practice, which could last several years. Most teachers know this, or learn it quickly. Some teachers need a few years of teaching experience before realizing the hard lesson that in spite of the strength and beauty of the dharma, and even the power of transmission, it takes time to dissolve the stronghold of ego.

The teacher must invest in the student's *becoming,* knowing well that this process is likely to leave in its wake a trail of tears, arguments, and false projections and an intense internal struggle as the teacher encourages the ego to relinquish its dominion over the student's identity. Teachers cannot trust the *personality* of the student, but instead must place their faith and commitment on that within the student that longs for truth and that is committed to realization and union in spite of what may be decades or even lifetimes of resistance. The teacher makes a *long-term* investment in the disciple's eventual development. It is a high-risk undertaking because the teacher is unlikely ever to see the full fruition of his or her efforts; but it is also low-risk in that the disciple's eventual surrender is assured—although "eventual" may be so far in the future that one cannot conceive how and when it will occur.

Far from enjoying a life of leisure and glory, the true teacher gives everything to students. Just as a mother might throw herself in front of a moving vehicle to save the life of her child, on the level of the spirit, the authentic teacher literally sacrifices his or her own life for the needs of the student. While the false teacher takes the student's energy and uses it to augment his or her own power, the true teacher's aim is only fulfilled upon the disciple's surrender to God or Truth.

According to the great seers of karma, when the master takes on a disciple, he or she is obliged to that disciple until the disciple is fully liberated—even if this process expands beyond a given lifetime. Yogi Ramsuratkumar once said, "I do not seek for happiness. I only want to do my Father's work. If even one being has benefited from my life, that is enough. It has been worthwhile. And when this body dies, the soul that may remain, may it be born again to do my Father's work."

The paradox is that at one level we are all serving the same One. It is our destiny, yet can remain unconscious for a long time. When we earn the trust of the master, it is like receiving a personal referral from the company vice president to the boss. This referral is based not upon the teacher's personal likes or a system of favoritism, but upon the quality of our work. It is this quality of work, or practice, which initiates a rigorous process of reciprocity between the disciple and Divinity/Truth. When, through the recommendation of the teacher, this force of Divinity "perceives" a quality of consistent effort, persistence, sincerity, and capability on the part of its "employee," it pours its energy toward that student, in effect giving her a substantial "raise" in terms of benefits as well as responsibility. This is what is referred to as the Burden of Love, the glory of sacrifice. As our capacity increases, so too do our responsibility and burden, yet that "burden" carries with it unfathomable gifts of integrity and love—the gift of giving.

Codependence versus Objective Dependence

Codependence implies a quality of grasping in relationship to the teacher based on unfulfilled and unconscious psychological needs; objective dependence is a fully conscious gesture of the recognition of one's own interconnectedness with, and ultimate dependence upon, the ultimate source of Truth—in this case represented or personified by the teacher. More often than not, both forces operate simultaneously. Depending upon the disciple's own maturity when entering the relationship, early stages of studenthood (which could be brief or go on for a number of years) are likely to be dominated by a more childish dependence that will be most apt to give way later to gestures of autonomy and independence. Assuming the student stays with the relationship through these challenges and learns the stage-appropriate lessons of individuation, this may yield to an experience of objective dependence, or surrender.

Mutual surrender is a process in which teacher and student surrender to each other, each in his or her own way and to the extent of his or her own capacity, ever deepening that surrender until the distinction between teacher and student disappears fully in essence, remaining only in form. Mature surrender takes place between two adult human expressions of God. The teacher surrenders first, but the process is not complete until the student has followed. Surrender cannot be an act of weakness or submission. It is not relinquishing one's own responsibility. Instead it is an expression of profound and complete self-responsibility and self-salvation within the context of the student–teacher relationship. When this quality of strength and human maturity is offered as a sacrifice to God or Truth, a magic far beyond the occult begins to emerge. It is the magic of Love found only through complete release.

The truth of the matter is that we all surrender to something. While we cry out about the dangers of surrender to the teacher, we forget that we are already submitting to the bondage of egoic limitation. We understandably feel safer surrendering to the known and familiar prison of our minds than to the unknowable mystery of the master; it is safer to the ego to remain incarcerated within its own confines and to live and die within its own box. But in terms of the life of the soul, not allowing the walls of limitation to crumble in the process of surrender from the self to the Self—as expressed through the conscious relationship between master and disciple—is suicide.

MEETING THE TEACHER
Defining Criteria for Teacher *and* Student

It is due to the previous birth's virtue that I found you;
the traces of times before followed us and showed You to me.
I called out in a language unknown to the mind,
and was drawn once again to see Thy beautiful flowering face.
—S. V. BALAKUMARAN, "YOGI RAMSURATKUMAR LALEE"

Neti, neti." *Not this, not this.* Having suffered yet another minor disillusionment with Guruji in Rishikesh, I was getting a very good idea of what I *didn't* want in a teacher. And so, having completed my pranayama exercises by 5:00 a.m. in the concrete cell that was my room, and then bathing in the icy-cold Ganges River because I was promised it would remove all my past karma more quickly than any available therapy, I sat by the bank of the eternal river and made lists. Lists of what I wanted in a teacher, and lists of what I didn't.

"I want a teacher who speaks English, or at least some Germanic language I can learn easily. I want a teacher who is Western, or at least one who understands Western psychology and knows how to work with it effectively. I want to study with a woman, if possible, or a man with a hell of a lot of integrity. I want my teacher to have few enough students that he or she can work with me personally, but not so few as to make his or her credibility questionable. I want my teacher to take interest in my particular life circumstance. I want a teacher who will provide practical tools for integrated spiritual understanding instead of telling me that good and evil are illusions, and there is nowhere to go and nothing to do. I want a teacher who doesn't demand celibacy for prolonged periods of time and who understands deep sexuality. I want a teacher who respects marriage and child raising. I want a teacher who is alive and who talks. I want a tradition that is juicy and immersed in life instead of just observing it. I want a teacher before I am thirty."

Just as it is often recommended that individuals wishing to find a romantic partner make extensive and detailed lists in order to be clear about whom they hope to attract, I made lists every day, sometimes building upon and refining the list from the day before, sometimes starting anew. I was not trying to define the ultimate criteria for authentic mastery as much as I was attempting to get clear on the criteria for *my* teacher. Upon completing the day's list, I took the paper and floated it down the sacred Ganges, praying silently: "If something other than this should be Your Will, so be it . . ."

Determined to follow the guidance of my as-yet-unrevealed heart, the calling arose from within to travel far south to the village of Tiruvannamalai, where the great saint Ramana Maharshi had once lived. As a woman alone, with no experience traveling in India and no reservations on the overbooked, sold-out transportation options, my task was challenging. I paid fines for jumping on trains without a ticket and spent nights standing when there wasn't a place for me to sit or lie. I bribed a counterfeiter to make me a ticket so I wouldn't be stuck sleeping in the railway station—only to find I was to share my train berth with a sleazy and drooling old man. I ate unidentifiable, fly-encrusted foods—or I fasted. I traveled on crowded, steamy buses and bicycle rickshaws. Finally, I made my way to my destination. When I arrived after three days and three nights, I felt there was nothing in the external world I couldn't conquer if I applied myself well. There was no material task more challenging than the one I had just been through, and what remained was the immaterial mountain.

For the next several days I literally sat in a mountain—the holy Mount Arunachala, said by figures as credible as the great Ramana Maharshi to contain mystical attributes and powers. Meditating six to ten hours a day in a cave where the Maharshi had spent years of his life, I began to experience a quality of intimacy with "God" I had never felt before. My God was suddenly personalized, and near. Like a friend. "Why, if you love me and are even willing to hang out with me like this," I would ask, "aren't you bringing me a teacher who will teach me how to be nearer to you? What else do you want from me? Please reveal to me my destiny. I'm all the way over here in India on a one-way ticket, and I need some help—and now would be much better than later."

I wish I could say that the very next thing that happened was my teacher arriving at my doorstep with a spiritual engagement ring and asking me to be his disciple, but instead I became involved with a final set of spiritual snake handlers. A young male seeker from England had sustained a minor awakening for a period of months and had decided it was time to collect disciples. Thus far, he had successfully courted only the worship of his beautiful but psychotic girlfriend. I was lonely and pained with the intensity of my longing, and they were recruiting lost souls. During the three demented days I spent with them, disheartened by having gotten into yet another tangle with spiritual frauds, a friend of theirs asked me if I knew a Western man by the name of "Mr. Li" who came to town each year with a group of students to visit his teacher, the local God-mad saint Yogi Ramsuratkumar.

This piece of information struck an inner cord. A teacher who was willing to serve the function of disciple in front of his own disciples was something I had not yet come across in my seven years of searching. It suggested the possibility that someone in a position of power might actually be motivated by something other than egoic self-aggrandizement. It hinted of a promised humility, and although I was told that Mr. Li's guru was a madman who chain-smoked and didn't speak with anybody and probably wasn't even worth a visit, I resolved to investigate the situation.

Nothing in my life and everything in my life had prepared me for meeting my teacher. Although I had been working my way toward that meeting since my birth, particularly during the seven years of teacher-hopping that preceded this event, I could never have imagined the consequence of that initial meeting.

It was late morning when I staggered down from the mountain cave where I had already meditated for five hours. Arriving late to the darshan (literally, "sighting of the master," but often used to refer to the meeting between teacher and students) of Yogi Ramsuratkumar, I walked in to see the Yogi holding the hand of a middle-aged Western man dressed in Indian garb. Both the Yogi and the man manifested the oddest series of twitches and erratic body movements, as if neither was in control of his expression. And when the Yogi smoked his cheap Indian cigarettes, I never saw him exhale. What was I seeing, I wondered? Spiritual madness? Mild retardation? Was I watching some kind of healing flowing from the Yogi to this man who looked like any of my friends' parents at the synagogue we attended in my childhood? I contemplated these questions while scanning the room for a character called Mr. Li.

After watching this strange healing for more than an hour, it dawned on me: *this* was Mr. Li! But why did he have a Chinese last name if he was a Jewish-American with a Hindu guru? No

matter. After the darshan, I immediately approached him, intro-
ducing myself to the end of my life as I had known it.

"Where are you from?" he all but barked at me.

"California," I told him. "Originally from Maryland."

"At least it's only California," he sighed. "I thought you might
tell me that you were a citizen of the universe."

I asked him if I could attend one of his teachings.

"Why not?" he half-grumbled.

I also mentioned to him that people who ran Yogi Ramsuratkumar's darshan had invited me to lunch, apparently mistaking
me for a member of his group, and that when I tried to decline
they wouldn't hear of it.

"Never refuse a free lunch," he said.

For some people, meeting the teacher is quite dramatic; and for
others, it's less so. It is not unlike meeting a potential intimate
partner. Sometimes the meeting includes the full set of fireworks,
honeymoon period, eventual fall from grace, and then relationship building. Other times it comes on slowly—someone you
knew but had never really considered in that way, or someone
you had built a friendship with and then one day started to see
differently. It is often easier when the meeting is more dramatic, as
the thrill of new romance may carry the potential student beyond
the confines of excessive doubt and skepticism. But it can be
more beneficial for the connection to grow slowly so that one is
not flooded by excessive emotion, and the situation can be considered carefully and with discernment. For, as we all know, while
sometimes strong and dramatic attraction indicates the magnetic
affinity of souls, at other times it is a surefire sign of complemen-
tary neuroses and inevitable disaster. Knowing my own tendency
to fall hard and fast, when I finally met my teacher, in spite of

an intense rush of feeling, I told myself I would wait six months before asking him if I could be his student, just to make sure the feeling was real. In the end I waited only six weeks, but at least I was aware of my tendency.

Our psychological tendencies and dispositions are likely to play a significant role in our initial encounter with the teacher. Each doubt, fear, hope, and conscious and unconscious projection, and every bit of character strength we possess, will directly influence this meeting. We can be assured that when we meet the teacher, one eye will look through a lens of clarity while the other sees through a filter of mistrust and skepticism.

For example, one woman told me that she initially went to live near her teacher-to-be solely because she was in love with one of the teacher's close students. A pragmatist by nature, she found the devotional practices around the teacher to be excessively sentimental and the teacher's tough personality not only uninteresting, but distinctly distasteful. Yet during the first couple of years she spent living in proximity to her teacher for the sake of her lover, she witnessed a consistency in the teacher's integrity she had not known previously, as well as that quality in his students. As the years passed, she was surprised to find that a profound love had grown, a love that eventually yielded into devotion and finally to a deep bond between student and teacher.

Another man I spoke with had been spending time moving between three exceptional teachers for fifteen years, never committing to any one of them because he never had the "right feeling"—the feeling he expected and wanted to have upon meeting his teacher. When I asked him about his father, he told me that his father had divorced his mother shortly after his birth, only six months into their marriage, and for many years had affairs with a variety of women, never committing to any one of them. His mother had a series of boyfriends but never remarried. Furthermore, he told me, when his father was on his deathbed, he was unable to share even a single moment of emotional intimacy with his son. In light of this poor attachment in childhood, it seemed likely that this man would have difficulty experiencing the set of feelings he imagined he should have in order to know he had met his teacher.

In my own case, when I finally met my teacher, I found myself intoxicated not only by a true vision of his divinity, but also by my unconscious projected fantasies of a savior, the perfect human, the good father. My tendencies toward extremism and zealousness made me want to throw myself fully and indiscriminately at the teacher and the teachings, and then sort out the psychological complexities later on in my studenthood.

The coincidences are too sublime, the feeling of being "found" is too precise, and the accounts of meetings over centuries and across cultures are too exacting to let the meeting between teacher and student be ascribed to chance. My own teacher did not meet his teacher until three years *after* his own initial awakening, when he was already functioning as guru to a large body of students. Yet he insists that his teacher was the source of the entire process of his search, his awakening, and the eventual meeting between them, which resulted in a course of formal discipleship that lasted more than twenty-five years until his teacher's death in February 2001. My own experience of receiving an inner "call" to travel across the entire Indian subcontinent so as to arrive in Tiruvannamalai five days before my teacher's arrival—just in time to meet a couple of charlatans who would lead me to him—hints to me of this greater karma between student and teacher.

Criteria for Teachers

Because it is not easy to evaluate another's enlightenment or mastery from an unenlightened state, criteria for identifying an authentic teacher are difficult, if not impossible, to define. Yet we can gain some insights into what to look for based on what others further along the path suggest.[1]

In the interviews I conducted with them for my book *Halfway Up the Mountain,* many scholars and teachers—including John Welwood, Andrew Cohen, Claudio Naranjo, Arnaud Desjardins, Charles Tart, Georg Feuerstein, and Joan Halifax—set forth their criteria for identifying authentic teachers. They recommended considerations such as: Does the example of the teacher's life demonstrate what I wish to become? Is the teacher completely free, and if not, what are his or her strengths and weaknesses? Is the teacher genuinely humble? How refined is the teacher's attachment to money, sex, power, and fame? What is the teacher's track record? How much impurity is there? How much of something else is mixed in with the spiritual gift? Some further, though by no means definitive, criteria are considered here.

To Whom Does the Teacher Bow?

When meeting a teacher, we may be wise to ask of them: "Who is your teacher?" "Who gave you permission to teach?" Or in the words of Arnaud Desjardins, "To whom or what do you bow?"

There is a distinct difference in quality between a teacher who considers himself (or less commonly, herself) as God or the embodiment of Truth and one who considers himself a servant of God or Truth. Even if it is ultimately true that we are all God, the angle from which we perceive this great truth is often the defining characteristic between those who are likely to abuse power and those who live in awe and serve the great Mystery.

When we ask "To whom does the teacher bow?" we are inquiring into the source of the teachings the teacher represents.

The lineage of mastery of most of the great traditions consists of an unbroken chain of transmission originating in ultimate Truth and passed down from an initial teacher or master to his or her successor, who then passes it on to subsequent successors. In non-theistic traditions, the individual may not "bow" to any one person, but will often practice in the service of a principle, such as "enlightened consciousness" or "Truth as represented by Buddha nature." Such "bowing" is a position of conscious surrender and deference to a greater source of knowledge that exists without as well as within ourselves, and should not be confused with weak submission.

"To whom does the teacher bow?" also means we must consider and evaluate the response. Some teachers are indeed granted permission to teach, but the individuals who grant the permission may not be a source we respect. Some teachers equate their popularity with how many "enlightened disciples" they can send out to teach. A popular teacher might proclaim ten or twenty or thirty teachers as lineage holders—a questionable proposition in my estimation. In other cases, the individual interprets something the teacher did or said as giving him permission to teach, perhaps through some "private meeting" that may or may not have occurred, or through a dream. Or the individual receives transmission through a sacred channel, medium, or object. This may sound absurd, but I cannot recount the number of times when I was living in Tiruvannamalai that people relayed to me messages they had received from "The Mountain." Who could refute "The Mountain"?!

In my own experience, it was crystal clear from the first day I met my teacher that he bowed to his master, Yogi Ramsuratkumar. From the very beginning, the sincerity of his discipleship and the primacy of his studenthood was evident. This crazy-wisdom master, who was renowned in the West, flawlessly assumed discipleship in the presence of his guru. His deference was not feigned, but was the expression of utter attention, intelligent reverence, and mature humility. At the time, I knew nothing about his source. On my initial visits to Yogi Ramsuratkumar's ashram, all I could perceive was a crazy old man who smoked cigarettes continuously, and who thousands of people seemed to agree was a great saint. It was only after I had spent the greater part of my first year of apprenticeship to my teacher under the guidance of his teacher, in whom I witnessed a degree of integrity and palpable majesty I never dreamed truly existed, that I knew I would never be able to doubt my teacher's source—the genius of Love that resided at his fountainhead.

From the perspective of ego, the idea of being the spiritual teacher, or guru, is extremely attractive. However, if we are fortunate, through our spiritual practice we will come to appreciate the nearly unfathomable responsibility the role of spiritual teacher requires. It is a responsibility that has nothing to do with power and self-aggrandizement; on the contrary, it demands complete surrender to the imposing task of directing the evolution of another person's soul. The function of the authentic teacher is to be an utter humiliation to the ego, entirely contrary to what ego imagines such a role would bring. When the reality of this perspective dawns, assuming teacherhood in any circumstance— much less without a lineage to back oneself up—becomes a highly undesirable prospect.

Does the Teacher Serve the Student's Best Interest?

Is the teacher self-serving or other-serving? Look closely, as sometimes behavior that appears oriented toward others is self-serving, and behavior that seems egotistical and self-aggrandizing is actually profoundly humble when viewed from a deeper context.

Mel Weitsman, roshi of the Berkeley Zen Center, says that for him, being a priest means serving the *sangha* or "community of practitioners," not promoting oneself or trying to gain something for the purpose of one's own self-interest. How rare such qualities are—particularly among false prophets, whose behavior is almost entirely self-serving, though usually disguised with a philosophy of "I'm doing this for you [the disciple]" or for God.

Georg Feuerstein suggests:

> *Accepting the fact that our appraisal of a teacher is always subjective so long as we have not ourselves attained his or her level of spiritual accomplishment, there is at least one important criterion that we can look for in a guru: Does he or she genuinely promote disciples' personal and spiritual growth, or does he or she obviously or ever so subtly undermine their maturation?"*[2]

We can ask ourselves: *would the teacher be genuinely pleased if I surpassed his or her knowledge, or would this be perceived as a threat and met with jealousy?* I can unequivocally say the former about my own teacher. Nothing would thrill him more than the unlikely event of my transcending his own knowledge, and I can take refuge in the clarity of that conviction. In the nondual world, there is no need for competition, as Truth, God, and Love are infinite. There is more than enough available for all who allow themselves to partake.

What Are the Teacher's Students Like?

> *Do the teacher's long-time students exemplify qualities that I would like to emanate if I became a student of this teacher?*

I once accompanied my teacher on a visit to the community of another teacher who was a close friend of his. Although the other teacher's students were of a variety of ages, sizes, classes, and races, I was struck by an energetic similarity between them that was so distinct as to render them uncannily similar to one another. As I excitedly shared my vision with my teacher, an amused look came across his face.

"Oh no!" I exclaimed, realizing that the same was true of my own teacher and his students. Sometimes teachers make great claims, yet one cannot see good results in their long-time, senior students. If a teacher proclaims he or she has enlightened dozens of students, but those students do not impress me in any way, this tells me I should carefully consider involvement with the teacher.

Discernment here can be tricky. On the one hand, we must be careful not to judge the teacher's students superficially, appreciating the fact that significant and enduring transformation often takes a long time to arise—and it probably looks quite different from what we imagined when we first engaged in the spiritual path. But on the other hand, we must trust our own powers of discrimination in discerning the effectiveness of the teacher's work with his or her students.

This was one of the primary factors that led me to leave one of my Buddhist teachers. She was continually using the example of her right-hand woman as an illustration of the fruits of mindful practice, but all I could see was a clumsy, self-obsessed, and slightly paranoid (though well-intentioned) woman who was locked into a "good mother" projection with her teacher. I carefully examined this teacher's students over time and found little in their spiritual development that inspired me.

On another occasion, I went to hear a teacher—one of numerous individuals crowned as "enlightened" by a contemporary Indian master—expound upon the "easy path to realization." His articulation of dharmic principles was impeccable, but it was clear that the principles he could so fluidly articulate had not found any real integration in body or psychological disposition. I said to him, "I've met so many people here and abroad—'enlightened' students of your teacher—who speak just like you do, and yet their lives do not demonstrate anything that I would personally like to emulate. How do we account for this discrepancy?" He told me I was not seeing clearly.

The way the teacher's long-term students appear *energetically* is probably how you will become if you choose the path of student-hood with that teacher. This could be a very good thing, as often students of strong teachers are bright, energetic, and aware. Then again, depending upon the teacher, the students may be excessively intellectual, touchy-feely, provocative, passive, or impersonal. You can ask yourself: Do I admire this teacher's strong students? Do I aspire to express my own personalized vision of this tradition in the form they do?

This is not a right-or-wrong issue, and it skirts the domain of personal preferences. For example, one extraordinary contemporary teacher asks his students for one or more years of celibacy and discourages child raising within the community. This runs against my personal preference. If I felt beyond the shadow of a doubt that this was my one and only teacher, he strongly requested this behavior of me, and I felt that I could live my dreams without having a child, I would consider it, but such issues should not be dismissed lightly. We must be careful when signing on with a teacher who will make significant demands of us that we may later regret, remembering that we ourselves are ultimately accountable for all of our spiritual choices.

Criteria for Students

The best way to attract a teacher who fulfills the criteria for authenticity is to meet the criteria for authentic discipleship. It is so much easier to point the finger outward than inward, yet we find no deep satisfaction until we claim the power of self-responsibility.

Frances Vaughan suggests:

> In order to choose a teacher or group with some degree of self-awareness, one could begin by asking oneself some questions. In considering involvement with a self-proclaimed master, for example, one might ask: What attracts me to this person? Am I attracted to his or her power, showmanship, cleverness, achievements, glamour, ideas? Am I motivated by fear or love? Is my response primarily physical excitement, emotional activation, intellectual stimulation, or intuitive resonance? What would persuade me to trust him/her (or anyone) more than myself? Am I looking for a parent figure to relieve me of the responsibility for my life? Am I looking for a group where I feel I can belong and be taken care of in return for doing what I am told? What am I giving up? Am I moving towards something I am drawn to, or am I running away from my life as it is?[3]

There are other criteria that can help us to take inventory of our own capacity for discipleship.

Am I Willing to Commit?

> Deep studenthood is like marriage, only even more serious. It must be entered into with a commitment to a serious, ongoing course of study and relationship with a spiritual teacher in order to fulfill the responsibilities of relationship and work through all major obstacles.

In the student-teacher relationship, the major obstacle is the *maya,* or illusion, of our own false perception. The teacher is our spiritual partner, and the work requires a moment-to-moment willingness both to be in relationship with truth and to handle everything that creates a wedge between us and that possibility. True discipleship is a twenty-four-hour-a-day, lifelong affair. The investment is all-consuming, but the payoff is greater intimacy with truth.

Am I Responsible and Reliable?

> *Successful discipleship requires responsibility and*
> *reliability in a very pragmatic sense.*

Our relationship with the teacher is not only an affair of the heart, but one in which we must put our bodies on the line and express our commitment through practice and action. We may ask ourselves: Am I willing to participate with consistency in a relationship with my teacher? Can I be depended upon? Do I show up on time? Do I follow through with commitments? Do I tend to fulfill the agreements I make—do I meet deadlines and accept responsibility? If my answer is "no" to one or all of these questions, am I willing to radically alter my habitual behaviors in order to become a conscious disciple?

Am I Willing to Overcome my Childishness?

> *Here we ask ourselves: am I willing to honor my teacher in*
> *her or his teaching function instead of insisting that she or*
> *he fulfill the role of good mother, father, lover, or friend?*

Any of these qualities of relationship *may* emerge through the course of an extended discipleship, but they are gifts and should not be expected. The teacher loves the student and may even feel a personal fondness and affinity for him or her, but not in the sentimental way people care for each other within an ordinary context. Overcoming our childish relationship with the teacher involves a willingness to see with increasing clarity the mass of projections we make on the teacher—and on God Itself.

Daniel Moran, a teacher in the lineage of Arnaud Desjardins, speaks of the day he realized he had unconsciously taken to wearing the same brand of pants as his teacher and had even developed the habit of keeping his hand in his pocket and resting his weight on one leg—*just like his teacher.* This phenomenon is more common than we would like to think. Mature men often imitate even the hairstyle of their teacher, and women assume a similar taste in fashion. There is nothing inherently *wrong* with such behaviors, but they can serve as humorous reminders of the ways in which our relationship to our teacher remains childish in certain aspects.

What Is the Quality of My Connection with My Teacher?

> *Do I feel I am with a savior? Good father/good mother?*
> *Friend? Mentor? Lover? Do I idealize this teacher or am*
> *I moved to reduce him or her to my own level? Does my*
> *respect for him or her arise from an authentic inner place,*
> *or do I feel intimidated, swayed by others' opinions? Am*
> *I starstruck by his or her charisma and power?*

There is no one correct answer to this important question about the quality of our connection, but if we inquire deeply within ourselves, we may gain increasing insight into what draws us to the teacher.

The presence of an authentic teacher does not necessarily mean that he or she is *our* teacher, any more than the presence of a good man or woman means that this is the person we should marry. Nor is our unwillingness to engage with the teacher necessarily indicative of resistance, even when the qualities of relationship are generally healthy and positive. I remember meeting the Indian saint Mata Amritanandamayi (Ammachi) on several occasions in between my various relationships with teachers who were much less developed than she. I was continually struck by the breadth of her compassion. I felt as though I was in the presence of a true master, and I even tried to convince myself that I was her disciple. Yet in my heart of hearts, I knew it wasn't so.

"The disciple recognizes the guru and the guru recognizes the disciple. A sacred commitment is made on both sides," writes Arnaud Desjardins.[4] We are not only searching for authenticity in the teacher but for a quality of mutual recognition that is as mysterious as the nature of love itself.

Am I Ready for the Responsibility of Discipleship?

Spiritual responsibility means we take responsibility for all of our spiritual choices, including the choice to place ourselves in the hands of charlatans who then disappoint us, and the freedom that results from the courage to accept true help in the face of ego's stormy, temperamental resistance.

On a lecture tour in Johannesburg, South Africa, I was asked by a young woman, "You speak so passionately about the need for a teacher, suggesting that my own longing and need will attract the teacher, yet so few teachers come here, and many of them aren't of high quality. Do you really think that principle applies to us here in South Africa, as well?" Another woman came to a talk I gave in Northern California and asked if I knew of a good teacher in her town, or at least in Marin County, because she didn't want to have to drive over one of the large bridges in the San Francisco area to get to her teacher.

While these women claimed to want a teacher, they may not have been prepared yet to make the significant effort authentic discipleship requires. The great yogi Milarepa started out practicing black magic and traveled across landmasses, endured tremendous dangers, and then had to build seven houses before his teacher would fully accept him as a disciple. I believe that a woman in South Africa, or in the countryside of Pakistan, or in the remote regions of the Kalahari will somehow find what she yearns for spiritually, provided her intention is strong enough.

A common mistake is for people to assume that once they commit to a spiritual teacher that they can abdicate responsibility for themselves, but the precise opposite is true. Even within the context of practicing surrender, or obedience, we are still fully responsible for all of our choices and actions. Because we are often engaging with strong energies and potent practices, we are called to further integrity and impeccability in our lives, a far cry from the stereotypical, blissful, abandoned relationship with the guru that is sometimes fantasized about and portrayed in the media.

———— ⌘ ————

Criteria can offer invaluable guidance in our attempts to discern between various teachers, paths, and practices, and to clarify our own motivations as students. But criteria are limited. As we will come to understand more clearly in the following chapter, every circumstance is inherently distinct—determined by its context, which includes countless seen and unseen variables in both the student and the teacher. Therefore these criteria should be taken as guidelines that we continue to refine and revisit throughout our lives as conscious students of the path.

9

BREAKING THE RULES

*Where is your sword
Discrimination?
Draw it and slash
Delusion to pieces.*
—BHAGAVAD-GITA

*Twenty years from now you will be more disappointed
by the things you didn't do than by the ones you did.
So throw off the bowlines. Sail away from the safe
harbor. Catch the trade winds in your sails. Explore.*
—MARK TWAIN

H ad I followed the unwritten rule book regarding how a spiritual master should talk, look, and act, I never would have become my teacher's student. Not only did he announce at the first public meeting I attended that he was not taking any new students, he just didn't do the "guru thing" in the way the mind imagines one who goes by that title should. To begin with, his name was Lee and not "Ananda." He was Jewish and not Hindu. When I met him he had dreadlocks and sang in a blues band, and told us we are trying to become *human,* not divine. From the external appearance of things, and even from the rules in the unwritten guru handbook, he just didn't make the grade. Yet by that time in my search, I had been worn out by Divine Mothers and Advaita masterminds whose understanding—though far superior to my own—simply could not quench the depth of my thirst. I had lost interest in the rule book.

Six weeks after our initial meeting, I walked into a nearly unfurnished room at the outskirts of Tiruvannamalai to attend a public talk Lee was giving to the itinerant Western seekers in the area. He had left India weeks before but had returned unexpectedly at his guru's request to complete the paperwork for the purchase of some property. Unbeknownst to me, my soon-to-be teacher had already identified in me dynamics that years of psychotherapists and spiritual teachers and shmurus had either been unable to perceive or were too unskilled to confront effectively. With such a carefully constructed psycho-spiritual resume behind me, bearing numerous degrees documenting my intellectual knowledge, and with a litany of mystical experiences and meetings with "high beings" to back my spiritual resume, I had remained conveniently sheltered from the gravity and depth of my own self-deception.

I arrived early for the talk and sat down across from Lee in the only other chair in a room that would soon be filled with skeptical seekers curious about the American crazy-wise master who had come to town. I anxiously awaited any interaction with this eccentric and unlikely individual. I had already identified him as the most likely possibility to actually help me fulfill the only aspiration that really meant anything to me. I also knew that he wasn't going to make it easy—that there was a lawful "payment" I would have to make with the currency of my soul for an exchange of that level to ensue.

"Do you want to know what is really going on with you?" he asked coolly and unsentimentally, before even saying hello.

"Yes," I stuttered, caught completely off guard, my gut instantly registering a preview of the dreadful news to come.

"Are you sure you really want to know?" he challenged, demanding I be fully responsible for whatever was to follow.

"I am sure."

At that, he delivered a forty-minute personalized sermon detailing in word, gesture, and tone every overt and unconscious nuance of the false personality structure I had effectively hidden from myself for all the twenty-five years of my life. He unveiled endless manifestations that no Buddhist teacher, psychologist, mentor, or healer had ever come near reflecting with such precision. He ranted about aggression, zealousness, grandiosity, seduction: the very things each of us most fear to hear about ourselves—aspects so seemingly repugnant that we are willing to live and die shrouded in deep lies to avoid hearing the bare reality of those truths. My teacher-to-be revealed them to me one by one, sparing nothing. Minute after eternal minute, one lie after another was exposed, and with each I felt as if another strip of my inner protective skin was literally being peeled away. I was being skinned alive from the inside out, and a thin layer of psychic salt rained over each fresh wound.

The truth being hurled at me was so shocking that I was only remotely aware of the room filling up with high-minded Western seekers surely unaccustomed to the unconventional display of mastery before them. Their occasional gasps gave evidence that they were stunned by merely inhaling the secondhand smoke of the guru's purification. But I could not be bothered with their reactions, for in addition to the egoic shockwaves frying my system, I was simultaneously experiencing something entirely unprecedented in the whole of my life until that point: I was experiencing objective love.

I had been loved many times before, and had, myself, passionately loved: men and countries and food and children and sex. But this was unique. It was truth's love of itself as yet unrevealed. A love that can only arise through clear seeing—void of motive—that expresses itself in the form of service to the other by exposing falsity. No one I had met before in my life had possessed the capacity to see me for who I was, as well as who I wasn't, and was willing to express it at the risk of intense reactivity. Yet to react would have been to refuse the gift, and I knew it. Words that invited to be interpreted as insults—many of which had not even earned a rightful place in Webster's dictionary—became bullets of psychic love shattering false constructs and destroying egoic pride. The ego was humiliated by the same language that caressed the soul so famished with longing. I was utterly naked.

A few days later, I received an unexpected invitation to have lunch with several Westerners who had taken up residence in Tiruvannamalai, most of whom I did not know but was aware had attended Lee's talk. Wary of the motivations behind their invitation, I arrived to find myself the object of a thoroughly calculated intervention. Word had spread among the "spiritual tourists" that I had fallen under the spell of a teacher who was a benign charlatan at best, and an abusive patriarch at worse. Gossip had spread like wildfire regarding Lee's verbal "assault" on me days before. These spiritually correct aspirants were alarmed by the unspiritual vocabulary with which I had been addressed, while oblivious to the inner experience I had undergone. They had come together in a shared need to protect me—but from what?

I listened one by one to the concerns they expressed. He had been inappropriate, uncompassionate, unnecessarily mean, degrading, attacking. On one level, I couldn't blame them. He was guilty of all such crimes to my ego, but this is precisely what I wanted a teacher *for*. I had been begging teachers for years to wage such an attack on the lies I had insisted upon for a lifetime; I knew these lies kept me from the very thing I most longed for: my Self. After sitting through three hours of their anxieties—insisting of myself that I listen carefully just in case I had been mistaken about the only thing I knew to be true in life—

I thanked them for their concern and absolved them of any guilt they might feel having released their sister-seeker into the lion's jaws. I was ready to engage the student-teacher relationship.

The Use and Misuse of Criteria for Defining Spiritual Authority

My teacher did not follow the rules, a fact that caused great distress not only to my family and friends but also to other seekers who insisted upon a more conventionally "ethical" path. The rule book my teacher, his teacher, and even his teacher's teacher adhered to contained only one rule: *do whatever is necessary to serve the disciple.* It's the rule that absorbs all rules, and has equally been co-opted as an excuse for untold crimes. But ultimately there is little value in playing it safe. Reality isn't safe, and neither are Truth nor God. And there is no way around the fact that you have to play to win.

Nonetheless, the "rule book"—whether scribed on paper or engraved in a spiritually moralistic mind that is already replete with long lists of the rights and wrongs of which teachers are capable—does have its rightful function. It offers protection to new students of the path, teaching the ABCs of spiritual discernment. Often, people who have no conscious interest in spirituality suddenly find themselves in the company of a Buddhist master or neo-shaman or spiritual mentor of some sort, and they have no idea how to evaluate whether or not they are with an authentic teacher. The "rule book" offers some guidance in making the most basic distinctions.

Furthermore, an ethical code can serve as a useful checkpoint for individuals who want to become teachers but who may not be sufficiently prepared to do so. In certain Western Buddhist circles, efforts have been made to set criteria for those serving in the function of teacher in order to avoid the most common abuses, in the areas of money, power, and sex. Many would-be teachers would benefit enormously from a deep consideration of such lists of rules, particularly in the West, where a pervasive feeling of deep psychological unworthiness and powerlessness has resulted in a disproportionate craving for power and domination over others in all walks of life, including spirituality. Excellence in any field, however, always lies beyond the scope of rules and enters into the domain of objective creativity. The individual who wishes to apprentice to and eventually attain such mastery will have to transcend all confines in order to dance with infinite possibility.

A major problem with a set of fixed criteria for judging spiritual mastery is that the student, understandably concerned with protecting her- or himself against the dangers of corrupt authority, quickly attaches to the suggested criteria as if they constitute an objective moral code, thereby limiting the student's own possibility of perceiving authentic authority that doesn't match up with the given definition. As Murshid Samuel Lewis said in the documentary *Sunseed,* "A concept of spirituality has nothing to do with spirituality. It has to do with concepts."[1] Criteria for a spiritual teacher are ultimately only criteria, whereas a teacher is a living process.

Another problem is that the *contents* of consciousness are used to evaluate the *context* of consciousness. Transmission—the greatest function of the master—is an impersonal force as well as an indefinable and unquantifiable process. It does not choose its carriers based on their adherence to the subjective ethical code of human beings in the Western world in the twenty-first century. It operates according to its own dictates, decrees that stem from a source far beyond conventional reason or even ordinary timespace. This is precisely what most genuine aspirants on the path are seeking in a master—someone who embodies the *way* of mastery, not a particular form of it.

At best, criteria for spiritual mastery offer highly generalized guidance that points out which direction to look when considering a teacher: a framework for making rudimentary distinctions. At worst, a set of defined criteria is a rigid and subjective moral code that ego creates to protect itself from those techniques in the master's bag of tricks that might undermine its autonomy. This complex form of defense is, of course, elegantly structured by ego to appear virtuous, moral, intelligent, and honorable, always in the name of the "higher good."

Everything and Its Opposite Are True

So what is the aspiring spiritual student to do? I suggest considering a few areas of generally agreed-upon criteria for evaluating spiritual mastery, as considered in the previous chapter, while cautioning the seeker that although they are generally decent ideals to uphold, spiritual discernment in each circumstance remains essential. All of this is encapsulated in the famous Zen teaching: "Not always so."

Looking, Talking, Acting Spiritual

Although it may not be written in the rule book, many people have an idea of what a teacher—particularly a Western teacher—should look, talk, and act like. We may be unaware of the degree to which we hold these biases until confronted with a teacher who is much younger than ourselves, has a significant speech impairment or a physical disability, or dresses in a manner we find objectionable. We may think we are flexible regarding the language the teacher uses until we find that every fifth word out of his mouth is a vulgarity, or that he regularly tells crude jokes in public seminars, or that instead of talking about God and Truth he goes on about sex between grasshoppers or a love of gambling. We may believe ourselves to be open-minded regarding various human manifestations on the part of the teacher until we discover that she chain-smokes, wears thick makeup and spiked heels, drinks heavily, or is a lesbian. To pierce the illusion of manifestation, we must continually ask ourselves if we are certain that our ideas about how an authentic spiritual authority should look, talk, or act necessarily reflect true spiritual mastery.

To the mind, if the spiritual teacher is a man, he is basically modeled after our projected images of Jesus Christ, God, or a gray-bearded Himalayan master. If the teacher is a woman, she resembles the Great Mother archetype, whether of Celtic or East Indian origin. She is large, warm, embracing, and has a voice that is compelling and melodic at the same time as it is yielding. Such masters are about as common as perfect husbands and perfect wives, and imitations of such projected ideals are a dime a dozen. In other words, not only is expecting teachers to conform to such criteria unrealistic, meeting these criteria may be cause for caution!

More often than not, our ideas about what spirituality looks like are precisely what stand in the way of our experience of it. If we are not willing to see beneath the superficiality of our egoic desire for spirituality to *appear* a certain way, we are in no way prepared to enter into apprenticeship with an authentic spiritual authority.

Enlightenment

Most people assume that having achieved "enlightenment" or "awakening" is a necessary condition to qualify one for spiritual teacherhood. But what do we mean by "enlightenment"? If there is a single issue people in the field of spirituality disagree about more than any other, it is who is enlightened and what constitutes their enlightenment. The issue is of such importance that I dedicated major portions of *Halfway Up the Mountain* and *Eyes Wide Open* to its consideration.

The teachers I most admire tend to focus less upon a fixed state of consciousness as the marker of readiness to teach others, and more upon qualities of proven reliability, unwavering commitment, and undisputed integrity. Teachers who gain the respect of both peers and students are more committed to sharing the teachings than they are to augmenting their own power and authority; they are unlikely to become corrupt in areas of sexuality, money, and power, even when such commodities are freely offered to them; and they are willing to admit to their own mistakes, even at the cost of their personal pride and reputation. Teachers I respect less grant their students permission to teach shortly after a shift in consciousness that marks the most basic level of awakening, well before it is clear whether that state will endure. While I believe there is such a thing as awakening from the dream of false perception, this "enlightenment" merely marks the beginning of a new level of spiritual work—the "kindergarten" of spiritual mastery.

Beyond these, there are many qualities that comprise effective teacherhood. For example, someone who has a solid psychological structure and the backing of a strong lineage, even when his or her realization is relatively shallow, may make a better teacher than someone who has had a powerful awakening but is not backed by a lineage. The lineage itself—the stream of transmission passed from living master to living master over thousands of years—offers tremendous protection to those who surrender to its ultimate authority and respect its lawfulness. When I meet a teacher who is self-proclaimed rather than sanctioned to teach by a senior teacher who is part of a lineage and tradition, I am wary, though I do not disrespect his or her function.

Simply to state that one must be enlightened to teach is reductionistic as well as extremely difficult to evaluate from an unenlightened perspective. From countless trips to the spiritual marketplace, I can say with conviction that I would readily avail myself of the teachings of those who do not proclaim their own awakening, or who even claim the lack of it, before I would apprentice myself to the majority of Western teachers who advertise their enlightenment in magazines across the world, guaranteeing to deliver enlightenment to their disciples on a metaphorical money-back guarantee.

Taking Ourselves Too Seriously

We may need to break the rules sometimes simply because we tend to take ourselves and our spiritual lives far too seriously, and we need to see what happens if we veer off-course for awhile. As serious spiritual aspirants, we often get wound up so tightly that God or Truth can't even find a crack in our shell of virtue through which to enter. Having a sense of humor in relationship to the spiritual teacher allows some space for our own humanness, as well as for the teacher's humanity, while creating some breathing room.

One time when I was attending Yogi Ramsuratkumar's darshan, sitting across from him about thirty feet away, my leg fell badly asleep. At that very moment he called me up to ask me a question, and without thinking twice I jumped up to rush over to the dais where he sat. As soon as I took my first step, I fell wildly off-balance, staggering toward the front of the room like a drunkard, my hands reaching in front of me preparing to catch my fall. I looked up at the Yogi and his attendant to see the most baffled looks on their faces as I headed toward them, utterly out of control. Finally, I shifted my course just enough to crash into the wall beside the Yogi. The 250 people watching this event, as well as the Yogi and his attendants, were in hysterics, though it took me about a month to find it funny.

A friend of mine had a similar experience while studying at a Zen monastery in Japan. The environment was rarified and extremely formal, as is characteristic of traditional monasteries. As she stood up to bow to the master at the end of a formal meditation period, she realized her whole leg had fallen asleep, and instead of moving forward, her body went backward and she fell straight through the thin rice-paper walls of the *zendo,* winding up with half of her body outside in the garden.

One afternoon several years into working with my teacher, he called me over and asked if I wanted some feedback on my spiritual practice.

"Of course," I told him.

"Are you *sure* you want feedback?" he asked once again.

"Yes!" I repeated.

He asked me one more time and then told me, "Look, if you want to proceed on the spiritual path as rigorously and quickly as you insist you want to, you need to *RELAX*. Relax, relax, relax. You've just got to chill out. Relax. Calm yourself. Have fun. Relax . . . Relax. Relax, and then relax!"

"I don't know *how* to relax!" I told him.

"That's precisely the point. I'm not talking about month-long inner vacations, but about learning to relax within yourself. As much as I abhor the inner child, when you find yourself agitated, tell yourself, 'It's okay, honey. Everything is going to be fine.' You just need to *relax!*"

Author Regina Sara Ryan told me another story that happened when she was a Catholic nun in her twenties. Nunlike in her personality structure, as a young woman Ryan did everything "just so." She was the "star nun," as holy as they came. One day during a sewing period when the novices were supposed to be observing silence, they were instead chatting away, gossiping, and enjoying themselves. Just then the Novice Mistress walked in, and the nuns fell immediately to their knees in acknowledgment of their sin. The Novice Mistress looked at each of them in turn, asking, "Sister, did you break silence?"

"Yes, Mother," one replied.

And on to the next one and the next she went, each one saying, "Yes, Mother."

When she finally got to Regina, the young nun looked up, ashamed. "Yes, Mother, I broke silence," she admitted.

Pausing for a moment to take in this response, the Novice Mistress let her stern face break into a smile. "Glory be to God!" she proclaimed. "You're finally becoming normal!"

Spiritual life *is* serious—so serious that if we really want to fulfill the enormous task of becoming more deeply human, we must learn to laugh at ourselves, to relax, to break the rules now and then, and to be all right with it. Spiritual practice is hard work. Relating to a teacher can be difficult, at times deeply frustrating. So sometimes we need to laugh at the ludicrousness of our own projections, play with our own neuroses, create relationships with others around our shared absurdities in relating to the teacher, and bring a little bit of laughter into the intensity of our discipleship.

If we are going to risk a relationship with authentic spiritual authority, I suggest we realize we are entering into the sphere of limitlessness, in which narrow definitions and rigid criteria can be useful, but can also be blinders that restrict our capacity to see the range and depth of possibility the master offers. Then again, if we want to play it safe (which is particularly common when we have been scorched by corrupt teachers or corrupt parents), criteria might be just what we need for a time until we are able to trust our own intuitive sense more fully.

The fulfillment of conscious studenthood involves both knowing the rules and knowing when to break them. When we know the rules, we are informed seekers with an increased capacity to detect fraudulence and deception, and we are more likely to find ourselves in the company of teachers worthy of our attention. When we know how to break the rules, we do not suffer the limitations of our own spiritual morality and intellectual rigidity.

10

SPIRITUAL MONOGAMY
VERSUS "SLEEPING AROUND"

*We cannot "fool around" if we really want our teacher to
take us seriously. In spite of what may be strong emotional
feelings toward one master or another, we must look clearly
at our own personal history in order to see where we are
likely to err in our approach to the spiritual teacher.*
—LEE LOZOWICK

I f only I could say that I met my teacher, was enlightened
shortly thereafter, and we lived happily ever after. But the
story is not so simple. Meeting the teacher is the end of one
story and the beginning of another. And while the lies constitut-
ing my personality structure had been revealed, neither had they
been undermined nor replaced. I had fallen wholly and spiritually
in love with Truth in the form of my teacher, determined for the
first time in my life to enter into a "spiritual marriage" between
student and teacher; yet my teacher was insistent that he was not
looking for new students. He told me the sacrifices involved were
far greater than most people are prepared to handle, and repeatedly
warned me, "If you are wise, run the other way as fast as you can."

Meanwhile, upon realizing I would not be talked out of my
vision of the teacher, one of the local Westerners decided I should

at least be given a good education on the topic, and thus gifted me a copy of William Patrick Patterson's *Struggle of the Magicians*. I opened it and read the following:

> *Awakening through the grace of vision, born usually*
> *of deep disappointment with ordinary life and himself,*
> *the student is magnetized to seek. Influences, conscious*
> *in origin, enter his life. A book, a poem, an image,*
> *an impression, a person—some representation that*
> *transcends the personal, the ordinary, speaks to him.*
> *There is a flash of awakening. He responds, resonates,*
> *the world suddenly appears greater, more mysterious.*
> *Jubilant, inspired, he identifies, imagines himself a*
> *spiritual being, and seeks a teacher. His expectations*
> *are as great as his "spiritual" dream of himself, his*
> *capabilities. He doesn't see that aligned against his*
> *permanent awakening are massive mechanical forces,*
> *both personal and collective, societal and natural, all of*
> *which contrive to keep him "in place." Nor does he see*
> *that only a very small part of him, his essence, wishes to*
> *awaken; his personality has no desire to awaken. And so*
> *it obfuscates, lies, and defends.*[1]

I didn't doubt that *other* people's personalities didn't want to awaken, but surely mine did. I was a naive student blinded by spiritual infatuation: so resolute, in fact, that I made a vow to be Lee's student for the remainder of my life even if he never once acknowledged himself as my teacher. I had heard a famous Zen story about an archer of low caste, who, upon being rejected as a disciple by the master archer, took a stone and placed it on an altar in the forest and worshipped it as his master. Through the intensity of his devotion, the "stone master" transmitted to him the secrets of mystical archery. If need be, I was determined to do the same.

Meanwhile, totally unbeknownst to my conscious self, I initiated an intricate plot to win Lee's affections. I was accustomed to getting what I wanted if I was clever enough. I decided that since the thing my master loved most was *his* master, if I endeared myself to Yogi Ramsuratkumar and proved myself deserving of his affections, my teacher would see that I was worthy and would have to accept me as a student.

When learning to swim, it is more clever to begin in a shallow pool than to throw oneself overboard into the sea, but my naiveté knew no bounds. And how could it, as nothing in my cultural upbringing had prepared me for such an event? On the contrary, I had learned to control, manipulate, overpower, and assert my authority and independence. Yet beneath all the manipulations was a hungry heart, and a sincere one, and the masters wasted no time capitalizing on my aggressive sincerity to teach me a critical lesson.

The first part of my plot—to win Yogi Ramsuratkumar's affections—succeeded, though through no doing of my own. He not only offered me his affections but lavished them upon me until the lathery cloud of bubbles surrounding me was so thick it would have taken a cannon to burst through them. He drew me into his inner circle, bestowed upon me a special place by his side, and gave me the job of chanting for him every day. He allowed me to drink from his cup and left me so intoxicated that at times the sacred mantra ran through me nonstop for days at a time. My absorption in God rendered *everything*—including much-needed sensibilities—dormant and ineffectual. He provided me the status and recognition that had dominated my egoic ambition for decades, if not longer, inflating it to such extremes I could not help but see the absurdity of it and experience the futility of its emptiness. In a way that only a true master could, he saturated my soul with benediction while simultaneously deep-frying my ego.

There was only one problem with my plan: it didn't work. When Lee got wind of what I was up to, he congratulated me sincerely enough on having gained the attention and affections of one of the most renowned living masters in South India—and let me know in no uncertain terms that as long as I was working under the guidance of Yogi Ramsuratkumar, he would have nothing to do with me. He told me that even if master and disciple are ultimately One—as was the case with him and his master—they are still two in form, and each works in a highly refined and specific energy field that must be respected. He had no intention of interfering with his master's work with me and told me that if I wished to even be considered as a student of his, I would have to get Yogi Ramsuratkumar's full permission to leave—without a single gesture of control or manipulation on my part. He added that since I had gone to the trouble of making such a mess, I may as well cash in on the benefits and stay close to Yogi Ramsuratkumar, both in order to receive the personalized grace that had been made available to me in spite of my manipulations and to learn the lesson I needed to be released by the Yogi. Lesson Number One: When Entering a Traditional Guru-Disciple Relationship, One Master Only—unless otherwise specified.

To fully appreciate the extent of the bind I found myself in, and why I would expose myself to this test of faith under such unusual conditions, requires some background information.

Yogi Ramsuratkumar was so uncommon, so far off the spectrum of my previous comprehension of what can arise within the container of a human body, that it took six months of spending at least four hours a day with him, seven days a week, to finally comprehend that he was indeed a *man*. If, after being by his side for hundreds of hours over many months, I didn't see him as a man, how did I see him? He was more like a ghost—the shell where a human being once had been. A nearly transparent figment of the imagination. I experienced him as a fluid process rather than as a person: like a geyser of compassion, a continual outpouring of radical and obscure blessing oozing out from and through this porous frame of a look-alike human.

I respected his authority because it wasn't subjective. It is said of his teacher, the Southern Indian saint Swami Papa Ramdas of Anandashram, "Ramdas plays football with the planets." Yogi Ramsuratkumar was no different. He played human beings with the precision of a world-champion chess player moving pieces on a board. At the same time, he was innocent to the point of expressing himself with the purest of childlike mannerisms. Yet the moment you doubted his mastery, it came out and cut you with a sword. To question whether or not he was enlightened is as irrelevant as asking whether or not Picasso ever got a degree in fine arts.

Yogi Ramsuratkumar showed no sign of being willing to release me—quite the opposite. A few days after Lee departed, the Yogi called me up during his public darshan to speak with me, asking me how long I intended to stay in India. I told him I wasn't quite sure, but that I had thought perhaps another six weeks. (Surely I could learn my lesson by then, I thought.)

"Mariana is not going to stay here for six weeks," he exclaimed in his inimitable squeaky voice. "She is going to stay here for six years!"

At that, he waved his hand to motion me back to my seat among the crowd and began to laugh madly. When Yogi Ramsuratkumar laughs, the whole world laughs. Whatever it is, it's funny in the truest sense of the word. We both laughed, hysterically, myself in a mindless stupor, tears streaming down my face for no apparent reason, until darshan ended an hour later. Then I went back to my room and sobbed for much longer than I had laughed.

There I was, having found in a Jew from New Jersey the teacher I had been seeking for seven years, and now I was about to be held spiritual hostage by one of the greatest living masters on the Indian subcontinent—only he was not *my* teacher. Did he really mean I would be there for six years? What about Lee? Was I willing to endure six more South Indian summers with heat so intense that boils erupted on my body? To endure physical and spiritual conditions in which even a twenty-five-year-old woman was likely to turn wrinkled and gray within a couple of years? To search amidst a dreadfully limited pool of eccentric spiritual tourists for the man I had not yet met but so desired to be the father of my future child?

And that was just the beginning! What about the teacher I longed to be with across the ocean? Would he take me after six years, and would I even survive the sadhana ahead with an individual so powerful that his laser glance could burn a hole in my soul such that I could physically perceive my body being scorched? What if the Yogi didn't allow me to leave the country to renew my tourist visa and I became an "illegal alien?" How about my friends and family? They thought I was strange before: how was I to explain I was now captive of a God-mad saint who rarely spoke and explained nothing? A saint so potent I implicitly knew beyond a shadow of a doubt that if I even tried to escape, the cosmic forces he commanded would crash a bus, make my passport disappear, or create an avalanche to block the road?

Within weeks I had gone from being a naive young seeker, fully in (perceived) charge of her life—confident in her capacity to control, achieve, succeed, and seduce—to a still-naive young woman, but one who had been taken at her word by two of the most radical and powerful masters of their respective continents. I was now a marionette whose strings were held by two but whose free will was paradoxically the key factor in determining the form in which her destiny would unfold.

The question of spiritual monogamy is a topic of significant interest to most serious students of the path, and the subject of frequent scorn among committed spiritual tourists. A useful, though not definitive, means by which to explore this topic is to consider the relationship between lovers as a metaphor for the student-teacher relationship. We model our relationship to God or the Beloved or the teacher based upon the template of our human relationships. If we want to learn to be lovers of God, we can discover our weaknesses by looking at our patterns in intimate relationship, and we can deepen our capacity for intimacy with the One by practicing it with human beings and with the teacher.

The Problem with "Sleeping Around"

In California and other New Age centers, the term *polyamory* is widely used to indicate a lifestyle choice in which a person chooses to have love relationships with many people instead of one. Sometimes the individual has a "primary relationship" accompanied by secondary relationships; at other times it appears more as free love; and in still others the individual may not be involved in a relationship at all but adheres to a philosophy of open relationship.

There is an interesting parallel to spiritual monogamy here, because while you might find the occasional individual who manages to live a polyamoric lifestyle in a clean, honest, and conscious manner that is sustainable over many years, this is the exception. In Western culture, where our conditioned psychological template for authentic intimacy and healthy sexuality is fragile and confused, it is difficult for most people to successfully manage one intimate relationship, much less many. The same principle applies to the question of "monogamy" in relationship to the spiritual teacher.

When people hop from teacher to teacher, they may have an experience of striking intellectual or bodily intoxication, but the relationship usually remains limited in both breadth and dimension. A great teacher for a day is like a dharmic psychedelic that yields profound inspiration and insight—then fades as quickly as it arose. The experience is real; it just doesn't last. Many people are nectar junkies, and who could blame them? The first taste of the teacher's nectar is often sweet and intoxicating and goes down smoothly. But if we stick around long enough for it to hit the bloodstream of the ego, we may find that the divine medicine tastes like poison. Rather than endure the often-unpleasant process of digesting the teacher's full transmission, many people unconsciously opt for a series of mini-transfusions of nectar, which temporarily satiate ego's belly but rarely satisfy the soul.

Though it is not always the case, many people who hop from teacher to teacher stay with one until either the teacher or the process instigated through the teacher's presence begins to threaten the ego in a significant manner. The unconscious fear of egoic annihilation—which is the eventual destiny of any individual who commits to a solid and rigorous path of spiritual discipline under the guidance of an authentic teacher—creates too much pressure for the psyche to endure. Of course, the individual in this position does not think, "My ego is threatened." That would be far too vulnerable a stance for the ego to admit. Instead, the mind may suddenly give rise to thoughts such as "I'm not quite sure I agree with the way this teacher talks about men/women." "I don't like the way this teacher plays favorites." "Maybe the teacher is not as great as I imagined him to be." Or the ego's discontent may simply be experienced as an inner itch— the need to move on.

The difficulty in learning discernment, of course, is that while any of these thoughts may reflect the ego's escape plan, they may also be accurate and indicative of very real underlying issues. The individual's growing capacity for discernment may finally be allowing him or her to see the deep cracks in the teacher's structure. I experienced this personally on a number of occasions, such as the time when I told one of my pseudo-gurus that I dreamt he was not a real teacher, and he told me that if such dreams ever came again I must instantly wake myself up! There is no clear way to know whether such doubts are symptoms of egoic resistance or not. However, if one has been teacher-hopping for many years and is confident that one's preferred teachers are indeed good teachers, then the failure to commit to any of them for an extended period of time may be a sign of hidden egoic resistance.

The Value of Monogamy

In the domain of human love, there are qualities of bonding, surrender, and depth that cannot be known until they are experienced through years of devotion and commitment to one's beloved. The same is true of the relationship with an authentic spiritual teacher. I have read books by people who deconstruct the value of the monogamous and committed student-teacher relationship with razor-like clarity. I have listened to discourses refuting the value of the spiritual teacher that were delivered with such charisma and intelligent articulation that even one who knows otherwise is impressed by such intellectual savvy. Yet the fact remains that most of the individuals espousing these views have had difficult experiences that shape such opinions. They may have been badly burned one time too many by a would-be spiritual authority. They may have early unhealed wounds inflicted by a parent or some other authority figure that now express themselves as intellectual opposition to the principle of spiritual authority. As Sufi sheik Robert Frager believes, "A lot of Westerners who are critical of the authority of the teacher don't know what they are talking about because they've never had a relationship with a real teacher."

In spiritual monogamy, two primary processes occur: One, the teacher comes to know in great detail the nature of our deepest gifts, as well as our personalized resistance to Truth. And two, the transmission provided through the medium of the teacher enters our psyche with increasing depth and potency, gradually penetrating its way through the psyche's nooks and crannies.

In the first process, whether we see the teacher as an individuated expression of the Divine itself or as a finger pointing to the moon, the student-teacher relationship is very intimate, even if ultimately impersonal. The teacher observes the student over many years, making suggestions and giving directions according to the former's increasing awareness of how the student is best served in light of the nature of his resistance. Meanwhile, the student learns to trust the teacher to the degree that his confidence in the teacher's direction overrides the convincing assertions of the ego. The relationship becomes co-creative as teacher and student work together not only for the purpose of the student's ultimate adherence to Truth or God, but so that the fruits of their relationship are used to serve and heal humanity.

In the second process, related to transmission, the context of enduring spiritual monogamy allows for the full benefit of the subtle and invisible forces of Truth to eventually penetrate the fortress of the student's psyche. In the same manner in which a canyon is formed by what began as a small stream flowing over millions of years, what is once felt as but a hint of transmission flowing from teacher to student becomes an unceasing stream of benediction and clarity, gradually wearing down the hardened rock of the false identity structure. Given enough time and consistency, the hardened ground will eventually erode. As long as the student continues to make him- or herself even the least bit vulnerable to the teacher and the teachings, transmission will have its way.

It can be extremely difficult to trust this process when, some-times for years at a time, no visible results can be seen; but the absence of concrete and linear evidence does not imply a lack of progress. In a lifelong marriage there are years during which a deep-ening of love can be felt and other periods during which it seems as though little is happening. This is equally true of the committed relationship with the spiritual teacher. During these "dry periods," we are carried along by faith, conviction, commitment, or whatever other forces of will and willingness we can muster.

Whether the student courts transformation in the context of Buddhism, Sufism, Christianity, Judaism, or potentially even an unknown or obscure tradition, he links himself to a force so pow-erful it has the potential to give birth to an awakening to Truth and surrender to God. No one tradition is superior to another. The transforming potential is the student's committed intention and loyalty to that source, which initiates a powerful alchemical process of transformation.

Exceptions to the Rule

Every aspect of the student-teacher relationship will include exceptions. Even once-extraordinary human romances sometimes end in divorce, and vows meant to last into eternity are interrupted or severed. The same is true of the student-teacher relationship.

At times student-teacher relationships end in divorce—either pleasantly or less than such. In most cases, the strong student needs a teacher who is at least a few paces ahead of her own development, and some students outgrow their teachers. Other times, either the student's needs or the forces of the Universe shift such that a transition away from the teacher, or to another teacher, is called for. One woman I interviewed, for example, was with a great Western teacher for nearly a decade when he invited another teacher to speak at a conference he was hosting. The moment the other teacher walked into the room, the woman knew he was her true teacher. She consulted her teacher on this matter and received his full support in "changing partners"—a rare, pleasant divorce.

Teachers also die, and sometimes the rightful response on the part of the student is to remain with the teacher even when he or she has left the body. Another student, however, may need or desire a source of ongoing feedback and transmission from a living master and must make the necessary energetic shifts to adjust to the new situation. Still another student will experience this as a time to learn to walk on his or her own two feet. This can be a difficult decision for the student to make: accurately assessing whether he or she has reached a sufficient degree of spiritual maturity to correctly interpret feedback from the now-disembodied master—and live as a spiritual "widow" or "widower" of sorts—or whether, in spite of an inner loyalty that does not die, it is time to move on or to be independent.

Another variation on traditional spiritual monogamy is found in many religious and spiritual traditions, where an individual has a root teacher accompanied by various other respected teachers who serve to support the function of the main teacher. Tibetan teachers operate similarly. Sometimes this model works very effectively, and other times less so.

Sometimes teachers send their students to study with other teachers. This is particularly common among Buddhist and Sufi masters. Perhaps there is some area the teacher is unable to break through with the disciple, or perhaps another teacher possesses a particular quality or skill the teacher would like his or her student to learn from. Sometimes the reason remains unknown, such as in the case of a woman I interviewed whose teacher not only continually sent her to spend time with other teachers but never acknowledged himself as her teacher—this despite her unwavering certainty of this fact and two decades of dedicated discipleship. Then there are rare cases such as that of the Sufi sheik Llewellyn Vaughan-Lee, who carries forth the lineage of Irina Tweedie. "Mrs. Tweedie," as she was called, came to understand that Vaughan-Lee was not an immediate disciple of herself, but of *her* master, B'hai Sahib. But as B'hai Sahib had long since left his body, Vaughan-Lee's rightful access point to his master was through Irina Tweedie. Both willingly adjusted to the needs of this situation.

Still others are not destined to have only one principal teacher throughout their lives. I have a number of friends—both long time and diligent students of the path, as well as respected teachers and spiritual leaders in their own right—who have had a number of powerful relationships with a small number of spiritual teachers throughout their lives, accompanied by periods of deeper self-reliance. It is clear to me that they are not "escaping" but rather following the deep dictates of their own soul's unfolding.

A further exception to the rule of spiritual monogamy is that a seeker may "sleep around," even for decades, because he simply has not found a teacher who works for him. Some people live their lives without finding their teacher, or find them only late in life. There are classic stories of those who travel the East and the West in search of their master, eventually giving up their search entirely—only to then find the teacher at the equivalent of the local laundromat. Irina Tweedie, who was to become one of the greatest Sufi masters, met her teacher when she was fifty-two. Who could second-guess such forces?

Lastly, there are those who really enjoy the game of teacher-hopping and are content with what they receive. They are like spiritual hummingbirds who make a life out of sucking nectar and may even catalyze some useful cross-pollination in the process. Vishnudas, a German by birth, was one such individual I

came to know on my various trips to India. It seemed that no
matter which teacher I visited to conduct my research, Vishnudas
was there. He had worked out a one-man musical performance,
with bells on his ankles, guitar in hand, and a harmonica and
microphone attached to a headpiece. He sang traditional Hindu
guru bajans (songs of praise to the master) to American rock and
folk melodies, filling in the name of the "guru of the hour" in
appropriate spots. He had been doing this for years, and I often
wondered if in his ecstasies he sometimes mistakenly sang the
wrong name. I suppose he would say with a chuckle, "They're all
one anyway." Another friend, deeply devoted to Truth, has been
visiting various teachers for many decades and actually serves the
function of sharing and disseminating information among spiritual teachers and to serious students of the path.

The exceptions are valid; still, a lifestyle of "sitting around"
with a variety of spiritual masters is often as effective as a life of
sleeping around with different men or women. An endless stream
of physical love affairs will bring a lot of excitement, emotional
"highs," and some profound encounters (as well as a healthy dose
of cynicism), but we are unlikely to learn much about the depths
and possibilities of love. Similarly, sitting with many teachers is
likely to bring about a heady dose of ecstasy and some deep dharmic insights, and it may leave us with the impression that we are
going somewhere, yet we are likely to end up with very little
aside from a bagful of spiritual trophies.

———— ⊗⊗⊗ ————

Despite the potent possibilities of monogamy, it is wise to take as
much time as one needs before jumping in. A committed relationship to a teacher not only bears similarities to marriage but
is potentially even more serious, as the implications of such a
commitment may well extend even beyond the life of the body.

Many teachers will wait a long time before asking their students for a monogamous commitment, and some may never ask at all, but sooner or later the conscious disciple benefits from making a firm decision. While the disciple's ego may interpret the teacher's call for commitment as an expression of the teacher's personal greed or hunger for power and dominance (and in the instance of the false teacher this may well be the case), the authentic teacher is committed to the student's best interest, courting his or her commitment so the student may receive the benefits of the vow of ultimate surrender. Even so, the decision must come from the student, and in its rightful time.

11

GURU GAMES AND CRAZY WISDOM

The real function of the spiritual friend is to insult you.
—CHÖGYAM TRUNGPA RINPOCHE

With the torrential flow of grace that now ceaselessly gushed over and through me—the result of Yogi Ramsuratkumar's benediction and unwavering commitment to my liberation—I began to drown. And drowning wasn't pleasant. I was going down gasping, sputtering, calling for Mommy, begging Moses to part the sea and let me feel the dry lands of egoic security once again. When I hear neophyte spiritual seekers asking for annihilation, to drown in grace, to die into God, I find myself wondering how many have had even a glimpse of what they're asking for. I, too, once believed that all I wanted in life was to drown in an ocean of love, and I still do—but who among us willfully allows herself to be thrown overboard into the ocean with a boulder tied to her feet?

One evening during this part of my story, I sat on the stone wall outside the local Arunachala temple, the rocks still steaming from the 120-degree day that had by then cooled down to a "moderate" 112 degrees. All eighteen feet of material in the traditional Indian *sari* I wore were sweat-saturated many times over as I poured out my woes to my friend Astrid. Originally a secretary from Denmark, Astrid had come to India twenty-five years earlier on a two-week guided tour. She met Yogi Ramsuratkumar, realized he represented her greatest transformational possibility in this lifetime, renounced a life of materialism and greed, and had not stepped off the Indian subcontinent since.

I lamented to Astrid that her beloved Yogi Ramsuratkumar had taken to severely messing with my mind. For days or even weeks at a time, he would shower me with his personal attention. Out of a sea of thousands of disciples, he singled me out, asking me to sit by his side and sing to him, giving me blessing-saturated bananas or oranges to eat that expanded my state of consciousness exponentially, and visiting my house to bless my room or give me special messages. To receive the master's personal attention in this way is to be viscerally reminded that each of us, personally, is completely and unequivocally embraced by God, ultimately held in the lap of the Great Mother, suckling the breast of grace at all times.

Then, in a seamless and unannounced transition, he would ignore me—utterly. The desolation I felt at such times was in exact proportion to the exultation I had felt when he showered me with his attention. Not only did he no longer garland me with his *malas* of literal and metaphorical roses, but I ceased to exist to him. I watched him as he directed his penetrating eyes in my direction, but instead of seeing *me* he saw through my body to what was *behind* me. I had never known such feelings before. Through the simple withdrawal of his glance and acknowledgment, the bubble of my egoic inflation was instantly popped, and I felt reduced to literally *nothing,* an existential nonexistence.

When I finally fell low enough, I would begin to grovel, telling God I was willing to trade in my narcissistic demand to be important for the mere acknowledgment of my existence—some small sign that I was not essentially hollow.

Whether it had taken days or weeks to get there, at *precisely* the moment I was brought to my knees and made to bow down in humility, to acknowledge the false identifications that separated me from all of humanity and from the cosmos, Yogi Ramsuratkumar would call me to him and once again shower me with the personal affections of the Divine.

And so it went for months, with not even a faint sign that I would be allowed to leave India in the foreseeable future. The nature of this dynamic, combined with whatever other notes the Divine was playing on the splintered keyboard of my soul, was such that I slipped into what I much later learned was a mystical depression. Divine joy intertwined so intimately with divine sorrow that both became forms of despair. For to allow myself to get drunk on the divine nectar was to agree to experience unbearable emptiness when the nectar was withdrawn.

I shared my aching heart with Astrid, the only person I thought might understand what I was saying without reducing it to some psychological issue that would require further inner-child work. When I finished my story, she smiled sympathetically. "I know it feels personal," she said, "but it's the oldest guru game in the book. They've been doing it for thousands of years precisely because it works. It doesn't matter what you tell yourself—when the guru plays that card, it works. Don't be too upset with yourself for taking it so seriously." Then she added, "It takes most people at least a couple of decades to come to terms with it. And besides, it's good for you."

By this point I was in regular correspondence with Lee, giving him blow-by-blow accounts of my antics and tribulations with Yogi Ramsuratkumar. Though the two of them lived six thousand miles apart, it was completely predictable that when Yogi Ramsuratkumar adorned me, Lee stripped me; and when Lee encouraged me, the Yogi ignored me. Lee would do things like write me a letter telling me what a great boon Yogi Ramsuratkumar's blessings were for himself as my teacher, and when I wrote back telling him how delighted I was to hear him say he was my teacher, I would receive a letter telling me I was presumptuous to call him my teacher before Yogi Ramsuratkumar had agreed to let me go. Or Lee would write about how strong my practice appeared to be, then follow it with a letter about how I was flushing diamonds down the toilet through my childish antics.

And so the months passed. With pristine clarity I remade my vows to the path, only to be immediately beset with an animosity toward God that is still embarrassing to admit. Fortunately, I had come across Sufi master Irina Tweedie's book *Daughter of Fire* in a local ashram library. It had literally tumbled off the bookshelf as I walked by, dried flowers mysteriously falling from its pages onto the library floor. The book detailed Mrs. Tweedie's daily trials with her master, which not only bore many similarities to my own but actually seemed more unbearable than what I was experiencing, thus providing me with a strange sort of relative comfort.

I am hardly suggesting that everyone who gives themselves wholly to the student-teacher relationship will experience such duels and agonies as I did. Most people won't. Many Buddhist teachers, and most who function in the role of spiritual teacher, do not intentionally confuse and disrupt the ego in this way. They know that such extremes are not for everyone, or they trust the practice itself or the influence of the lineage to provide the necessary opportunities for egoic disidentification. Still, the ego is the same for all, and I have come to appreciate that in the vast majority of circumstances, the process of dismantling egoic identification is at best momentarily difficult, and at "worst" outright agonizing for extended periods of time. According to an old Persian saying, "The ego will not go in gladness and with caresses. It must be chased with sorrow drowned in tears."

While even someone with no psychological or spiritual orientation could see through the simple ploy Yogi Ramsuratkumar used on me, through its use he revealed to me the fickleness of ego, the tendency toward a conditional relationship with God, the experience of God's glory and God's heartbreak, and the simultaneous reality and falsity of duality. He knocked my Humpty Dumpty ego straight off the wall so that even "all the king's horses and all the king's men" couldn't put it back together in quite the same way again.

The legendary story of Marpa and Milarepa is a classic illustration of a crazy-wisdom teacher playing guru games.[1] Once a black magician who came to realize with great remorse the nature of his misdeeds, Milarepa found his way to the renowned master Marpa, offering him everything he had in exchange for the great teachings of liberation. Though Milarepa was eventually to become his greatest successor, Marpa could never outwardly acknowledge him as such. Instead of giving Milarepa esoteric teachings, Marpa asked him to build houses of weighty stones with his bare hands. When Milarepa had laboriously completed a house, hoping to finally have earned the teachings he had come for, Marpa found some fault with it or realized he had asked for it to be built it in the wrong spot. He would then tell Milarepa that in order to receive the teachings he would need to rebuild the house in another place, disassembling the walls and transporting the stones one by one. Milarepa built nine houses, stone by stone, his body ever bruised, his hands torn, his back half-broken, his mind distraught, and his will nearly shattered.

If that were the entirety of the story, one might assume that Marpa was an exploitive, domineering, patriarchal, uncompassionate teacher. But Marpa's wife tells the story that while by day he made demands on Milarepa that seemed ruthless and cruel, at night Marpa returned home teary and distraught over having to kindle the painful fire of purification that was so necessary for his most beloved disciple to endure.

By the time Milarepa had built all nine houses and had "earned" the teachings, he had already received the transmission he sought. He attained it through the intensive purification process he had undergone as a result of his trust in and reverence for Marpa, and his unwavering desire for ultimate surrender.

Crazy Wisdom

"Crazy wisdom" (wisdom gone wild), refers to a quality of inner freedom that knows no bounds. It is a term commonly misunderstood to represent, and thus defend, spiritual teachings and practices that flirt with the boundaries of moral behavior. But crazy-wisdom teachings are always designed to serve the disciple's freedom from the insidious rigidity of egoic identification. Crazy wisdom is ruthless and raw in its insistence on uncompromising freedom, and thus at times its outer expression is cutting, confrontational, or simply bizarre. Still, at other times it is mild, ordinary, and even invisible to the eye. Its priority is to undermine the stronghold of ego identification; if necessary, the crazy-wisdom master will employ unconventional means to effect that outcome.

Arnaud Desjardins points out that true wisdom is always crazy to the ego. Since the ego does not understand authentic wisdom, even a mild intervention that cannot be absorbed by the ego's conceptual framework is quickly labeled as "questionable" or even "crazy," when instead it simply lies outside the ego's capacity to classify and file into its system. Thus it is important not to mistake the inner wildness of crazy wisdom for a set of external behaviors; to do so reduces crazy wisdom to a concept of extreme behaviors rather than an expression of unrestrained freedom born from within.

Disciples of the great Indian mystic Mother Mayee, for example, spent countless hours walking the beaches of Kanyakumari with her, carefully searching for particular types of garbage that were of interest to her. These they would collect, carry in sacks throughout the day, and then burn in a fire in the late afternoon. Many disciples had theories about why they did this, but none could be sure. They knew only that they trusted her and did what they were asked, and in a seemingly unconnected, nonlinear, and inexplicable manner, their lives were transformed.

As it is concerned with conventional morality, the expression of crazy wisdom can be disturbing to the mind, challenging conditioned notions of ethics and morality. It is wise that this is so, as far too many self-proclaimed messiahs have incorporated highly questionable behaviors in the service of so-called awakening. Unfortunately, such behaviors on the part of charlatans have created skepticism regarding the field of crazy wisdom—a manner of teaching that has been in existence for thousands of years. In a culture full of dubious spiritual authorities, few Western crazy-wisdom masters today are afforded the privilege of making use of their full bag of tricks. They are well aware that a single lawsuit brought against them by one unhappy ego could result in their losing the opportunity to continue their teaching function; thus they choose to accept the "oppression" of their mastery in service of remaining available to their students.

There are three major spheres in which crazy-wisdom teachings and guru games raise questions for most people: sex, money, and drug and alcohol use.

Sex

Having seemingly committed every other error in the book, I can say with great pride and amazement that I have never had sex with a guru. Not that all sex with gurus leads to negative or difficult consequences—in many cases it doesn't—but it certainly raises a red flag of caution, or at the very least of potential complications, and it should. As anyone who has seriously engaged spiritual life in Western culture knows, the issue of sex is a big deal.

In ancient Tibet, sexual intercourse was an accepted means of spiritual transmission from teacher to student. Drukpa Kunley, known as "The Divine Madman of the Dragon Lineage," was a famous and cherished fourteenth-century Tibetan Buddhist master who gave spiritual transmission through sexual relationships, earning him the reputation of being "the Saint of five thousand women." It is said that prayer flags demonstrating great pride were hung on the homes he had visited. Of course, times have changed dramatically. Now such a man would be jailed, but was he really not a saint?

If we consider the powerful process of union that occurs in sexual encounters, it seems conceivable that when a human being abides in conscious, dynamic union with the Divine or Truth, the transmission from teacher to student could arise through physical union with the teacher. It involves the same principle as a contemporary Zen master conveying the final transmission to his successor by having both himself and his student locked in a closet together for two days, forehead to forehead, their heads bound together with string.

Western culture is wholly unprepared to accept, much less approve of, such behavior, and most teachers—both Western and Eastern—are equally unprepared to embrace the full responsibility of providing "transmission" in this form. Many are simply unprepared to manage their sexuality with integrity in the face of the overwhelming love projections they receive from their students. I raise these points not to endorse regular sexual encounters between students and teachers but to release the consideration from a "spiritually correct" perspective based on conventional morality. More often than not, sexuality can be misused in the name of crazy wisdom, yet we still must consider evaluating each situation from a "context-specific" perspective.

Often in Western culture it is difficult to know whether teachers' chosen sexual practices—for themselves and for their students—are a function of their spiritual work, their personality preferences, or their psychological weaknesses. What appears to be important is that the teacher be honest about his or her sexual practices. Then it is up to the student to decide whether or not these behaviors are acceptable to him or her.

Criteria that might be useful in evaluating a teacher's sexual practices include whether they involve us personally—either because we are personally intimate with the teacher or because the teacher's suggestions negatively affect our sexual relationship with our intimate partner; whether they involve children—ours or anyone else's; whether the results seem to be helpful or harmful; and whether the teacher appears to have integrity, both in sexual relationships and his or her teaching work in general.

Sexual relationships between teacher and student are usually, though not always, the result of a mutual process and agreement. It is rare that a teacher will engage a sexual relationship with a student without the latter's full and willing consent. Of course, the teacher has power and influence in the situation, and he or she should take full responsibility for how this power is used or misused in terms of seduction and eroticism. But if we choose to become involved, we disempower ourselves when we place the full responsibility on teachers should our sexual liaisons with them not turn out the way we imagined. This circumstance hits very close to home for me, as my partner, spiritual teacher Marc Gafni, was at the effects of false complaints of sexual harassment by individuals with whom he had mutual sexual encounters, a subject detailed in the epilogue of this book.

As spiritual apprentices, we should be aware that erotic transferences onto the teacher commonly arise at some point in the student–teacher relationship. If we can see them for what they are without judging them or taking them too seriously, we can use them to empower our conscious discipleship.

Money

Those of us who are attracted to intensive spiritual practice but still crave playing the wild card that characterizes crazy-wisdom teachers and traditions might find guru games interesting. Interesting, that is, until the teacher asks us to tithe 10 percent of our precious income to the zendo.

Although he was a penniless renunciate, it is said that the late Indian master Swami Nityananda used to employ large crews to build temples and roads. At the end of the day, he would routinely direct them to the side of the road and have them lift up a rock, under which they would find the exact sum of money they had earned according to the amount of work they had completed. A suspicious tax collector, perplexed by how a master who wore only a loincloth could generate such sums of money, approached Nityananda one day demanding to know where the money was coming from. In response, Nityananda brought him to a nearby swamp, opened up the jaws of a resident alligator, and pulled out a large wad of bills. The tax collector never challenged the master on financial issues again.

A senior student of a great Zen master left the monastery with his master's full blessing in order to build his dream house. He labored at it for three years, and when he had completed the final details of his mansion he invited his teacher for a housewarming party. His teacher arrived, made a full survey of the house, thanked his student for building him such a fine estate, and moved in!

When some curious, skeptical guru seekers came to a weekend seminar to check out my teacher many years ago, he spent the first two lectures speaking little of spiritual topics but instead making one sales pitch after another for books, tapes, T-shirts . . . telling people that the way to his blessing was through his wallet—that he wasn't there to offer the teaching, but to make money. The curiosity seekers were scandalized and shortly left. He did not speak that way for the rest of the weekend.

G. I. Gurdjieff kept his students always at the edge of financial ruin, generating one financial disaster after another. When questioned about why he did this, he said it was absolutely essential because if people feel too comfortable they don't grow.

Again, crazy wisdom can be used or misused, which is why it is such a challenging path. The crazy-wisdom master will employ money, or any other available commodity, to offer students an opportunity to free themselves from the attachments or aversions that keep them bound to their illusory perceptions. Even though in essence money is only symbolic, it is also *very real*. It is instructive to observe ourselves supplicating God to grant us ultimate liberation, then cringing at the thought of donating a hundred dollars to buy some new meditation cushions for the meditation hall.

In a psychological sense, the act of trading money for teachings is symbolic of the energetic exchange between teacher and student. In many cases, paying for immaterial goods actually helps people. It is classic psychological economics that when we pay for something, in our desire to "get our money's worth" we are more willing to pay attention, apply ourselves, and make ourselves vulnerable to whatever "service" we have purchased. When something is free, people don't trust it. I learned this firsthand when I moved to a small town in England and established a massage practice. At first, I tried to attract clientele by setting up a chair at the local market and offering free ten-minute massages. Not only did people not sit down, they walked around me. But when I put up a sign offering ten-minute massages for three pounds (five dollars), I was busy the rest of the day.

Material riches are a metaphor for true power and objective wealth. The only true power and wealth are internal, but most people will settle for money, fame, or relative power, or at least for the fantasy of it. Of course, the unconscious belief is that the material wealth will somehow miraculously translate itself into ultimate happiness, but this can only be found through that which we could refer to as union, compassion, surrender, or God. It is interesting to entertain the possibility that all the corrupt, patriarchal dictators in the world are actually seeking union with God, even if they are completely unaware of it.

On the reverse side of this issue, many people in spiritual circles operate with the idea that money, power, and fame are inherently corrupt, negative, and unspiritual. This limiting belief is primarily the result of Eastern philosophies and practices of traditional renunciation that have been poorly translated into contemporary Western culture. In the development of contemporary spiritual culture in the Western world, we must come to terms with money, power, and the constellation of conditioned belief structures that surround these forces. Our relationship to money, the teacher's relationship to money, our relationship to money in regard to the teacher, and what we do with all of that determines whether material riches and power are an asset or a detriment to our spiritual process. If we are conscious in our discipleship, we can use our relationship to money to gain valuable information about ourselves and appreciate the gift of our resources. To truly renounce is to renounce *false relationships* to things, not the things themselves.

It is also important to recognize that the teacher needs money to support his or her work. In traditional Southeast Asian Buddhist cultures, the townspeople and lay practitioners supported the local monastery financially as an expression of their acknowledgment of its essential function in the community. They knew that the monks and nuns were practicing on behalf of the welfare of all, with a level of rigor that they could not or did not desire to engage in themselves. They also knew that the practical way they could contribute was through their financial support. Each student must come to terms with his or her own response to the specific financial situation he or she encounters in relationship to the teacher.

Every time I see ads for "enlightenment intensives" charging hundreds of dollars in exchange for promised illumination, my third eye rolls. Even so, I cannot help but wonder whether the intention behind the attendees' enthusiastic longing really goes unheeded. In most of our lives, money comes and goes in waves, and powerful lessons are learned through putting our money and our bodies on the line.

For a few years, I spent time with a guru who was jokingly referred to as a teacher of "yuppie yoga." She attracted the rich and famous, and at her darshan, gifts of diamond rings, gold necklaces, stacks of bills, and property deeds would be offered. Perhaps the students' generosity served *them* in some way, perhaps these wealthy individuals needed to create a literal kingdom in order to entice them to worship, or perhaps the teacher attracted wealthy students because *she* wanted a queendom. These are not questions of objective morality but of refining our discernment, again and again.

It is impossible to create rules about teachers and money. Once again, what is true in one circumstance is false in another; or what is true in one situation may even be false in that *same* situation just a day or a week later, or for a different individual. All we can do is empower our own conscious discipleship by becoming aware of the variables, the dangers, the possibilities, and the necessity of risk.

Alcohol and Drugs

A great Chinese Zen master was known for drinking a cup of whiskey every night before bed, and for decades it remained a great mystery to the monks why he did so, though nobody had ever asked him. When he was on his deathbed, the monks realized they could not allow him to die without discovering the meaning of this practice, so one of the senior monks approached him and begged him to reveal its purpose.

"For many years I have had difficulty sleeping due to the pain of my arthritis," the master told him, compassion in his tired eyes, "and several years ago I discovered that if I drank a glass of whiskey I could sleep much better."

Chögyam Trungpa Rinpoche drank heavily and has been widely criticized for his alcoholism. At the inception of the Naropa Institute, the Buddhist college he founded, the school planned a fundraising event and invited wealthy donors from all over the country. Trungpa Rinpoche was expected to give the keynote lecture. Starting in the early morning on the day of the event, he began to drink. To the concern of his students, he consumed such extensive quantities of Japanese sake throughout the day that by the time he was scheduled to address the donors, he was doubled over and unable to speak. Infuriated and embarrassed, a close student glared from the audience at his drunken teacher, doubting his mastery and watching his behavior with scorn. At that very moment, Trungpa Rinpoche opened one eye, stared directly and soberly into the eyes of his distrusting student, and closed it again.

Many Zen and Tibetan masters and their students are known for consuming large amounts of alcohol. Many yogic, native, indigenous, and shamanic traditions involve the use of psychedelics and other drugs. In some cases drugs are used as a sacrament; at other times their use is a distraction or addiction justified with a spiritual rationale. Yogi Ramsuratkumar was known for chain-smoking a particular brand of local cigarettes. When I lived near him, visiting skeptical Westerners often challenged me, claiming he couldn't be a true master because of his nicotine addiction—one who controlled his senses would never engage in such self-destructive behaviors. I did not know the reason for Yogi Ramsuratkumar's behavior, but his implicit mastery, far beyond any teacher I had ever encountered, revealed itself to my satisfaction again and again. Thus I found it easy to allow such choices to be his own business. Once again, imposing contemporary Western moral standards upon a wisdom that has no convention and no bounds will limit our capacity for discernment.

As conscious disciples of the spiritual path of life, our task is not to make moral and rigid judgments about whether the intake of drugs and alcohol is "right" or "wrong" for a teacher or for his or her students. What we are called to consider is whether the teacher's relationship with us is compromised and whether we can tolerate the behavior. We may never know whether a teacher's drinking or intake of drugs is fully in the service of his or her practice or of his or her unconscious, or is perhaps is unrelated to either.

Furthermore, we should be wary of falling into the trap of imitating the teacher, indiscriminately deciding, "Well, he drinks two bottles of sake each day, and *his* practice seems to be going all right, so I guess that means I can, too." Many teachers gain poor reputations because their disciples imitate their habits, not because of the teacher's own actions. Are we willing to act in accordance with our own integrity and discipline irrespective of whether the teacher practices in the exact same fashion? The process of conscious discipleship is about empowering and taking full responsibility for our *own* practice, not morally evaluating the teacher's. Thus we must be ever cautious of the tendency to compromise our practice through unconscious mimicry.

Separation from the Yogi

It took me more than six months to solve the first crazy-wisdom *koan* my teacher gave me: to obtain Yogi Ramsuratkumar's permission and blessing to leave India and assume a life of practice back in America without applying any manipulation or control whatsoever. With my foreign entry visa nearly expired, I was aware that at the very least I would need permission to go to Burma to get an extension. I also knew that if I got that extension I was going to have to stay in smoldering India, far from my teacher's physical presence, for a *long* time. I became desperate to gain my release from the Yogi.

When we are desperate enough, the universe responds, though admittedly not always in the form requested. This time the universe kindly sent me a wall of mirrors in the form of people and circumstances that revealed to me what I had been unable to see about myself until that point. Among the messengers was a four-year-old twin girl who was jealous of the attention her sister received from Yogi Ramsuratkumar. I observed as she performed all kinds of antics to receive a mere morsel of love so that she, too, could feel special.

Though it had taken six months to arrive at this discovery, in a moment I saw clearly that it was not the quality of Yogi Ramsuratkumar's attention on *me* that was responsible for my divine jail sentence, but of mine on *him*. I had begged for the Kingdom of Heaven, and it was his obligation to see to it that I obtained those riches by any means necessary. I saw plainly that while I had been clear within myself about who I wanted for my teacher, I had not *acted* clearly because my ego was unwilling to forego the delicious attention it was being fed by Yogi Ramsuratkumar in favor of spiritual monogamy with my teacher. The ping-pong match the two masters played, with me as the ball, demanded I take full responsibility for my own conscious discipleship. I was finally willing to cease the childish behavior that had made me feel like a prisoner; in reality, I now understood, I had handed my captors the keys to my cell.

In that moment of insight, I knew Yogi Ramsuratkumar would allow me to leave India to proceed in my life with Lee. He did not have to let *me* go; I had to let *him* go. When I did, he responded in kind *almost* immediately.

Almost . . . but he wanted to be sure I had learned my lesson, or perhaps see if I wanted to play for the bonus, as well. The next morning, the moment I stepped into the darshan hall, Yogi Ramsuratkumar called me up to speak with him; he always knew without asking when I needed to do so. Earlier that morning he had received my one-sentence, noncontrolling, nonmanipulative request to leave India. I had told him in the note that I would like to return to California, pick up my car, drive to Arizona, and ask Lee if I could become his student.

"This beggar [which is how he referred to himself] doesn't understand Mariana's note," he told me—he who understood the English language better than I did. I knew we were in another game: the game of "Playing Dumb." It was one of his favorites.

"I would like to go back to California, and then go visit Lee and ask to be his student," I repeated, just as the note said.

"What?" Yogi Ramsuratkumar turned to his attendant, telling her, as if I were speaking Atlantean, "This beggar doesn't understand."

"Mariana is asking you if she can return to California, at which time she will collect her car, drive to Arizona, and ask Lee if she can be his student," the attendant repeated. No good.

"What do you want?" The Yogi turned to me again, growing apparently frustrated by my seeming inability to communicate the simplest of messages.

Entirely at a loss, I sputtered, "I want to go back to America and do whatever Lee suggests I do!"—at which he raised his hands high in blessing, laughing in a way that makes the whole world joyous. This time, however, his laugh symbolized the end of the game and not the beginning.

"My Father blesses Mariana to return to America!"

The deal was sealed. At least that one . . .

We must continually remind ourselves that whether we are talking about the controversial aspects of crazy wisdom—sex, money, or alcohol and drugs—the real "craziness" is the paradox that exists within the dualistic perception of the human mind. Some force of divine intelligence opted to manifest a wisdom as crazy as human incarnation, complete with its mental madness and utterly distorted perception of reality, yet it also provided human beings with a longing to understand their condition. Who is the ultimate crazy-wisdom master?! "There is no one on this earth who is not looking for God," said the Persian mystic Hafiz. At the end of the day, we are all students of the crazy wisdom of life—persisting in our studies of money, relationship, sex, self-knowledge, disillusionment, confusion, and personal and collective unfolding.

12

OBEDIENCE

You must pay dearly, pay a lot, immediately, in advance, with yourself. The more you are prepared to pay, the more you will receive.
—JEANNE DE SALZMANN

At this point in the story that is my life, I had been sent by a God-intoxicated Indian saint to visit a crazy-wise Jewish teacher in Arizona in order to "do whatever he suggests." Most people, including my poor family, thought I was crazy. I am, by conventional standards. But true wisdom is crazy, authentic spiritual life is highly unconventional, and the game of radical transformation is one of fundamental risk.

I hadn't been at Lee's ashram for two weeks when he asked if I would like to take on a writing project for him.

"Sure," I said, having always done a lot of journaling, and having scribbled out an occasional sappy poem to a lover or a god.

"Great. Go talk to Sita and she'll tell you the idea. I've been wanting someone to do this for years, but nobody has been willing."

Only two weeks in and I had my first test of obedience from the master. I was elated—once again foolishly so.

I returned to him an hour later, highly agitated, certain a misunderstanding had taken place that he would clear up for me. "Sita said you wanted a *book* written."

"That's right."

"I don't write *books*. I've never taken a writing class, and I wouldn't have a clue where to begin. Books take years of work, and before that decades of accrued wisdom to even get to the point of envisioning oneself worthy of writing one in the first place!"

"Do you want the project or not?" he asked, apparently indifferent to my argument.

"Sure," I said with a gulp.

How the hell do you write a book?! I pondered half the night as summer's monsoonal rain beat on the tin roof of the kitchen-table-sized trailer I had been loaned to live in.

In the morning, I asked Lee if I should take a class at the local community college.

"Nope."

"Private tutoring?" I was still hopeful.

"No."

"Interview writers?"

"Negative."

I guess you write a book by writing a book, I thought with resignation, and I went about engaging my preliminary research.

Though I moved along at a snail's pace, I was rather proud of myself for doing it at all. But that wasn't enough for the master, whose job description includes enticing the disciple to fulfill his or her highest potential in the least amount of time without demanding more than is humanly possible.

The day before Lee was due to travel to India for five weeks, I found myself in the uncommon circumstance of driving him in my car to a bar in town to watch our ashram blues band perform.

"So, are you going to have the manuscript complete when I get back from India?"

His question sent my mind and body into temporary shock, and I nearly swerved off the road.

"Watch the road!" he yelled.

I veered back. "I haven't even begun the actual writing. Are you serious?!"

"Of course I'm serious."

To say that the following five weeks were as hellish as a Siberian winter would be an understatement. I slept about three hours a day, wrote sixteen to twenty, and used the rest of the time to fit in my various spiritual practices. I ate while I wrote, jogged to a nearby building when I needed to use the bathroom, and did not engage in idle conversation. When I felt so mentally deranged I couldn't bear it any longer, I would break down in tears of exhaustion, at which time a merciful sangha-mate would insist on driving me to the movies to watch a dumb comedy so my mind could rest. I would then return home to resume work until my eyelids could stay open no longer, wondering whether I was being tortured or liberated.

The mere mechanics of writing one's first book in five weeks was not the most difficult part. Far more confrontational was battling the ten thousand daemons that were preventing me from *believing* I could complete such a task—that I was smart enough, talented enough, worthy enough. But somehow I managed. In five (admittedly miserable) weeks of obedience to my teacher, I surmounted obstacles that years of therapy and meditation practices had not even touched. For more than a decade, Emily Dickinson's quote "I dwell in possibility" had hung on my wall, but now it was finally more than a distant romantic idea that belonged to another. When I finally let out my first exhausted sigh of relief after turning in my manuscript upon Lee's return, I found I had surpassed so many self-effacing belief systems about myself that I was disoriented about who I was. Freed through book torture!

As if the personal benefits of my transformational process and the overwhelmingly gracious response of readers were not enough, my very own family—after years of tolerating the outrageous adventures and bizarre ideas of their Buddhist-shaman-Hindu-anthropologist-therapist-influenced daughter—finally thought that this strange spiritual thing I was doing just might be a good idea. Not only were they impressed with the content of the book, but their outlandish spiritual daughter was now published and even appearing regularly on radio and television programs. The book was called *When Sons and Daughters Choose Alternative Lifestyles,* and my mother's first comment after reading it was, "You should have written that book years ago. You would have saved us so many problems!" We both laughed in recognition that it was precisely those years and problems that had taught me everything I knew about the subject. Even more surprising was my conservative Jewish, cult-fearing father's suggestion that my eldest brother might benefit from "spending some time at that commune of yours with that guru-fellow. It's sure done you a lot of good."

Exactly two weeks later, Lee gave me my second book title . . .

∞∞∞

If you really want to crash a spiritual cocktail party, all that's required is to raise the topic of obedience to the spiritual teacher. Obedience is poorly understood in the field of contemporary spirituality, conjuring images of "power over," control tactics, and manipulation. It is no wonder that this is the case, as countless abuses take place in the name of obedience, while those who argue against it do so primarily to protect the innocent from untrustworthy influences. Furthermore, not all student-teacher

relationships—particularly among the various Buddhist traditions—require obedience, certainly not at all stages along one's
path. Teachers who warn against obedience should be listened to,
and those who demand blind following should be scrutinized, but
many teachers of impeccable integrity in all traditions still choose
to work within this model because of benefits demonstrated over
many centuries.

Obedience is not a moral issue; it is a pragmatic practice—the
primary purpose of which is to facilitate with optimal efficiency
the aspirant's relationship to truth. Thus I strongly encourage the
reader to suspend preconceptions about obedience to whatever
degree possible and bear with me as we travel step-by-step through
a consideration of the labyrinth of obedience to the spiritual teacher.
If your particular tradition does not suggest obedience, I encourage
you to respect and follow that; use this chapter to augment your
own understanding of this complex issue and to appreciate why
individuals in other traditions would choose to engage in this practice at certain junctures along their process of unfolding.

Obedience to Whom?

Perhaps the highest expression of human incarnation is ultimate
and unwavering obedience to a force some call the Divine or God,
and others refer to as Truth. This force, "unborn, undying, never
ceasing, never beginning, deathless, birthless, unchanging forever,"[1]
can be expressed through a human being. The principal reason we
should even consider obedience to a spiritual teacher is to practice
obedience to the Divine or Truth within ourselves via one whose
own realization of the Divine is more transparent, and whose perspective is not obfuscated by the psychological blind spots that
can impede our perceiving the necessary steps to take in our lives
at a given time. Ultimate obedience to God or Truth cannot be

expressed with unwavering constancy until the human being is fully purified of all obstructions that deny access to that already-present force. We "borrow" or "rent" the guidance of the true teacher as a temporary stand-in for objective obedience in our lives until we ourselves are rightfully prepared to assume that function.

To place obedience to the teacher in its rightful perspective requires understanding the distinction between the guru and the guru-principle, or the personality of the teacher versus the teaching he or she represents. The guru-principle expresses itself through the personal form of the teacher, who expresses the teaching through his or her personality and culture. But objective obedience is only and always to the Ultimate.

As students striving toward the expression of our highest spiritual possibility, we are once again dealing with two seemingly opposing forces: one that longs for the true heart's release and will gladly do anything required toward that end, and the other the egoic insistence that the former should never occur. Under ordinary circumstances, the ego, fully identified with the body and programmed to believe it can and must preserve the life of that body, will obey only itself. Obedience to the teacher creates a circumstance that allows the student to learn three lessons: the distinction between egoic demands and the objective commands of truth; what it is to let go of control enough to allow something unknown to emerge; and the experience of trusting something beyond one's own limited mind. The spiritual student in obedience to the teacher is in "surrender training," preparing for the ultimate surrender to Truth, Life, and the Will of God.

Reasons to Obey

Modern Western culture was founded upon values of independence, freedom, and autonomy. Its members are taught that these values are superior to all others, and become confused and disillusioned when the proponents of these values act in a hypocritical and untrustworthy fashion. Women especially, who even in our "liberated" culture are subject to discrimination and marginalization, are likely to feel betrayed and oppressed. Given this cultural background and experience, suggesting that obedience to spiritual authority has value for spiritual transformation to occur may sound all but preposterous.

Few human beings have ever consistently experienced the guidance of the objective authority of the Self—either as expressed within themselves or in the form of another—much less the possibilities of living in obedience to that Self as temporarily mediated by one in whom it is expressed more fully: the spiritual teacher. The teacher has no investment in the deeply engraved defense structures that keep the individual aspirant from expressing that Self consistently in his or her own life.

To Practice Letting Go of Control

Those who are happiest in life are that way not because life gives them everything they want but because they have learned to let go of trying to force life to be other than it is. Instead of resisting life, they turn toward it in its full expression, continually letting go of the endless stream of conditioned egoic demands and expectations in favor of a mature acceptance of life and of their own humanity.

It is hard to trust that the universe has an Ultimate Intelligence that is greater than the intelligence of the separative mind (perceived by most of us to be "who I am"). Yet those who have even touched upon this revelation through mystical experiences or altered states of consciousness attest to its reality, and most of us intuitively sense that Love ultimately and mysteriously conquers fear, hatred, and resistance.

We should not underestimate how difficult it is to truly let go of the illusion of separation. The ego can generate convincing impersonations of letting go and imitations of freedom (as is readily exemplified in New Age spirituality), but each authentic letting-go—a true feeling, a moment of true presence, an unmitigated "yes" without personal agenda—represents to the ego a leap off a cliff. To make such a jump requires tremendous fortitude. Since the ego is convinced that even a small letting-go means death to the individual it has been put in charge of protecting, we must convince it that it can survive these leaps without incurring its ultimate demise. We do this by providing it with experiential evidence that it can, in fact, survive our small experimental leaps into the unknown. Our trust in and obedience to the teacher offer assurance that our "radical experiments" in letting go are ultimately useful and productive, and that our egoic mechanism is not running the show, once again asserting its own agenda.

When we finally begin to consciously allow the intelligence of Life to move us, the universe within and without opens. Imagined limitations are replaced with lived experiences of unlimited possibility. Others benefit from our contact with an energy that now fills us. We are more open and generous because we are no longer continually defending ourselves from engaging in relationships that once felt so threatening to the protective ego. When we release our limited control and embrace the unknown, we become privy to previously hidden secrets of the universe (though some can and should remain forever mysterious). Life opens radically, and true Self-expression begins.

Preparation for Death

We need to learn to let go not only to be able to experience life in its infinite range of possibilities but to prepare ourselves for the process of dying, for death itself, and probably for what comes beyond death. According to most Eastern mystical traditions, the moment of death is the most crucial moment of our lives. It is in that moment that our capacity to surrender fully to the Universe, enlightenment, the Source of All is tested. So important is the moment of bodily death that many branches of Tibetan vajrayana Buddhism focus an enormous amount of energy on practices to prepare for it.

In the moments just prior to death, the individual is forced up against the final wall of his or her resistance and intuits that he or she is facing the final opportunity to let go in this lifetime. Even earnest practitioners, however well motivated, often do not appear to be able to fully let go at the moment of death. A lifetime of conditioned mental habits and unconscious patterns live in and through the very cells of the body. The cells themselves, conditioned by the protective ego to ensure survival, are programmed not to let go. Although this concept may be difficult to understand, it is relevant to each of us: conditioned egoic functioning believes itself to be real and believes itself to be the body of the individual in whom it arises. The human being misidentifies with this force, forgetting his or her essential nature and believing that when the body dies, he or she dies. However death comes—accompanied by overwhelming physical and/or emotional discomfort; with great fear and exacerbation of attachments; when we are highly medicated and despondent; unsuspectingly while we're asleep—if we have not trained ourselves to let go in life, we will be *unable* to let go in death in spite of the best of intentions. The practice of obedience trains us to act in accordance with a greater dictate than that of our conditioning.

This principle becomes evident when we care for someone who experiences a difficult death process. I cared for a dear friend during her final months of life as an aggressive and extremely painful cancer consumed her. In the final weeks, it was obvious that her body could go on no more, that it was time to die, that every further day she hung on was a day of agony, defeat, and refusal to accept the task of death that life had set before her. But she could not let go. Through long, agonizing nights we lay on her bed together while she, unable to talk or open her eyes, grasped at life as if she were a hungry ghost refusing to accept the reality that it was already dead. For this reason alone, I told myself then, it is worthwhile to learn to let go while alive. Obedience to the master—misunderstood as it is—offers unparalleled instruction in this process.

It is highly likely that death is not the end of the life of the soul. According to sages in many traditions who for millennia have studied states of consciousness beyond the life of the body, when the individual dies, the Soul or Essence enters into a series of realms of consciousness in its journey of reincarnation. Tibetans refer to these realms as the *bardos*.[2] The individuated soul passing through the bardos is said to pass through any number of illusory distractions—both hellish and heavenly—as well as a variety of strong attachments and the reliving of difficulties in one or more former lives. The individual's greatest possibility lies in his or her capacity, developed during life, to be swayed neither by attractions nor repulsions, to let go and allow forces of consciousness larger than egoic attachment dictate the direction of the soul's unfolding.

Many people who have engaged in significant experimentation with deep meditation techniques and psychedelic drugs have had experiences that led them to this conclusion: that the only way to pass through difficult states is either to let go of them through detachment, or more powerfully, to allow them to transform themselves by surrendering into them. The ability to let go in this way requires tremendous presence, consciousness, and psychic strength.

The practice is the same in life as it is in death: to let go. Many people can learn to do this to a great extent through their own inner process and the circumstances life provides them. The advantage of working with a spiritual teacher is that the teacher can provide instruction in seeing and dealing with those attachments that are the most obscured in us and may therefore be the hardest to let go of when the body dies.

Letting go in obedience to the teacher is a risky form of practice if there are doubts about the teacher's integrity, but within a context of consistent and grounded practice, and under the supervision of a trustworthy guide, it can be very effective. With the exception of circumstances in which dangerous and unethical acts are committed, obedience can teach discrimination and help conscious disciples (as opposed to the victimized subjects) learn something about how they tend to relate to forces greater than their own egos.

The Teacher Holds Our Highest Possibility

The authentic teacher literally holds the space for our highest possible manifestation in the face of the limiting self-concepts we were taught by our parents and culture. The teacher, not bound by our limited self-concept, sees a possibility that often exceeds anything we had imagined for ourselves.

The authentic teacher is always watching for unexpected openings in which skillful intervention may catalyze a profound shift in the student. He or she is like a personal (spiritual) triathlon trainer, providing the willing student with exercises that strengthen spiritual muscles necessary to the student's progress in Self-development.

There may also be areas of potential development that the student has neither considered nor desired but that nonetheless offer opportunities for both gratifying self-fulfillment and service to others. In my own case, my teacher's request to write a book in a highly condensed period of time, combined with my willing obedience, began my whole life as a writer, which was an invaluable opportunity to overcome false belief structures that had kept me from fulfilling a role that had been my childhood dream. Such limited self-concepts keep us from expressing greater freedom and flexibility in all aspects of our lives and relationships, and deprive others of what we might otherwise offer. To be able to write enabled me to execute my greatest service in life, and was a gift offered by my teacher's wisdom combined with my willingness to obey his instruction, at least in that instance!

A teacher asked a student if she ever sang. She responded, "Never." Three years later, she was showcased at the Nice Jazz Festival—a high-profile event—still emotionally insecure but now singing blues to the masses and feeding thousands of hungry souls. For most students, the process is less showy but equally powerful. Perhaps the individual has a great capacity to serve others selflessly but has always been too afraid to express her warmth, and the teacher provides a circumstance in which the disciple can practice giving what she has to offer. Or someone is deeply desirous of an intimate relationship but is too full of self-hatred to allow one to develop, so the teacher arranges circumstances in less threatening arenas so the student can slowly build connections that pave the way for the possibility of a future relationship. The point is not *what* the specific exercise is but breaking through preconditioned limitations that restrict us and keep us from our highest potential as human beings. It often takes someone outside of ourselves to perceive this for us and direct us so we can work through stuck places.

On our own we rarely engage behaviors that are beyond our range of familiarity and comfort. The reason accidents, death, illness, war, and other tragedies are so powerful is that they are outside of our control and propel us into new realms of possibility. Conscious obedience involves a voluntary agreement to allow more of those opportunities to be created for us.

Ultimately, our highest possibility is that which some people refer to as enlightenment, surrender, or God. The spiritual path is a winding road strewn with obstacles and ever-deepening disillusionment as the depth of our own falsity, suffering, deceitfulness, and perceived separation is revealed. Under such circumstances it is difficult to remember our soul's deepest longing and to align our lives in accordance with that longing. The true teacher will remember for us, ever calling to us or simply existing as an external expression of our own conscious wish to live lives of freedom and surrender.

Reasons Not to Obey

As beneficial as obedience to a true teacher can be, it cannot and should not occur before its rightful time and circumstance. There are many reasons we choose not to obey, and they are best considered with understanding, respect, and patience, without judgment, and with an appreciation for rightful timing.

The Teacher's Level of Mastery Is Not Deserving of Our Obedience

One should never engage in obedience before one is confident in the teacher, especially if following the teacher's advice leads to life-altering choices. We may choose to study with a well-meaning and perhaps very good teacher, but the teacher may be one who is not realized to the extent that he or she is capable of directing our lives to the degree where such obedience benefits us. Claudio Naranjo tells the story of a time during his initial years of "enlightenment" when he was able to provide students with suggestions for major life changes that turned out to be tremendously beneficial. But his precision in providing direction eventually waned to such a degree that he stopped making suggestions altogether. There is value in obedience, but only to the teacher who clearly exemplifies the capacity to direct students well—and has an impeccable track record of doing so.

Before considering obedience to a teacher, we should focus our attention on becoming conscious students, for only through our own consciousness will we be able to accurately sense the degree of a teacher's mastery.[3]

Further Trust Must Be Built

Trust involves two processes: the trustworthiness of the teacher along with our capacity to discern it, and our own capacity and willingness to trust. Both must be in position for an effective student-teacher relationship to take place. If we obey the wrong teacher, we may find ourselves in serious trouble.

When we choose to obey because an adopted spiritual mandate tells us "Good students are obedient," our efforts are likely to be thwarted at some point. This is because our gestures arise from an ethic composed from without rather than a calling from within. Our efforts are more likely to be fruitful through smaller "experiments" with obedience to the teacher—following a teacher's minor suggestions wholeheartedly and without reservation and then observing the results. When we finally decide to place our cards on the table, we should be sure we are in the right game!

Obedience Is Too Hard

Obedience is hard—too hard for many. When somebody we trust asks us to do something that is either far beyond our imagined capacity or that we do not—and may never—understand, it is difficult. We cannot understand the ways and means of the mystery.

We can only be as conscious as we are able in any circumstance. Sometimes the risk feels too great; other times we are more daring.

Even when we do trust the teacher, it is difficult to obey when we simply don't *feel* like doing what is asked. I recall a time when my teacher asked for volunteers to serve cocktails at a weeklong trade show for a commercial photography firm at a conference center in Las Vegas. It wasn't even a mystical request; it was practical—one of his students who owned a company that produced trade-show booths had an important contract and needed help. The task was about as unappealing as anything I could conceive. I would rather have experimented with being a garbage collector or a homeless person. I told him that I did not *want* to, that if there were other volunteers I would rather not, but that if necessary I was willing.

In the end, one more person was needed, and he asked me to go, so I went. Through countless hours of serving beer with all the heartfulness I could muster (not because I was selfless but because I needed to make it bearable for myself), unanticipated conversations and interactions opened up. I was able to serve a few of those suffering businesspeople in a way that was priceless to them, and through "trying on" the identity of a trade-show cocktail waitress for a few days I was able to see how smug my ego had become in its identity as a spiritual practitioner and writer.

We May Not Get What We Want

Choosing to obey means that "I" may not get what I want. The question is, which "I" among the many within me is getting or not getting what it wants? Anyone who gets deeply involved in a life of spiritual practice quickly discovers the many opposing forces within himself that are at play in the soul's thirsty journey toward its source—and never are the forces of opposition and denial so evident as when one begins to work seriously with an authentic teacher.

The teacher's job is to devote him- or herself wholly to the "I" within the student that wants God or Truth. Nothing else. The teacher must skillfully work with the multiple aspects of the psyche that support and express that emerging truth, as well as with those that appear to counteract the student's true aim. But the teacher's ultimate loyalty must be to the "I" that wants only God or Truth. When the student is not identified with the "I" that seeks union, the teacher's requests are likely to clash with what the student wants to do or feels like doing.

There have been times in my discipleship when I knew my teacher was asking something of me that would support my deepest spiritual longing but I chose to respond instead to the wishes of other parts of me. Perhaps I was resistant, or perhaps there were other callings of my soul, or maybe there were needs to be satisfied at a different level of experience. Who can ultimately judge such matters? I suggest that we simply be conscious and honest in relationship to them. Responding to a student who was struggling with the clash between worldly desires and a desire for God, Arnaud Desjardins advised: "Leave *nirvana* for now, and cross the ocean of life."

Disobedience

Krishna Das, a renowned musician on the Western *kirtan* circuit, told me the following story. I appreciate it and respect his rendition of it not only because of its candor and honesty, but because both my life of practice, as well as coaching and counseling countless others on the path, has demonstrated to me that this is really all of us, each in our own way. The spiritual path is both transcendent and ultimate, and simultaneously deeply human.

In his early twenties, Krishna Das traveled to India in search of God. A contemporary of the Western mystic Ram Dass (Richard

Alpert), Krishna Das became deeply devoted to Ram Dass's teacher, Neem Karoli Baba, the Indian saint who is widely revered for his extraordinary realization, miracles, and compassion. Like so many fervent but inexperienced seekers before and since, Krishna Das devoted himself wholly to his teacher and his practice, leaving behind sex and relationships in a belief that they were obstacles to God, rather than acknowledging that his renunciation was the result of a mixture of his own fears and a genuine longing for God.

After three years of this informal "renunciation," Neem Karoli Baba, perhaps suspecting what was really going on in his still-youthful disciple, sent Krishna Das to the United States to sort out his foreign visa and to earn enough money to no longer have to live off others. As is common in such circumstances, no sooner had Krishna Das arrived in the land of power, distraction, and sexuality than his hormone-charged body predictably began to crave sex, fame, and a wide range of experiences. He began touring with Ram Dass and soon found himself in lust with a beautiful woman who came to live with him, the great energy he received from his guru now channeled into a powerful surge in his career and love life. A few months into this affair, he received a fax from India written by a close student of Neem Karoli Baba suggesting that he return to India.

As Krishna Das was but one of thousands of his master's devotees, he knew that such a personalized invitation was anything but casual. Still, by this point he was having *fun,* and although he swore he loved his master more than life itself—and as far as his conscious awareness was concerned, he wanted God more than anything (including really great sex)—he managed to convince himself that there were many important and justifiable reasons why he should wait just a little bit longer before returning to his life as a celibate monk in India. He wrote his teacher and rationally explained that he had not yet earned quite *enough* money to live in India as long as he would like to; that whereas he had applied for his visa, it had not yet come; and that he hadn't fulfilled *all* of the requests his master had made of him when he had sent him to the West. As any true master who respects his or her disciple's free will would, Neem Karoli Baba lovingly acquiesced to his student's wishes. Three months before Krishna Das was to return to India, his master died. Krishna Das never saw or spoke with his living master again.

Even as Krishna Das showed the maturity of one who has learned through life's hard lessons as he told me this story, some twenty-plus years later we could both sense the impact of missing the chance to see one's master a final time before death—particularly someone whose greatness was as rare as that of Neem Karoli Baba. In his process of ego inflation—which will touch every serious spiritual aspirant at one point or another whether it is expressed overtly or subtly—he missed an irreplaceable opportunity. Spiritual teachers are many, but truly great masters are rare, and they move within greater universal currents than the rational mind perceives. It is a painful truth that sometimes the lessons of disobedience can be more powerful than the lessons of obedience.

Even in the most conscious discipleship, there will be poignant moments when the voice of the teacher seems to be in direct conflict with a strong inner voice or sensing, and these are extremely difficult junctures in the process of studenthood. Some people are able to make great gestures of obedience to the teacher—whether they involve investing money or doing austere practices or taking on daring tasks. Still, there are other times when we have not discerned our teacher's trustworthiness accurately, and something within us tells us we should not follow this particular direction.

There was a time in my own process with my teacher when I was about to make a conscious choice of disobedience because

I was unconvinced of what he was asking me to do, even though his recommendations until that time had been flawlessly accurate. I was discussing my decision with him, asking both him and myself, "Why, if I know that the choice of disobedience is a mistake, would I choose to do it anyway?"

"Because you don't *know* it is a mistake," he responded. "Just go ahead and do it. Test me. Test yourself. Test your practice. You didn't come here to do your spiritual life perfectly. The reason you came here was to make conscious experiments *and* mistakes, and then to learn from them."

Mistakes are only mistakes when we do not grow from them. It is the very process of engaging and then wrestling with the principle and practice of obedience—not the flawless fulfillment of it—that deepens our understanding of what it means to obey the true Self that exists within each of us.

There are still other times, even in the life of a conscious student with an authentic teacher, when it is just not right to obey. Perhaps the teacher's suggestion is not the only right direction to follow, or more commonly, perhaps the teacher is suggesting something that the student will not be able to live with in good conscience in the long term. Returning to the example cited earlier in the book, I have seen too many female spiritual students agonize about, and then often renounce, having a child because it was not in line with their spiritual tradition or their teacher did not recommend it. Many of these women have lived to regret that choice. Again, mature studenthood—even in the context of a traditional and even obedient guru-disciple relationship—means that we are ultimately responsible for all of our spiritual choices and their outcomes.

If our experiments with obedience are successful, we will have occasional experiences during which we notice ourselves becoming free of ourselves. We will note that our experiments are worthwhile and effective. Then the teacher will ask us to do something else we don't want to do, and we will again question whether or not obedience is worthwhile. But if the teacher is trustworthy, over time we will gain a reference for the value of obedience and make further choices accordingly.

Blind Following versus Conscious Obedience

Because frequent abuses and disappointments occur between spiritual teachers and their students in the name of obedience, the process of conscious studenthood to any path requires learning the distinction between surrender and submission, between conscious obedience in relationship to spiritual authority and blind following. Blind following is the expression of childish and unconscious discipleship; conscious obedience represents the fruits of mature discipleship. Unfortunately, the latter often comes through one's repetitive mistakes with the former.

I was wrestling with the idea of obedience during the period when the infamous cult scandal of Heaven's Gate arose, in which cult leader Marshall Applewhite convinced thirty-eight followers that a spaceship, hiding behind comet Hale-Bopp, would deliver them to the next phase of their lives after they committed suicide (ultimately by consuming lethal doses of phenobarbital and vodka). One night I sat in the ashram office poring over articles about the event in various magazines and newspapers when my teacher came in and sat down. "According to the teachings of obedience you regard so highly," I challenged him, "if you asked us to commit suicide because a spaceship was going to take us to heaven, we should do it."

"That is the most preposterous and irresponsible thing you have ever said!" he snapped back—my teacher who had espoused such sublime teachings on obedience now enraged. "If anyone who calls themselves my student would actually do anything that stupid, they should closely reconsider what they are doing here." He got up, walked across the office and through the door, and slammed it behind him.

A crucial distinction must be made between obedience to something that feels outlandish *emotionally*—as in the case of the woman who was asked to become a world-class blues singer when she had never even performed in the elementary-school chorus—and acts of aggression and blindness that involve violence, damage to one's health or to that of another, disregard of children, and the like. Another friend's former guru instructed the man's wife to tell their seven-year-old daughter about an affair her mother had prior to her birth. The girl developed ulcers shortly thereafter and continues with stomach problems fifteen years later.

We ourselves are ultimately accountable for all of our acts of obedience and disobedience, and we must constantly ask ourselves if we think we can live with (or die with, at an extreme) any given choice. If the answer is no, it is far better to pass up a given opportunity to be obedient, remaining confident that if our intention remains pure and strong, another chance will eventually be given us.

Layla, a long-term disciple of the renowned Rajneesh, recalls her profound ignorance and naiveté when first engaging her master: regularly and indiscriminately, she offered her time, money, and emotional well-being at the whims of her teacher's senior disciples. Years after his death, she is once more considering involvement with a demanding spiritual teacher yet is understandably wary that she will again find herself in a compromised position. She is uncertain whether the maturity she has attained in subsequent years can withstand the temptation to capitulate to power in a childish way rather than from a conscious and informed perspective. She values the need for direct and personalized feedback from a spiritual teacher, but she still lacks confidence in her own capacity to engage a teacher in a manner that will promote more growth than disillusionment.

Layla's predicament is valid; yet paradoxically, it is her awareness of the dangers and temptations involved, combined with her years of unconscious obedience, that puts her in a position to finally be able to engage a process of conscious surrender if that is what she chooses to do. Her greatest assets on the path at this point are the discernment she has gained and her knowledge of her own weaknesses.

Submission versus Surrender

When people warn against the danger of surrendering to a spiritual authority, they are actually referring to *submission*. Submission, even when arising from sincere intentions, is what happens when the psychologically insecure and needy human being projects, and then clings to the notion of the spiritual teacher as savior or good parent, fully expecting that something outside themselves can and will take responsibility for relieving their suffering. In the Heaven's Gate example, my teacher's frustration at my interpretation of obedience was the result of my inability to make a distinction between blind submission and conscious surrender. Surrender, or conscious obedience, simply cannot arise when we are stuck in childish projections and behavior and are unwilling to think for ourselves.

True surrender discovered through conscious obedience is a position of power, never of weakness. It involves informed recognition and discernment—ordinarily gained only through years of spiritual work—that as powerful, independent, and highly functional as we may be, we still have blindness. This recognition, in the words of Gurdjieff, is that "human beings are machines"— that our functioning is overwhelmingly mechanical. Our true freedom lies only in the admission of this difficult reality, followed by a process of self-observation that allows Essence to overcome our machinations and eventually sustain a position in the forefront of our consciousness.

This is where the function of the spiritual teacher enters the picture. The teacher is someone who sits outside our mechanical functioning and makes suggestions for practices and activities. These may seem to be irrational and impractical, but they may nonetheless stimulate and elicit true Essence and authentic spontaneity.

Fleet Maull—Buddhist teacher and director of Prison Dharma Network—was at one time the personal attendant of the great Tibetan master Chögyam Trungpa Rinpoche. He stayed by Trungpa Rinpoche's side for days and weeks at a time and received direct personal teaching from him, as well as his master's intimate regard. Maull also secretly ran drugs to and from South America. While his life of promising discipleship flourished, his "other" life landed him in federal prison for fourteen years. He used the time of his incarceration to work as a meditation teacher and care for dying prisoners, but missed his son's growing up and years by his teacher's side that could never be recovered. A few years into his imprisonment, he received a notice of his master's illness and then his death. Instead of being by his beloved master's side as he died, Maull had to live it out in prison.

The shock of this event propelled him into a life of dedicated practice and conscious discipleship. In spite of having been literally held in the arms of his beloved teacher—physically caressed and encouraged to accept the love that was more true of him than his darkness—it was only upon incarceration that his true studenthood was initiated, and a life of mature practice began.

Away from the protective scrutiny of the physical teacher, Maull finally understood in a real way that the external teacher represented his own conscience, or innate wisdom, and was ever inviting him to realize his own basic goodness or "Buddha nature." After his teacher's death, he knew he would have to find this nature on his own . . . or not, and that the choice was his alone. He chose yes, and in retrospect expresses tremendous gratitude for how the predicament he got himself into became the greatest gift of his discipleship. During his long incarceration, he introduced hundreds to a path of contemplative spirituality and worked to reduce the suffering of many dying prisoners.

Maull was asked the obvious question: "What could somebody do to really understand what you came to realize, short of the extremes you went to?!"

"That is the million-dollar question," was his only reply.

───── ∞∞ ─────

Ultimately, we are learning to obey a source of inner authority. Thus the question becomes, at what point are we ready to begin following inner guidance in a way that is trustworthy, dependable, and will not compromise our highest transformational capacity? There is no answer to this question. While it may be true that we have gained a quality of inner mastery or reliability to a certain degree, if we want to go further we will have to surmount a still-more subtle level of the ego's barriers, and we do ourselves a tremendous disservice to assume too quickly that we are sufficiently prepared for the new level. The inner guru remains the ultimate authority, but the outer teacher is the one who awakens, trains, and refines the inner.

Furthermore, as one's practice and commitment to that which may be called Life, the Teacher, or the Lineage increases, new levels and realms of obedience emerge. For example, in Sufi sheik Llewellyn Vaughan-Lee's spiritual school, there are no written rules or practices, yet he suggested that in one's relationship to the teacher and to God there is a vast and intricate objective "ethical code" one must obey:

*The ethics on this path are incredibly high. You're
not even allowed, for example, to have a chair if you
don't use it—that's considered stealing. If you keep an
overdue library book, that is considered stealing. Maybe
somebody else would need it more. You're not allowed
to eat more food than you need because even the worms
could use it. But it isn't imposed. Nobody tells you that
you have to do it. It's not written down. But it becomes
the way you want to live because then you entangle
yourself less in the density of this world, and then you are
free. Then you have more time to be with your Beloved.
Things of the world don't hold you so tightly.*

Paradoxically, while we ordinarily think of obedience as giving up control, it can be a vehicle for true spontaneity. When we operate only under the dictates of our own will, we have relative freedom—we can do what we want, when we want to—but the range of what that "freedom" includes is still subject to the confines of conditioned beliefs about who we are. When we practice conscious obedience in relationship to an authentic spiritual teacher, particularly against our own personal preferences, we exercise the "muscle" of essence and freedom, which ultimately leads to objective spontaneity and obedience to inner authority.

The truth is that obedience to a teacher is a deeply personal issue, not a matter of conformity to a moral or ethical code. When we arrive at the moment of death, we won't get points for having been "good girls" and "good boys," for having obeyed Mommy-Daddy-Teacher. As conscious students, we benefit from gaining a deep understanding of the principles of obedience and then experimenting with them in accordance with our own wishes and perceived needs, making choices about who and what best serve our soul's true longing.

We will need to be able to live and die with the choices we make.

13

IMPERFECTIONS IN THE TEACHER

The purity of the guru is secondary to the purity of the student.
—ANDREAS BRAUN

Teachers will be imperfect. What you need to be
able to count on is them doing their job.
—ARTHUR DEIKMAN

I t can be both a challenge and a relief to consider the possibility that the teacher is imperfect, even highly flawed. Yet it is crucial to do so, or we will end up disillusioned with our teachers rather than facing the fact that human imperfection is an illusion. When students are afraid to entertain doubts about their teacher, I am slightly suspicious about their conviction. The capacity for intelligent skepticism—to doubt deeply and to follow that doubt to its end without spiraling into cynicism and negativity—can be a great asset on the path and is a skill that requires tremendous courage.

Paradoxically, deep doubt can lead to a sense of inner confidence in a way that few things can. That which survives doubt and ruthless questioning has the capacity to become a conviction that arises from within, rather than an adopted belief system imposed from without. When students are unwilling to look at imperfections, instead insisting on an idealized notion of perfection in the teacher, they can experience the slightest expression of imperfection as an internal avalanche so immense as to create a rift, if not a complete gulf, in their relationship with their teacher.

There came a point in my discipleship when I had doubts and frustrations about many things. I was bored with routine and practice, deeply discouraged by the dawning realization of how long integrated transformation takes, and wondering what I was doing with my precious life. I was rigorously contemplating questions such as: "Do I really want to live on an ashram?" "Am I sure I want to practice in the ways my teacher has prescribed?" "How would I feel if, by chance, I were to do this practice for the next twenty years only to discover there was some flaw in my teacher that I had overlooked?" And, "Am I certain my choice to work with my teacher so intensively is current, and not an outdated commitment based upon a previous conviction?" My teacher had taught me about the depth of our mechanical conditioning, about the egoic tendency to project and conform, and I wanted to make sure my whole relationship to him and the community was not just more of the same tendency. I trusted that the path I was on was a *good* one, but was I certain it was the *right* one for me?

So, I went to talk to my teacher about it.

"Why don't you just take a break from all of this for a time?" he suggested.

I was taken aback by this wholly unexpected suggestion and immediately assumed he was testing me. "Why are you saying that? Is this some sort of strange guru test?" I asked defensively.

"No. It isn't. Why don't you follow your doubts through to their end? Go away for a while. Greece is lovely this time of year. You could go to the beach. Or move to some city—London, New York. I don't know what you would like to do, but why don't you do whatever you want, for as long as you want, and see what happens? You can come back anytime."

"You're giving me a back door," I pressed further, still suspicious of his motivations. "I'm not going to fall for that guru trick. The better option is to stay here and work through this resistance."

"It's not about better or worse. It's about finding your own personal destiny within—or outside—the tradition."

"But what if I lose everything?" I argued. "My conviction. My years of practice. My trust in the tradition."

"That's the worst-case scenario. Although it would feel terrible for a time, you'd get over it. If there's something inherently false in me or the tradition or your practice, or something is not right for you, it's much better to find out now while you're still young than after twenty years of this."

His words were a song for my heart, still hungry for experience, though I had not dared to imagine that a beach in Greece could be part of the trajectory of my spiritual unfolding! I had given the tradition six years of my life, and I wanted to find out for myself if there was anything I was missing. I am adamantly averse to the "blind-sheep" phenomenon so commonly found among gurus and in spiritual groups, which gives teachers and their communities a bad reputation and leaves those who consider approaching such groups understandably wary. I wanted to be certain I hadn't unconsciously fallen into a blind-sheep mentality and to be sure I was with a teacher who fully supported my own experimentation and freedom.

Within a week, I went from being a semi-renunciate living on a desert ashram in a room the size of a cell, with almost no belongings save a few boxes of clothes and a laptop—slated to spend the rest of my life there if need be in my quest of ultimate liberation—to living on a hilltop in the pristine hills of northern California, the proud owner of a used car and a room with a view, and far from the scrutiny of a spiritual teacher. Upon my own request, I had been cast out into the sea of worldly life with no idea what awaited me.

Granted, the first couple of weeks were very odd—learning to use a debit card, navigating San Francisco traffic jams, grocery shopping and cooking for one person instead of forty, being alone. During my renunciate years, I had been on book tours throughout the States and research trips and conferences in Asia and Central America, but being back in familiar California ready to challenge the context of my spiritual practice was a greater culture shock than all those experiences traveling. I was in paradigm shock. But I knew what it was to be a traveler, and now once again I found myself with an internal one-way ticket. Where would it lead?

I was determined to discover and fulfill a latent and repressed desire I had experienced during my years of ashram life. I took my teacher's suggestion seriously, and I decided to challenge every spiritual ideal, practice, walk, talk, and internalized moral conviction I had taken on during my years of searching. I was ready to party: wine, men, salsa dancing, flirting with power and fame. I had done most of these things before, but now it was time to try them once again while carefully observing the results of my experiments from the perspective gained from years of dedicated and disciplined practice. "To experience consciously within limits" was my mantra, provided to me by Arnaud Desjardins— the words that his master, Swami Prajnanpad, had once used to guide him through the labyrinth of fame and desire.

But what were the limits? Each time I feared I had gone too far, I would consult with my teacher about my activities, only to be met with some variation of, "Don't ask me. You went out to discover that for yourself." And then, eventually, "Please quit confessing. You are embarrassing me!" He was right, and I was grateful for the freedom.

So I took another trip around the world. I was nostalgic for the life of a backpacking traveler. As I romped from exotic temples to coral beaches, I often thought of the journey as Le Tour de Emptiness—and not the spiritual kind of emptiness either. It was empty of purpose, conviction, fulfillment . . . yet that discovery itself became its value.

At one point during this journey, I found myself on Paradise Island—an exquisite half acre of unblemished perfection centered perfectly in the South China Sea in the Philippines. I had spent the morning with two friends and a Rastafarian boatman snorkeling in celestial coral reefs and prancing around the beaches of various local islands, and was now awaiting my lunch of freshly fire-baked rare fish. Sipping a fine Filipino beer and smoking my first cigarette in years, I was highly conscious of the fact that by conventional standards I should be on top of the world, having achieved the height of worldly pleasure and splendor.

Treasuring my fleeting nicotine high, I was contemplating the fact that no scenario could be more idyllic than my present one when suddenly the song "Suzanne," my favorite piece by my musical hero, the poet-songwriter Leonard Cohen, resounded in my ears. I thought I was having an auditory hallucination and inwardly smiled at the power of the mind. Here I was on a world tour designed around fulfilling unfulfilled desires within me, on an island bearing the name of "Paradise" that had no electricity, but somehow the deepest pleasures, including a cherished song by my all-time favorite musician, were filling all my senses. But then I noticed that the others with me were swaying to the music and I understood it was real. I was astounded by the brilliance of universal intelligence to have orchestrated such a personalized packet of experience for me, and I began to laugh hysterically—to the bewilderment of the others around me, who were of course oblivious to my inner experiments.

As I swooned in sensual contentment, the question of the hour was evident: Is external paradise what I want? Does it bring happiness? Is it the fulfillment I have been seeking since the age of five, if not since forever? As exquisite as I felt in my tailor-made paradise, and as unashamed as I was of my deep gratitude and appreciation for the opportunity to experience such pristine beauty, the answer was clear: No. Outer paradise does not create inner nirvana.

At another point in Le Tour de Emptiness, I was in Varanasi, India. I had gone there specifically to engage in a solitary two-week meditation at the ancient crematory grounds along the banks of the Ganges River—where it is said that the sacred fires have been burning bodies every day for ten thousand years, promising believers full liberation in their passing from this life to the next. I had planned to sit wrapped in a white shawl with the renunciate *sadhs* and contemplate death as hundreds of bodies were burned before me, inhaling the putrid smoke of burning flesh and turning toward, rather than away from, my inevitable future. Yet within hours of beginning this retreat, I was discovered by the local hustlers, who attempted to swindle money out of me for a pretend hospice, and I further attracted their wrath by trying to warn other foreigners against the scam, thus rendering any chance of uninterrupted meditation virtually impossible. Besides that, I experienced the burning of the bodies as very natural, so much a part and parcel of life that it did not unravel me nearly as much as the plague of crickets that had hit the city—millions of them—or the pre-monsoon rains that converted the already-sizzling city where men urinate freely on the streets into a pungent sauna.

Meanwhile, I had been given a challenge by two young Israeli friends I'd made along the way, who were also wrestling with the guru question. Intelligent and intense, these two suggested to me that if my relationship with my teacher was real, and that if I wished my present experiment to be complete, I should be able to throw my teacher out of my system completely without leaving a trace—and then see what came back.

I thought their challenge fair, so I made internal preparations and went down to the edge of the Ganges. There, I lodged myself behind a staircase in an attempt to find some relative solitude amid the Varanasi madness. I was ready to stay there all day, and all night if necessary, in order to engage in the task of throwing the guru out of my system.

I gathered all my courage and took the plunge . . . or tried to. It didn't work. I tried again, mustering more force, and then again, attempting an even deeper letting go. I was trying to throw my teacher out, but as I did, I felt I was throwing *myself* out, and it simply didn't work. It was like attempting to remove your own hands, or trying to pluck the subtle heart from the physical one. It cannot be done because there is a fusion, an interconnectedness so intricate that one does not function separately from the other. I intuited that the process of union and fusion between student and teacher had already begun; there truly was no separation. My teacher was in me, as part and parcel of myself. Not his personality nor my own, but as a fusion of consciousness itself. A sigh of long-awaited relaxation and a sense of profound contentment arose within me. I had gone as far as I was able to go, had stretched my capacity further than ever before, and had discovered something new.

Whether we participate in a relationship directly with a Hindu guru, a Zen roshi, or a Native American shaman, the teacher we want to be attending to is not the human personality but a human being who represents a body of teaching. Depending on the tradition, through practice or transmission or grace or alchemical physics, those teachings become part of us. The transformation they engender penetrates right into our cells, our consciousness, our very minds and bodies—and the thoughts and movements they produce as a result. The conglomeration of conditioning we once called "ourselves" becomes refined, changed, merged, and fused and infused with the body of teachings we often label the "teacher."

It needs to be reiterated again and again that we must take full responsibility for our relationship with the spiritual teacher. If we are going to go for perfection—whatever we imagine that to be— we should focus on cultivating our own perfection while doing our best to ensure that the one who is guiding us is reliable, sincere, and capable. The teacher is human and will inevitably have accompanying human imperfections. We simply need to decide how we will come to terms with this fact, and what is ultimately right for ourselves. When we get to the gates of death, there won't be anyone there giving out gold stars for disciples who were good little girls and boys in relationship to their teacher.

What Is Your Bottom Line?

The question of whether the teacher is perfect is not really the issue. It is safe to assume that spiritual teachers will not comply with our mental concept of perfection and therefore will eventually "betray" us, or at least betray our projections and expectations of them. We *will* become disillusioned at some point. It may be more useful to consider whether the teacher transmits the teachings that he or she is responsible to with impeccable integrity. The questions, then, are these: How much do imperfections in the teacher interfere with this transmission? And does the teacher's clarity outweigh his obstructions to a significant enough degree that we as students can trust him to make our investment of energy and learning worthwhile?

To ask whether the teacher's imperfections are too significant to make it profitable for *us* to study with him or her is
distinct from making an objective evaluation of his or her teaching capacity in general. For this reason, we should be careful not
to evaluate a teacher's value for someone else too quickly, or to
become righteous about our own choices. Whether the teacher's
imperfections are worthy of amnesty or not is really not a matter
of right or wrong; the issue is what best serves a given student's
needs. It is again a circumstance for which the rule book just does
not suffice, because the issue is a deeply individual one.

Ultimately, it comes down to this: What is our bottom line?
What can we handle and what can we not? Drugs? Sex? Prud-
ishness? Puerility? Dirty jokes? Poverty? Inflation? Vanity? Pride?
Righteous indignation? Demanding rigor? We can rest assured that
somewhere there will be a "bottom line." There will be *something*.

For example, let's say a married Zen teacher has an affair with
another woman. On one hand, this does not necessarily mean we
cannot trust him in his function as spiritual teacher; it is likely
that our personal relationship to him and the transmission he
offers has nothing to do with either sex or his personal life. (Many
teachers who have demonstrated a great skill and integrity in
the transmission of spiritual teachings have been taken down and
even destroyed by sexual relationships that had little, if any, impact
on their students.) On the other hand, if we have been betrayed
in our own past and are using the relationship with the teacher
in an attempt to unravel and heal core wounds around betrayal—
perhaps through an unconscious erotic transference onto the
teacher—then the teacher's weakness or apparent lack of integrity in this arena may be an important consideration. This is not a
moral but a personal consideration, as no one is perfect.

Here is another example. Some teachers discourage the practice
of relationship, especially marriage and child raising, suggesting

that these constructs inhibit the optimal possibilities for awakening, at least within the traditions these teachers are conveying. If we find ourselves drawn to such a teacher and we aspire to have a family, we must ask ourselves such deeply personal questions as: Do I trust the teacher's assertion that an intimate romantic relationship and/or children would interfere with my path to God or Truth? Is my connection with this particular teacher so strong that I'm willing to sacrifice my wish for a relationship or family? If I do make this sacrifice, am I likely to resent the teacher in the long run? And, am I willing to attempt to negotiate with the teacher about this issue so I can proceed in my spiritual life in a way that includes my desire for a relationship or family?

In what domains do we personally require the teacher to teach in accordance with our own subjective and psychological needs and preferences so our studenthood will be fulfilling and worthwhile? In what areas can we accept either apparent or actual imperfections, and in which do we have limits? How much capacity do we have to tolerate our own ambiguity when it is unclear whether the teacher's behaviors are, in fact, expressions of imperfection or simply in conflict with values that are a product of our cultural and psychological conditioning? What do we *need* and what do we *want*? Are we willing, as Mick Jagger suggests, to sacrifice some of our wants in order to get what we need? The conscious student asks these questions of him- or herself until he or she gets satisfactory answers, then assumes responsibility for the outcome that follows.

Furthermore, when we hit our bottom line, how do we choose to engage with our teacher with respect to this blockage in the relationship? Do we attempt to repress it? Do we immediately leave? Do we consider attempting to talk about it and perhaps even to negotiate terms of some kind with our teacher?

I believe it is fine to respectfully disagree with one's teacher if he or she is accessible on a personal level; I think it is preferable to either angry and victimized reactivity or to remaining stuck in a childish need to be a "good disciple" in order to receive the love we imagine the teacher will bestow upon us if we do everything correctly. Gilles Farcet, assistant teacher in the lineage of Arnaud Desjardins, suggests having a "frank, open, and clear discussion" with the teacher regarding the issue in question.

I have repeatedly spoken with long-term "senior" practitioners who are frustrated because they feel that "dissent" in the form of questioning the teacher is not allowed within the community. It is true that there are many teachers who are intolerant of being challenged—some are great saints who are simply unwilling to appease disciples' psychological needs, and others are individuals with unconscious psychological "holes" that they are unwilling (unconsciously, of course) to allow to be uncovered. Still, in many other instances, disciples are simply afraid to risk confrontation, to take the leap into the well of emotion that comes when they challenge the fabric of their psychological relationship with their teacher—that tapestry of clarity and projection, godliness and humanness. They would rather assume that the teacher cannot handle being challenged, and even leave their studies with that person, than admit to the fear-driven projections of confrontation and rejection that can continue to dominate many years of their discipleship.

Imperfections in the Student

There is a story of a man who went looking for the perfect teacher. He finally found him and asked to be his disciple. The perfect teacher responded, "Has it never occurred to you that the perfect teacher requires the perfect disciple?" Even after our questions about the teacher's perfection have largely abated, they will continue to arise from time to time. But in order to sustain a position of empowered, conscious discipleship, at some point our attention must shift from the teacher's imperfections to our own. For truly, the teacher's imperfections, as long as they do not inhibit our own growth, are his or her own responsibility and problem to work out. Conversely, no matter how perfect the teacher and how well he or she can point us in the direction of our own liberation, we are and must always be fully responsible for our own imperfections.

———— ⬡⬡⬡ ————

After many years of apprenticeship to and apparent trust in my teacher, I passed through a period during which I questioned him and the community around him with intense scrutiny and unabridged criticism. He and I talked extensively through letters and in conversation, and I argued that I believed every student must exercise similar scrutiny to avoid the dangers of blind following. In response, Lee told me to question and challenge him and the community as much as I wanted, to the degree I desired, and for as long as I wished . . . and then, when I was finally ready to trust, to trust unreservedly and unconditionally in order to receive the full possibilities of discipleship.

Fullness sees fullness; emptiness sees emptiness. The eyes of mistrust see one facet of the diamond; the eyes of faith see another. But it is the eyes of discernment, aimed inward, that are the most indispensable of all.

"It is only in taking into account who you are as a disciple," suggests Arnaud Desjardins, "that you should consider what type of guru you can legitimately hope to meet, and what you are then entitled to expect." Our focus should be on our growth, our maturity, our responsibility, our increasing capacity to mine riches from mountains. When this is our focus, we will naturally attract spiritual authorities of equal integrity who are willing to continuously grow and take responsibility for their own actions. Armed with the willingness to accept our own imperfections, we know how to accept imperfections in others without blaming them or feeling victimized by them. Should we then find we are in the presence of a teacher who is unprepared to fill our spiritual needs, we can consider what it is within us that first attracted us to them. We can let these teachers go, if necessary, and forgive them for their human imperfections without becoming disillusioned, and without needing to reject all spiritual authorities because we feel let down by the failure of our own projection of perfection.

⸻⸺

Neither perfection in the student nor in the teacher is a requirement for a fulfilling and effective life of spiritual practice. Sincerity and discrimination are required, as is, ironically, a tolerance for *imperfection*. At the end of the day, expressions of human integrity—including reliability, tenacity, mutual devotion, forgiveness, and faith—far outweigh any projection of imagined perfection.

14

THE SOURCE OF TRUE POWER

You receive exactly what you give . . . you take all, you accept all without any sense of obligation. Your attitude toward life is the attitude of one who has the right to make demands and to take—who has no need to pay or earn. You believe that all things are your due—simply because it is you. None of this strikes your attention, yet this is precisely what keeps one world separate from another.
—JEANNE DE SALZMANN

I t was a sizzling, irritating afternoon sometime in those first months with Yogi Ramsuratkumar—the days before he was discovered by the whole world and we still sat with him in a small group. My mind was obsessing over my own spiritual inadequacies, my eyes fixated on a spot on the ceiling. I was begrudgingly contemplating the fact that as wondrous as this saint who sat before me appeared to be—his realization so undisputed that the great Shankaracharyas, the keepers of the Hindu faith, had traveled from all corners of the subcontinent to honor him on his birthday—the reality remained that he was he, and I was me, and there wasn't a hell of a lot in common between us. He had surrendered his mind, vanity, pride, selfishness, greed, and attachment to serve humanity, while I became infuriated when the guy in the local cow-shack coffee shop charged me seven cents for a cup of coffee for which he charged the Indians only five-and-a-half cents. The Yogi sat wrapped in blankets enduring the 120-degree heat, pouring out compassion to all he encountered, while I could not travel to the market without internally, and sometimes externally, cursing rickshaw drivers, beggars, vendors, leering men, and whichever sun god in the Hindu pantheon had thought up the Indian summer. The Yogi was preoccupied with the healing of all beings in the cosmos—seen and unseen, animate and inanimate—while I was obsessed with myself.

Suddenly my focus was jolted back to Yogi Ramsuratkumar, pulled by the force of objective command. As I turned toward him, I saw a look on his face that blazed straight through my chest, instantly burning to ash all my mental garbage. I quickly looked behind me to see what extraordinary expression of manifest reality could possibly have catalyzed the most naked expression of beauty I had ever seen. There was no one behind me. I looked again. No one. Nothing . . . "Holy shit," I gasped internally. "He is looking at me."

He was looking at me. He was *bleeding* love at me. Not a sappy, sentimental love. And not the all-encompassing, impersonal love of a god to all of his children. What I saw was the deeply personal, intimate, direct expression of a heart broken open upon seeing itself reflected in another. It was a love that included every "sin" I had ever committed—a love that was fully aware of each wicked, demented, and vindictive thought I had ever directed toward another or myself; of all my imagined and actual inadequacies; of all my crimes of ignorance and unawareness; even of the ways I would continue to hurt people in the future out of my own blindness and fear. Love without reason. Love without conditions.

I had traveled thirty-two countries and five continents. I had had lovers of exotic creeds, met mystics of all traditions, found God in secret pockets of nature few people even believe exist . . .

but I had never witnessed anything remotely like this, much less directed toward me. It was my Self, seen for the first time in the reflection of the Other.

Although I tacitly understood that it was still the beginning of the beginning, I knew that love could never rightfully be denied again, no matter if it took the rest of my life and beyond to come to rest in that knowledge. That evening, eyes still puffy from the tears of joy I had shed, hands still shaky, I took out my twice rain-soaked, cheap Indian notebook and scribbled an insufficient tribute to a moment I knew would fade—still, the reality of a truth once perceived could not be denied, and therefore I knew I would be responsible to this truth for the rest of my life and needed to preserve it in writing:

> *I was moved to tears. It was due to the feeling, deep,*
> *deep within, that my soul is now being taken care of: a*
> *deepest knowing that I have been found. Even now I cry.*
> *Never alone again. Never alone again. A past of imagined*
> *craziness, believed inadequacies . . . erased in an instant.*
> *It is all gone. Now come years and years of hard work*
> *and a new kind of suffering, but if I do not cease to know,*
> *to believe I am being held, it will be different.*

Five summers later, in 1998—I remember as though it were now—I am sitting in the funky, fifteen-foot trailer that is as old as I am and that has become my bedroom and work studio. It is stationed in the sandy parking lot of my teacher's ashram in Arizona. I am wearing a damp yellow bikini I hose down each time it dries out. I pass hour after hour with the table fan on, my fingers on the keyboard while my pores sweat out the Arizona desert heat. The pores of my still-distrusting mind sweat out the old, false beliefs that I am inept, inadequate, lacking in knowledge, and incapable of manifesting the high capacity my teacher insists I am capable of.

It is my fourth book. This time Lee has asked me to write about "the error of premature claims to enlightenment." I am once again certain that *this time* he has surely gone off his rocker, and I tell him as much. *This time* he has utterly overestimated the abilities of a twenty-nine-year-old woman. Given that since the very day I met him he has systematically destroyed every false idea I had about what enlightenment is, what spiritual life is about, and even what it means to be fully *human,* how the hell am I supposed to now write about enlightenment, much less about those who claim it prematurely? I tell him that this time he is being completely unrealistic, and, as he has each time before, he tells me I don't have to do it. And this time, once again, I choose conscious trust in his seemingly limitless faith in me over my conditioned, ego-engraved convictions of personal inadequacy.

As I begin to ascend the internal Everest that this particular book represents to me in my writing career, the daemons of denial wage warfare with the Self upon the battlefield that is my body. My only grace is my stubbornness, as my obstinate but still-moving fingers gesture to universal intelligence a refusal to capitulate to perceived limitation, trusting my teacher to estimate my capacity more accurately than I can. Frustration is my daily companion as, at many points in the writing, I find myself not only at a loss for words but at a loss for some piece of knowledge necessary for the book—at which point I demand of whatever universal force commanded my teacher to ask me to write this book that it supply the required information. Although I cannot prove it, I tacitly comprehend the fact that the book has somehow already been written in an unseen world and it is my job to midwife it into concrete reality.

I would love to say that at these moments I choose to appeal to Saraswati—Goddess of Wisdom—to bestow knowledge upon me, and she then descends in a beatific cloud, caresses my fingers, and reveals all knowledge through them. But it is not like that. At these moments, all there is to do is endure tremendous tension in the body, use all internal weapons to keep the daemons even inches at bay, keep the fingers on the keyboard, and literally *insist* that whatever gods or gurus or whoever the hell runs the show write what is needed to serve the reader. I curse the gods. I tell them I don't even know if I believe in them but that they must work regardless. And then knowledge comes. It does not shower itself in glittering rainbows of grace; it comes up in hacking coughs and gasps. But it comes.

I finally perceive the source of this knowledge, and with this realization comes a sober, unsentimental, humbling awe for the guru function and how it operates in and through my life and body. I understand that the seed of the Divine, or Truth, lies dormant within us, awakened to greater or lesser degrees. The guru or true teacher is someone in whom that seed is more awakened than it is in myself. In the meeting of student and teacher, the more-awakened force sparks the lesser-awakened, much as a flaming candle ignites the wick of an unlit candle upon contact. Whenever that moment occurs, whether the process is conscious or unconscious, transmission has taken place. The teacher has catalyzed the dormant energy of truth within the student. At that moment, the process is both complete and is only beginning. For whereas the transmission is alive, it has yet to emerge and be integrated. A lifetime or lifetimes of false conditioning obscure its transparency and consistent expression. The whole process of spiritual sadhana, or practice of purification, awaits the student who is committed to allowing the transmission of truth to express itself through the vehicle of his or her own body.

My teacher has not asked me to write books to serve humanity, though that is a graceful and beneficial side effect to the degree it occurs. Taking orders from his Boss—whether we call that authority universal intelligence, transmission, Truth, or Love—he has requested this clearly difficult and painstaking task of me to serve the unfolding of my optimal capacity in incarnation. In my rare moments of true prayer, I have asked both Yogi Ramsuratkumar and Lee to give me *everything* as quickly as possible. I have told them I will endure whatever pains and sufferings are required in order to serve according to the highest possibility available to me in this lifetime. I have let them know that I might scream and fight and resist and probably act in ways that appear as though I am retracting my vows, but that they should ignore all of it and persist in the shared task we have agreed upon.

And they have persisted, according to my request, in giving me work at the highest level my body-mind can handle, insisting that the seed of transmission express itself. I have gradually come to recognize that once these seeds of transmission have been expressed through the written word, and particularly after I have shared them with the world at large, I become responsible to that knowledge. This comes as a great and largely unwelcome surprise to the ego, which still wishes to enact spiritually adolescent and self-gratifying behaviors. I do not fulfill this new obligation much of the time, but this does not lessen the demand. The tension between my former self, with its habits and tendencies, and my true capacity is as uncomfortable as it is creative and will ever nag me until I fulfill my highest possibility: a thorny blessing I would never wish to be otherwise.

The benefit of the manifest teacher is that he or she can orchestrate a highly individualized transformational "packet" according to the needs and abilities of each student, a packet that diminishes the power of obstacles and augments the student's strengths. Whether the teacher supports the student in becoming a famous rock star or a loving parent, a true teacher would never take away the student's own power, capacity, or objective autonomy; he or she does precisely the opposite. The authentic teacher serves as a fountain that directs power into our lives. The fountain flows endlessly, in excess and abundance, yet we must make ourselves increasingly receptive to that outpouring, lest we continue to squander the resources of transmission available to us while complaining that grace and transmission are not present in our lives. Or, in the words of George Bernard Shaw, we will become "a feverish, selfish little clod of ailments and grievances complaining that the world will not devote itself to making [us] happy." A weak teacher will energetically feed off the student's energy; the true teacher will dig the well within the student's psyche until it is overflowing to the point that its abundance saturates everything in its vicinity. It can be no other way.

We Are All Slaves to Something

We are all slaves to something. Understanding this point is essential if one is to comprehend and appreciate the value of the spiritual teacher as manifest in the world and the precious possibility of conscious interrelationship that exists between teacher and student.

Whether we believe that the infant is born as a "blank slate" and conditioned at birth (or during the perinatal period), or whether we resonate with the wider perspective of karma—which implies coming into the world with preconditioned tendencies accumulated through an unspecified quantity of lifetimes through which the individuated soul journeys before its eventual return to God—the fact remains that the human or egoic mind is shaped and sculpted by an indeterminate number of factors and influences. What we understand to be "ourselves" is a set of tendencies that have engraved themselves so deeply upon the psyche as to create and recreate repetitive sets of experiences we come to know as our "personality." Some people have personalities that are more pleasant to live with than others, but as wonderful or awful as any particular personality might be, it remains largely mechanical and predictable.

When we understand this, we come to appreciate that no matter how much relative freedom we have and how good our lives have become, until we have the capacity to function free from even the most subtle attachment—positive or negative—to our conditioning, we remain slaves. Sometimes we must fulfill our worldly desires before we are willing to acknowledge the emptiness that remains—the "wound that only God (Truth) can heal" in the words of Lee Lozowick. A classic historical example is the life of Siddharta Gautama, also known as the Buddha. Destined to rule the kingdom into which he was born and to have all riches, women, pleasures, and even knowledge at his beck and call, he saw with unwavering clarity the inevitable facts of suffering, old age, sickness, and death, which prompted him to relinquish all forms of outer wealth in favor of the "Kingdom of Heaven" within.

When we finally comprehend that we are indeed slaves to our own limitations, we naturally look for help from someone who is not enslaved to the same degree we are. The teacher who has discovered even relative freedom has necessarily undergone tremendous inner purification—"trial by fire"—and possesses knowledge of how to endure such heat and use it to fuel the mysterious process of alchemical transformation.

I once read a news clip about a train that caught fire as it was entering a tunnel in the Alps. While everyone else was panicking, one man who clearly saw the predicament told the others, "Our only chance to survive is to go toward the fire and then go around it." Even though the passengers didn't have to go directly through the fire to be saved, only twelve were willing even to approach it. Those who followed the man's advice and went in the direction of the fire got out alive, whereas the remaining 150 died in the very fire that paralyzed them with fear. The egoic mind's insistence on saving itself without external help is equivalent to those who feared to walk toward the fire. The true teacher is the one who calls us to move toward the fire and the one who will stay by our side to assure our safe passage.

We are all slaves to something—generally a combination of our personal ego and cultural and collective egos that express themselves through conditioned mechanical behavior. If we want to be slaves to truth, we must become humble apprentices to it. In the context of conscious discipleship, this comes through apprenticeship to the teacher. The seed of true power is within. The teacher waters that seed through transmission, and through his or her skillful means prunes the growing plant to perfection in order to feed the masses. The true teacher will only and always direct us to an essential knowledge of, and contact with, our own personal power.

Master as Disciple

I was recently asked by a Jewish cantor whether I thought it was more difficult to be a master or a disciple. I told him it is harder to be a true disciple than a false master; but it is harder to be a true master than a true disciple, for the true master is simultaneously both master *and* disciple. True masters continue to have the full responsibility of discipleship in relation to their own master, as well as all the responsibilities of masterhood in relation to their disciples. The true master *is* a true disciple. One who claims to be a master but is not also a disciple *in some form* leaves his or her mastery open to question.

The source of the teacher's true power is his studenthood, not his or her teaching function. This is an interesting proposition, for the teacher's function, appearance, and even outward attention will largely be expressed through his teaching function. Still, the locus of the teacher's internal attention is his or her own studenthood, and all actions he or she performs are an expression of that studenthood.

Spontaneous awakenings do occur, and there are occasions when an authentic teacher has not had a living teacher. In such cases, "discipleship" is to a deity, a body of teachings, or ultimate truth itself. Arnaud Desjardins addresses this distinction in the question: "To whom do you *pranam* [bow]?"

The purpose of "bowing" to the other—even if the "other" is the teachings, the lineage, the tradition, the ancestors, or the ineffable—is both for protection and to keep ourselves grounded and humble. The lineage and the living or once-living teacher who comes to dwell within as one's conscience offer the student profound karmic protection and mediate the forces of denial and sleep that may arise even amid profound awakening.

To be humbled in relationship to the teacher and lineage is a far cry from powerless submission. It demonstrates respect for an intelligence far greater than that of the ordinary untrained mind. To "bow" to another represents a humble willingness *not* to know or understand everything while refusing to capitulate to cynicism regarding the precious possibility of human incarnation.

Ultimate Equality

At the level of Essence, everyone is equal. Period. It is the law of nonduality. There is no need to argue this point, nor to react against it. To do so would be to refute the sages and mystics of every tradition in every time, as well as the truth we all know within if we dare to admit it. It just *is,* and every true teacher knows this. If they don't, then they're not true teachers. At the most essential level of existence, the teacher is no different from the student.

There was a moment just weeks before my mother's death when I knelt beside the couch where she lay, surrendering to the inevitable. We were both devastated by the imminent loss of one another as we sat together waiting, loving, grieving. In a moment of shared acceptance of a reality neither of us could deny, I told her, and we both understood, that while at this moment it was she who was lying on the couch and I who knelt beside her, no sooner would I turn my head or blink my eye than it would be me there, my yet-to-be conceived child kneeling by *my* side. And then it would be my child's child . . . so utterly the same. Beyond equal, to the point of One. And still, it was two. She fulfilled what she was able to, given her karma, will, incarnation, and circumstances; and I would fulfill what I could given mine.

Within nonduality is duality; within equality is hierarchy. If we return to Ken Wilber's concept of holarchy, we can describe it as concentric circles upon circles of ever-greater inclusion in a process of relative evolution on all levels, while simultaneously everything is already complete. To make a distinction between different levels has nothing to do with morality, good and bad, higher and lower. It is only the multiple levels of psychological wounding that convince us that the existence of relative levels of power and knowledge is dangerous to us.

The Guru Is None Other Than the Conscious Self

The Upanishads teach that "the guru [or true teacher] is none other than the conscious Self." This simple statement reveals a truth that, if understood, undermines all false notions and misunderstandings about the true teacher and his or her objective function in the world. The false guru is the unconscious self, the sincere but weak teacher is the self striving toward unitive consciousness, and the true teacher is the conscious Self. The true guru or teacher is not *my* separative self, *my* personality, or *my* conditioning, but *the Self,* housed in the body and mind of the teacher's own humanity. The teacher is not limited to a separative identification, and thus abides in connection with the same Self that is consciousness Itself. We love the teacher because we love our own Self—not in a narcissistic and self-aggrandizing manner, but because we love Truth or God as expressed through the teacher. We respect the teacher for having made that bravest of leaps—to die to their identification with the egoic mind. We bow to them as a gesture of remembrance of our own intention to make that same leap of surrender.

In many forms of psychological work, we project onto the therapist those qualities of our psyches that we have disavowed because our conditioning and wounds have limited our range of mental and emotional experience and expansion. As therapy progresses, healing occurs through reclaiming the disowned aspects of ourselves. The student-teacher relationship works in a parallel manner, albeit on a different level: we project onto the teacher our highest Self, eventually (ideally) coming to embrace this full possibility for ourselves. In the student-teacher relationship, the teacher ideally is in essence that which we project onto him or her, as well as an ordinary human being. In fact, we may only come to consciously perceive such a vast possibility for ourselves by seeing it lived through another.

When we finally come to appreciate the teacher—not the personality but the expressed essence—as none other than our own Self manifest in another, all subjective power differentials collapse. Relative distinctions become relegated to the realm of form. The teacher remains a construct that is ultimately imper-sonal while at the same time expressing itself through the personal as a most intimate connection between the authentic teacher and the conscious disciple. Respect becomes an organic response to the relative circumstance of less-learned in relationship to the more-learned.

Power ignites power, force feeds force, and divine reflects divine. To discount this possibility because of an intellectual con-tradiction, an outdated psychological fear, or crimes of ignorance committed by others or by ourselves is to deny ourselves the option of engaging with a vehicle that will carry us to the foun-tainhead of our own true source of power. Perhaps we will not choose to walk the road of the student-teacher relationship, but the conscious disciple of truth benefits from the availability of all paths of integrity.

15

FOR THE GLORY OF LOVE

Don't ever listen to the so-called swamis who tell you
that you have to become old and dead in order to make
spiritual progress. They can say such things only because
they have forgotten what it means to have a heart.
— THE AGHORI VIMALANANDA

Yoga is falling in love, not a choice of a carrier.
— IRINA TWEEDIE

I t was an "average" day during those initial months of anguished purification in India, if anything around a God-mad saint could be considered average. The scene was in full play: Yogi Ramsuratkumar, master of masters, on his simple wooden platform, the same rags and blankets he had worn during five decades of living as a beggar-saint on the streets of Tiruvannamalai now covered by layer upon layer of jasmine and rose garlands. His devoted attendants sat nearby gazing lovingly at their master, alert to the subtle shifts in his every mood or need, their insides melting as they endured the searing burn of divine heat invisibly transforming subtle layers of their interiors. Disciples and visitors sat in rows several feet away, approaching the Yogi to make their requests for enough money for a daughter's dowry, or for a miracle cure for a loved one's cancer, or to express praise and adoration for the gifts already given through the glory of God as manifest in the form of the personal beloved.

And there I sat, playing my part as disciple, supplicating God to allow me to taste a morsel of the sublime divinity that sat before me. My inner moods shifted continuously. At one moment, I assumed an arrogant stance of condescension toward the visitors who came before the most transcendent, compassionate, and gift-bestowing expression of humanity they likely would ever set eyes on, asking for favors as mundane as for their child to pass his university entrance exams. At the next, I would be plunged into feelings of essential unworthiness as I pleaded to this One who appeared to be outside myself to bestow upon me a spiritual possibility I believed I lacked. Then would arise gratitude and praise for the glory of God transmitted so evidently, yet mysteriously, by this form before me.

In a moment, and clearly to no credit of my own, my vision took a 180-degree turn. Suddenly, the Great Game, the cosmic love affair, the grand explosion of duality, "the play of consciousness" (as Swami Muktananda referred to it) was palpable. There was no division, no separation, no "other." Only supreme, unwavering equality. Each of us was simply playing out our specified role in the divine script at this moment of manifest existence. Yogi Ramsuratkumar played the part of the great Yogi—feted, worshipped, adored. But it meant nothing, even and especially to him. The cast featured his noble attendants as the select of all disciples, renouncing personal desires and fulfillment in service of the great one. The rest of us played the crowd—supporting actors, extras, wannabes—perceiving ourselves either as gracious recipients of others' sacrifices or under-recognized pious disciples of God: seekers of the truth who imagined ourselves to be separate from the Great Oneness.

The forms were as diverse as the actors in the play, the differences simply lawful expressions of the infinite manifestations of duality—the differentiated aspects of the Divine Mother with heart, lungs, eyes, kidneys, and so on inseparably intertwined to form the whole of Her body. This vision of manifested supreme equality arose with such heartwarming delight that it caused me to nearly double over in laughter. At the same time, it brought about unprecedented calm, trust, and acceptance in the place where I commonly experienced separation, contradiction, and disparity.

———— ❦ ————

The question is always the same: if all abides in Oneness, why is there apparent separation and difference? Why forms? Why "higher" and "lower?" If God is One, indivisible, everywhere, in all things, whole, unified, why all this mess? Philosophers and mystics in every tradition take their guesses. One appealing answer is that separation exists purely and wholly for the glory of love. People who argue about the limitations of a tradition in which the student doesn't eventually "graduate" and surpass the teacher surely have never sampled the flavor of love for the teacher.

Love makes us grow like few things do. From time immemorial, people have been motivated to do things for romantic love they would not do for any other reason: to grow, to transform, to sacrifice selfishness, pride, and even their own limited identification in order to join with another in a greater whole. Divine love catalyzes these same processes on another level. The projection of our higher self as expressed through the living form of the teacher symbolizes our own highest possibility, and the externalized locus of this attention can pull us toward our Self, push us from beneath, arouse our conscience, or simply bring us running toward it through the longing its own beauty kindles in us.

The *Ras Lila* depicts the great love games surrounding Lord Krishna, who played his flute so beautifully that when the *gopis,* or cowherd girls, heard it, it "made the love-god, Ananga, grow stronger within them":

> *Some Gopis had been milking, but in their great eagerness*
> *they left their milking and rushed to Him. Others had just*
> *put milk over the fire to boil, but they left it. Still others*
> *left without removing the wheat-porridge which they were*
> *cooking over the fire. And all of them went to Him. . . .*
> *Some Gopis were serving their husbands his meals, and*
> *they left that. Some were giving milk to their babies, and*
> *they left that. . . . Still others were eating their own meal,*
> *and they left that.*"[1]

The Form of the Master

My very first vision of my teacher was seeing him in the role of disciple, receiving benediction and direction from his teacher. In truth, it was the fact of his discipleship that initially drew me to him. After years of chasing false gurus, hearing that a Western spiritual master was coming with twenty disciples to visit his master got my attention. I was intrigued by the possibility of a teacher who might possess enough integrity and humility to reveal himself in the surrendered role of disciple before his own students. At the time, I did not know that his discipleship was one of the most potent forms of teaching he used with his own students. He was not a teacher who asked students to submit to him while he took off in private jets to Hawaii, but one who lived in visible surrender to his teacher while serving others in a parallel manner.

Forever imprinted in my mind is an image of Lee dressed in a baby-blue traditional Indian *kurta,* hands folded in a gesture of pranam to his master as the Yogi walked out of the darshan hall one day. It was the look in Lee's eyes that got to me, even though at the time I did not understand the implications of what I was seeing. It was a look of utter and abject adoration, a surrender arising from completeness, a whole-bodied submission to the awesome expression. of One in the form of the personal Beloved. Lee's eyes and yearning heart followed his master's every step as the Yogi walked past him and out the door. I recognized clearly in that moment that no matter who this man would become to me, and in whatever crazy-wise manner he might express himself in his function as teacher, I had already seen that he was first a Lover. His connection to the teachings and to his teacher was that of a disciple, and my longing heart and doubting mind were thus reassured.

In a private talk addressing Yogi Ramsuratkumar's students, Lee told them:

> *If we are afraid to love the human master, we are denying ourselves one of the sweetest and most tender aspects of relationship. When we bring the Beloved into our bodies, hearts, and minds, there is a literal rain of nectar in the body itself which is neither metaphorical nor mystical. The body itself becomes an ocean of nectar and sweetness that is the result of the Beloved's blessing in our hearts. When we bring the Beloved into our hearts, bodies, and minds, we become pervaded, permeated, and soaked in the ocean of the Beloved's blessings. This is a quality of devotion that many of us miss out on because we are afraid to love the human master.*

Reflecting upon his own decades of discipleship, Arnaud Desjardins, teacher to thousands, suggests:

> *Don't insist too much on the impersonal side of the guru. Don't be afraid to take the human side of the guru to heart. Because he is your guru; he is the form for you to*

*be led beyond form. Of course the guru stands for the
impersonal, whether the guru is man or woman. . . . We
have to see and feel, "He is my guru, the mouthpiece of
Reality." And when we are convinced, then don't hesitate
to take completely into your heart the physical form of
the guru. Don't make the mistake of saying, "This is the
divine aspect of the guru, this is the human aspect of the
guru.". . . Don't hesitate to take the human being of the
guru into your heart.*[2]

When You Meet the Buddha on the Road, Invite Him In!

"I thought if you meet the Buddha on the road you're supposed to
kill him." This comment is often directed to me as a challenge in
the various talks I give on the value of conscious studenthood. It's
usually accompanied by a look both poignant and slightly smug
that suggests this insightful observation will close the conversation. I have found that rarely do the people who utter it have any
actual experience with the high-sounding dharma they expound.

It is true that we must eventually "kill the master" in the sense
of allowing the sense of "otherness" to be destroyed, and to allow
the voice of the guru, or teacher, to arise within us and guide
us along the way. But at the same time, we *cannot* kill the guru
because the guru as an expression of the guru-principle is eternal.
This is a tacit reality, a lived principle attested to countless times
by individuals even in traditions that do not use words such as
"guru" or "master." We can kill Jesus, but not the Christ; we can
slay the body of the master, but not God. The personal guru is a
teacher contained within a human body accompanied by a particular personality, but the Guru is Consciousness itself.

To "kill the Buddha" means to kill the projection of separation between ourselves and the Buddha, not to kill the human being who embodies Buddha-nature. Far better to kill the projection and then invite the one who has fully and radically realized and embodied his or her Buddha-nature to come live in our house, fully internalized but also respecting the teacher who lives outside of ourselves and who ignited the inner teacher that lives within us.

If I met the Buddha on the road I would certainly not kill him! I would cook up a tremendous feast and invite everybody I care about—and even those I despise—and let us all be fed until our minds and hearts and bellies were overflowing to the point that we could do nothing but share the glory of our own richness with others.

Nonduality versus Enlightened Duality

It happens, no doubt, that, when the good and faithful servant enters into the joy of his Lord, he becomes intoxicated with the immeasurable abundance of the Divine house.

—HENRY SUSO

Nonduality is the path of oneness. It is the realization of the essential non-separation of all things. The context of the non-dual teachings is the essential emptiness and illusory nature of all phenomena. This is the key to achieving the furthest reaches of self-understanding available within the human experience. Yet in spite of the realization of essential Oneness and the "illusory" nature of all phenomena, there remains the outer world. "Form is emptiness," the Buddhist scriptures teach, "but emptiness is also form." There remains a world of physical and emotional suffering, of mass environmental destruction, of war, of profound loneliness, isolation, and widespread dissatisfaction and depression ranging from the personal to the global. Georg Feuerstein suggests that it is not the forms of life that are illusory; rather, our *relationship* to those forms is based upon an illusory, or false, perception.

"Enlightened duality," a term Lee Lozowick coined, describes the principle and practice of an abidance in nondual realization that is then expressed through all facets of dual experience, infusing and transmuting that duality within the context of Oneness. In enlightened duality, apparent separation is acknowledged. Even suffering that is based upon misperception is still recognized as suffering. The teacher and student exist independently at the same time as they are one. In lived enlightened duality, nothing is denied. Everything exists, yet all is seen through a recognition of its essential nondual nature.

Nondual realization is, in itself, unchallengeable. However, when the teachings and insights of nonduality interface with a wounded Western psyche, mistaken perceptions arise. Human beings commonly seek enlightenment from a conscious or unconscious urge to have their personal suffering alleviated, a drive that exists alongside a true longing for re-union with Truth or God. All too often, however, the Westernized ego—informed by a psyche that is programmed for independence, disconnected from the body, and wounded by betrayals—co-opts the insights of emptiness, non-meaning, and illusion and uses them to build a solid spiritual-intellectual fortress. This fortress, paradoxically, separates the insightful one from his or her own very real humanity and that of the individuals he or she holds most dear. What is expressed as nondual realization is often the *memory* of a nondual insight.

The greatest masters in the world, in spite of their realization of emptiness and void and illusion and non-separation, are masters of love. This is what they teach, and this is what they express through their humanity. Arnaud Desjardins tells of his first encounters with such masters more than four decades ago when he was a young seeker of truth:

> Long ago I had the chance to meet some well-known Tibetan gurus. Still at that time I was dreaming of mysterious esoteric teachings, occult powers. But I found these masters to be so simple, with such humility, even if their only teaching was compassion, compassion, compassion. According to my feeling, this is one of the greatest teachings: to insist upon compassion.

The sixteenth Karmapa was dining with students in a lovely restaurant high above the city of Hong Kong when he suddenly got up from the table and went outside. After some time, a concerned student went out to see where the master had disappeared to and found him weeping uncontrollably. Shocked by the scene of the enlightened master sobbing like an inconsolable child, the student appealed to him to share the source of his anguish. The Karmapa explained that he had been sitting there in the elegant restaurant, enjoying the refined company of mature students of the dharma, when suddenly his attention had been drawn to the city below. He began to consider all the millions of people who were suffering endless expressions of human misery and affliction. He then reflected upon how few of them would ever have the fortune to come into contact with the great teachings, which represented the only real possibility for them to be relieved of their suffering. This awareness was devastating, and it was for them that he wept.

Great disciples of all traditions are Lovers. Their tremendous efforts of will, sacrifice, discipline, and selfless service are enacted not for the purpose of self-fulfillment or personal satisfaction, but as expressions of Love. Mother Teresa repeatedly taught her nuns that they were not social workers, but Lovers: "Your vocation is not to work for lepers," she told them. "Your vocation is to belong to Jesus." In *The Woman Awake,* Regina Sara Ryan writes:

> *Mother Teresa held her source and her payoff as no secret. Her work was not to help the poor, although that is what she was always doing; her work was to serve Her Beloved Jesus, who had first loved her. Her work was her faith—in knowing that the sick, the poor, the deformed, the destitute were the faces and forms of her Beloved, and that her God was not separate from humanity.*[3]

Practitioners of all traditions may express their realization and understanding through an abidance in emptiness or through an appreciation of form. Regardless of the degree and consistency of their realization, and irrespective of the language they use to describe their intention, true disciples of all traditions have willingly submitted themselves to serve as slaves of Love. Through their sacrifice, Love begins to dominate and consume them, pouring forth from a fountain whose Source is everywhere and thus cannot be depleted. Such Lovers often choose, or are chosen, to engage the form of the student-teacher bond in order to apprentice to the multifaceted forms of love—personal and impersonal, form and formless—that are revealed within the context of that relationship.

What Can I Give?

The teacher, the tradition, and the specific practices of the tradition serve simultaneously as means to an end and expressions of that end. There was a period in my discipleship when, frustrated to the brim by the recognition of my egoic motivations to practice (to get love, to gain approval, to arrive somewhere), I decided, after years of unwavering obedience, to not practice the disciplines my teacher and my tradition recommended. I wanted to see what would happen. To my surprise, what happened was nothing. I felt completely loved, connected to my tradition, and free of guilt—which prompted me to consider why one would practice at all. I shared my reflections with a trusted senior practitioner, who suggested I not draw any quick conclusions but simply wait and watch.

One day several weeks later while walking in the hills near my California home, I found myself feeling extraordinary contented and grateful to my teacher, life, God. Overwhelmed with appreciation for my precious birth and the intersection of my life with the great teachings and an authentic teacher—extraordinary gifts to receive—I became filled with a desire to give something back. The response to this desire was immediately obvious: practice. Practice was revealed to be both the means to an end and an expression of that end. For although my life remained full and plentiful even after relinquishing my practice for a couple of months, it was clear that the present bounty of my experience was the fruit of years of internal resolve. Even more importantly, I understood that a lifestyle of consistent practice is the most natural and respectful way to acknowledge the gifts we receive the moment we encounter the teacher and the spiritual path. To respect the body through conscious eating and exercise, to study the great mystics, to spend time daily in meditation or contemplation, to pursue ever deeper knowledge of our own existence—the means, the end, and the expression of that end are one and the same.

The question of the student-teacher relationship takes a radical shift when we turn from a consideration of *What can I get from the teacher?* to *What can I offer as a result of my practice?* We are so accustomed to thinking of the teacher as an "other" who is going to give us something we don't already have, rather than as a symbol of what we have already been given through the transmission that occurs immediately upon our association with a body of teachings. We think of the teacher as someone who *owes* us something, rather than as an advocate of the soul, a "cosmic cheerleader" who urges us to express the fullness of our own divinity. We think of the teacher as someone who must serve us, rather than someone who assists us in learning to serve the liberation of all humanity on whatever level we are called to do this.

One day when I was ranting to a senior practitioner about the decrepit condition of my spiritual practice and my teacher's refusal to express his love for me in the way I thought he should, she asked me to consider the possibility that I was never going to get anything more from my teacher than I had already been given. "What if what he has already given you," she challenged, "is the full extent of what he is ever going to give you? What if what you have now is all you are ever going to get? Could you live with that?" My mind had to do a backbend to wrap itself around this new perspective, and when I finally managed to, I saw that she was absolutely correct.

What if we already have everything? What if our lives— including our difficulties, strengths, sorrows, and confusion—are already so saturated with grace that there is really "nowhere to go and nothing to do?" What if we have already been fully found, and everything is *really OK,* even if we sometimes fail to realize it? What if the very fact of finding the path—of walking the road of an endless unfolding into eternity—is all there is, and we are already doing it, and will continue to do it, and have already arrived even as we walk?

If we have already been given everything, the only tasks that remain are to acknowledge our gratitude and then express it through our own giving with as much consistency as possible. This profound shift in the underlying attitude of our discipleship— from one of trying to "get," to one of seeking to give—marks a mature phase of conscious discipleship in which the apparently distinct roles of teacher and student merge in the shared task of service to God or Truth through service to humanity.

Love in Separation

When there is only oneness, there is no one to love. No Lover and no Beloved. There is Love, but not the *play* of love. One particular expression of discipleship that some individuals choose to live out involves consciously choosing to express the distinction between guru and disciple in order to live a life of enlightened worship and enlightened love. The gopis were no different from Krishna, but chose, or were chosen for, the role of enlightened lover for the sheer joy of worship and adoration. They chose to forgo immersion in impersonal Oneness for the experience of love in separation—to live their yearning through the very cells of their body. The Sufis refer to this as "the path of longing." The Sufis' passion for the God within is consciously projected onto the externalized Beloved, and this passion increases through a process of purification, prayer, practice, and praise until the heat of it becomes a fire that turns all obstacles to ash as they surrender to the fire. Some describe an experience so delicious it is painful, so exquisite it is agonizing, so joy-filled that it grieves, so hot that it sears the heart in ecstasy. The longing itself becomes the fulfillment, and the possibility of actual union is avoided at all cost, as it would eliminate the sought-after longing.

Layla and Majnun is a great Persian love epic of an unconsummated longing between lovers. In it, Majnun says:

> *Oh Lord! Let her berate me, castigate me, punish me—I do not care. I am ready to sacrifice my life for the sake of her beauty. Do You not see how I burn for her? And*

*although I know that I shall never be free of this pain, it
does not matter. For that is how it has to be. And so, dear
God, for Your own sake and for the sake of love, let my
love grow stronger with each passing hour. Love is all I
have, all I am, and all I ever want to be!*[4]

Upon completing years of a purification process under the guidance of her Sufi master that few people would ever wish to know
existed, much less endure, Irina Tweedie wrote in her journal:

*From now on I will have to live with the Glory and
the Terror of it [Love]. . . . It is merciless, inescapable,
sometimes nearer, sometimes receding into the distance,
but never far away, always just around the corner on the
edge of perception; a throbbing, dynamic, intensely virile,
intoxicating "Presence" so utterly joyous, boundless and
free. . . . It is said that the river takes no rest, the wind
knows no fatigue, and the sun can only shine and shine
forever. The child plays for the joy of playing. It does not
think of the benefit; all its joy is in playing. Yoga is falling
in love, not a choice of a carrier. . . . I know that there is
nothing left to do for the devotee who has surrendered
himself. For from then on He takes over and the will of
the devotee becomes the will of the Beloved.*[5]

To live such longing often involves a long process of apprenticeship to Love. Egoic desire and pure love are often intermingled
within the psyche: human love and divine love each playing off
one another. Yet even mundane or selfish or conditional love,
when attended by the conscious intention to know ultimate Love
and Truth, becomes the training ground for divine Love.

I learned this lesson one day when Yogi Ramsuratkumar called
me to him, handed me a small stack of papers, and asked me to

read them aloud, one by one, to his disciples. First was a poem Lee had written to him. It expressed the poet's intention to praise, to serve, to love without reserve, without expectation of fulfillment, for the sake of love itself. The next was a poem I had written to the Yogi—a poem also of intention and hunger and desire, but of my own wants and needs and demands of God. Then he had me read two more of Lee's, then one of my own. Then Lee's, then my own. Most of the hundreds of disciples who sat and listened thought I was being honored, acknowledged, recognized, and compared favorably to my teacher. Very few understood the chasm between the demanding nature of my own love and the selfless offering of my teacher's love as it was revealed in Yogi Ramsuratkumar's play. My love was for myself; Lee's was for God, a reflection of a vow to serve all of humanity. With gratitude, and touched by the compassionate wisdom through which the message was delivered, I understood the lesson.

In *The Hunger of Love,* Princess Sita writes to her Guru and Lover, Lord Rama:

> *The vow I made today, Beloved, has put me in chains,*
> *kissing Thee has cost me my life.*
> *Yet, I do not grieve, for these chains I wear are made of*
> *the finest silver.*
> *They bind not only my hands and feet,*
> *They also wrap around the chambers of my heart . . .*
> *Please hear Eternal Husband,*
> *I do not wish to be released from these chains.*
> *These chains do not clink or clatter,*
> *They do not rip into the skin or cut into the muscle.*
> *No, they tinkle with the sound of my vow to Thee.*
> *I do not long for freedom, for these chains enslave me*
> *In Your Prison of Love.*

I hope to die in these chains,
I long to leave my body with these chains
still wrapped around my full but broken heart.[6]

Who but a madman or madwoman would make such a choice? And why would anyone make it? Only because they were mad for love, the very madness that is the fire that has drawn the greatest lovers of all times and traditions to it. It is the fire of Rumi and Shams-i Tabriz, of Romeo and Juliet, of Radha and Krishna, of Camille and Rodin, of Heloise and Abelard.

We are all capable of a love as great as this; to think otherwise is a disservice not only to ourselves but to Ultimate Reality, which loves and longs to be loved by each of us equally. All of us are made of the same God and matter and possibility. Jesus and Buddha were made of the same stuff, only they made a different choice. Their choice is available to each of us in every moment, but the responsibility of making it is so terrifying that we shield ourselves from it as if it were the plague—even as we live forever unable to extinguish our longing for it.

I completed the first edition of this book almost exactly seven years after first meeting my teacher—now sixteen years ago—an event that followed seven years of chasing the charlatans within me who manifested themselves in the form of false or disappointing teachers. The years living in immediate proximity to my teacher produced a stripping-away of everything I once thought spiritual, replaced by a vision of ordinariness that is so veiled it appears altogether mundane yet is so refined it can be found in few places on earth.

In those initial years, I experienced a most unique love affair that bore similar qualities to other forms of love yet was fully distinct in its flavor. During those years, I underwent a wide variety of experiences in relationship to my teacher. I attached to him in an enormous spectrum of neurotic and divine ways. I was a dependent child attempting to gain the affection of a projected and unavailable father, and I experienced qualities of divine love too intimate to desecrate with words. I challenged his motives, actions, behaviors. At times I was angry with him to the point of being outright abusive. Sometimes I was an exemplary student, and other times an embarrassing appendage. I tested him in every way my imagination could fashion. I trusted and mistrusted, worshipped and cursed, surrendered and betrayed.

I am fully cognizant that the labyrinth the conscious student follows is one of the most challenging paths to Truth, but equally aware that it is an invaluable and important one for many serious spiritual aspirants. It is the opportunity to be in relationship with one "whose circumference is nowhere but whose center is everywhere," as Saint Thomas Aquinas said.

Whether with or without a teacher, it takes great courage, or sheer desperation of the soul insistent upon union, to walk into a living labyrinth and take up residence there—indefinitely if need be. I suspect those who do it have no other choice. Even if they cannot remember their true identity, they also cannot forget. It is less a matter of what we believe than a willingness to turn, without erecting barriers, toward what is already True. In the near or distant future, and certainly for many moments in between, we will all know reunion with our source, but some will know this sooner, and some much later. Conscious discipleship means that we step into the maze with full consciousness and complete self-responsibility, offering ourselves *now.*

I once believed that I would gain something from spiritual life, that enlightenment would be mine if I played my cards well. My teacher taught me that spiritual life is about giving instead of getting. I thought there was something in it for me, but in spite of myself I have learned that it is only about Love, and that Love is about God, and that relationship to God is about ceaseless praise of the One in the form of service to the many. The last great request the Indian saint Mother Krishnabai made of God was to be allowed to take the suffering of the whole world into her own body. She became ill immediately as she experienced the karma of the world eating up her body, and she died nine months later. Yogi Ramsuratkumar lived as a bleeding open heart, rarely sleeping, sacrificing himself each moment in an endless stream of pure giving.

Love is bondage and liberation, both at the same time. The true master is fully surrendered to Love in the form of his master and his disciples. The disciple likewise surrenders to Love in the form of his or her master and to the world he or she is ultimately called to serve. It is the sublime manifestation of the play of God through the expression of humanity. It is all and only for the glory of Love.

TOWARD A VISION
OF WORLD SPIRITUALITY

*There is an almost sensual longing for communion with others
who have a larger vision. The immense fulfillment of the
friendships between those engaged in furthering the evolution
of consciousness has a quality almost impossible to describe.*
—PIERRE TEILHARD DE CHARDIN

*Hundreds of millions of well-educated people are searching
for a "pattern that connects"—a compelling universal set
of spiritual principles by which they can live, yet cannot
find within the confines of conventional institutions.*
—MARC GAFNI AND MARIANA CAPLAN

The publication of this edition of this book marks sixteen
years since I first met my teacher in India; twenty-one
years since I was on the airplane to apprentice with my
Mexican shaman; and twenty-four years since my roommate's
sister walked into our Ann Arbor hippy home during college and
informed me that such a thing as "spirituality" existed. A life of
study, practice, and basic human maturation continues to change
me over time, and thus my perceptions of each element of the
path—from meditation, to yoga, to the question of the teacher, to
my deeper understandings of what is true—continues to unfold. I
hope that it will be this way until the day I die, and that my books
continue to reflect that development.

Yogi Ramsuratkumar experienced his "enlightenment" forty
years before I met him, and not only did not stop growing, but

kept expanding and changing like a comet arcing across the sky. The same is true of Lee, as well as many other teachers interviewed extensively for this book. As they pass through various developmental stages of life, as well as deepening their own spiritual experience and perception, they are changed by life.

Some people find and maintain an unwavering lifelong commitment to one path, one teacher, one set of practices. My teacher did that throughout his life, and I have great admiration for the unwavering conviction, clear-sighted devotion, and consistency of discipline he sustained for nearly four decades of practice. I used to believe this to be the only way, or at least the best way.

Others are changed by the seasons of life, the developmental stages of maturation, the changing circumstances of the paths and teachers they once committed to. One well-known author, after twenty-five years of devotion to his guru, discovered that the fruits of his spiritual gifts were to continue to research and to speak about how to preserve healthy child development in the technological era. Another spiritual leader I know, who was devoted to her guru for thirty years, left late in her life in order to experience living according to internal authority, while ever respecting her root guru and the tradition from which she came. After three decades of devotion to Zen Buddhism and direct service to his Zen master, Sazaki Roshi, poet-songwriter Leonard Cohen chose to leave the monastic life and practice of Zen. In *Book of Mercy,* he writes about leaving the monastery, entering the Santa Monica freeway in Los Angeles, and lighting up a cigarette—and how good it felt, though his indulgence incurred the wrath of many of his righteous practitioners.

One of the many fruits of decades on the spiritual path is that one experiences, with an increasing sense of conviction, the teaching propagated by Zen master Shunryu Suzuki of "not always so." There is not one clear-cut road of beliefs and practices to suit all human beings. There are well-trodden paths and religions that have proven to be helpful to many people in indescribable and irreplaceable ways. Yet whether we practice in one of these traditions or find our own unique path through the labyrinth of life, we each walk the path differently, in a way that only the inimitability of each of our beings can do—what Marc Gafni calls our "unique self."

I now understand that there are as many unique paths to spiritual unfolding as there are human beings. I remember when Llewellyn Vaughan-Lee, my Sufi "uncle," told me this. I was a die-hard seeker in my twenties. Although in theory it made sense, inside I secretly believed, "But my path is the best path, or at least one of the very best, and there is a best way to follow my path." Now, almost two decades later, it is clear to me that each human being follows a unique trajectory in relationship to spirit, truth, or God.

Many people stay with one tradition throughout their lives. Others go through phases of deep immersion in different traditions. Still others are *dual citizens*—they feel rooted in one religion or tradition yet simultaneously experience themselves as part of a larger World Spirituality. And others experience themselves as deeply spiritual yet feel confused about how to work in an intentional and effective way with all the spiritual options presented to them. These people are asking: How can I engage in a life of spiritual practice that is eclectic, yet uncompromised? Must I give up the religion of my birth in order to partake of the great teachings of the world's traditions? Is it possible to remain firmly rooted in my religion while partaking of the practices and approaches of other religions and spiritual traditions?

In this next phase of my writing and life, I am beginning, with my partner, Marc Gafni, a process of envisioning and enacting what Marc has called a World Spirituality. We are working with leaders of the great traditions to pave the way for the necessary evolutionary development of spirituality in the West. And we have opened the Center for World Spirituality, are writing a book outlining this vision, and run many gatherings and online programs to support the articulation and expression of this vision, as well as a World Spirituality Children's Program. The mission statement for the Center for World Spirituality reads:

Evolving a World Spirituality is the urgent need and great adventure of our time.

The yearning to articulate a World Spirituality is rippling across the globe in the hearts and minds of tens of millions of people. For some people, the classical religions have lost their power. They seek a path of practice and commitment that transcends the traditions. For others, their intuitive desire is to transcend and include the traditions. They seek to live as dual citizens, rooted in their tradition, even as they locate themselves as citizens in the broader community of World Spirituality.

A World Spirituality based on the shared truths held to be self-evident by all great systems of spirit and gnosis across historical time is urgently needed at this moment in history. Evolving an authentic life rooted in commitment and freedom articulated and lived in the principles and practices of World Spirituality is the next great step in spirit's unfolding.

The Center for World Spirituality is writing a series of groundbreaking books and creating new templates for spiritual practice, education, and community. The templates are at once rooted in the past, present, and future. Welling up from an integration of the leading-

> *edge emergent evolutionary insights taught by spirituality,*
> *psychology, and the sciences, World Spirituality paves the*
> *way for the next stage of evolution, seeding the ground of*
> *hope that is our collective memory of the future.*[1]

The spiritual path is never-ending. Patañjali, the mythic-human figure who channeled *The Yoga Sutras,* rests on a serpent called Ananta, which means "endlessness." The path has no end: it is a destination without a goal. As wide as we expand, the path is there to catch us, to hold us, to allow us to expand even more. If you ever meet a real saint, you see with your own eyes that the inner worlds are literally infinite. I believe that the evolution of humanity also has no end, and as this evolutionary impulse mixes with the spiritual possibilities available in our time, new developments can take place both in our inner world and in the collective.

The question of the spiritual teacher—the complexities, possibilities, necessities, and endless nuances—continue to live inside me, and my understanding evolves throughout the course of my life. Sometimes I fall deep into the remembrance of devotion and love for my teacher and my teacher's teacher, or I return again and again to the mantra I received as a young woman and remember the sheer power of the transmission of my lineage. Other times I am passionately concerned with how the teacher wakes up within us, the distinct lessons that are gained by listening to one's own inner voice, and the evolution of World Spirituality.

There arose a certain point on my path where, although I did not devalue or find fault with living strictly according to the dictates of the external teacher, I needed to experience life in accordance with internal authority—to learn the lessons of the inner guru and listen and respond to that direction. Jangalykyamane is the name of the yogic deity who symbolizes the "jungle physician"—the voice of the inner healer within us. This healer teaches us how to heal ourselves physically and psychologically; it also supports and guides us in our spiritual awakening and the accompanying challenges and pitfalls that arise at each stage of spiritual development. As a wise elder practitioner once told me, "There are two mistakes you can make in relationship to the ashram: one, not staying long enough; two, staying too long."

Again, I did not believe my inner authority was more powerful or more accurate than that of my external teacher. In fact, I thought it was likely that his may well have been the stronger voice. It was he who had taught me all of life's greatest lessons, and he and his guru, Yogi Ramsuratkumar, who had set the greatest graces of my life in motion. Nor did I believe that I had "graduated" from the guru in any way. Yet I still longed for the experience of being guided by internal authority while standing on the shoulders of all from whom I had learned on the path. I knew I had human needs and desires to fulfill to which only my inner guidance would lead me. One such outcome is the emergence of my beautiful family and our shared vision of World Spirituality.

Some paths argue that to live according to internal authority is foolish projection of the ego, while others assume that this is a healthy "outgrowing" of the guru. I don't think it is necessarily either, or that anybody can say what is true for everyone. The process I went through, and imagine I always will be going through, is my own spiritual individuation. My unique self, as formed by my teacher, asks me to move in the ways it is drawn and guided to, and to mine the wellspring of wisdom within in order to lead me through the challenges and graces of my life. There cannot be one way for everyone, and yet we can still strive to understand and appreciate the importance of spiritual discernment and its relevance to the labyrinth of the student–teacher relationship.

I pray that I have done my job well, and that this book will impact some lives in a meaningful and effective way. This would be my deepest satisfaction. I also hope to have made, and to continue to make, a contribution to the evolution of a World Spirituality.

EPILOGUE

An Unexpected Twist:
False Complaints Against Teachers

We do not seem to understand many of life's lessons until we experience them directly, either through our own suffering or from being touched by those very close to us. For example, we don't know death until someone whom we love has died; we don't know cancer until we have tasted it in ourselves or have witnessed the disease in a loved one; we do not really understand what depression feels like until it has visited us personally. Racism or any kind of religious, gender, or sexual-orientation oppression is the same way. We know it only when we touch it. The same is true for thousands of other life lessons and experiences. In this way, I have come to understand the multitude of discernments involved in false complaints against spiritual teachers, as in the case of my partner, author and spiritual teacher Marc Gafni.

My hope is that this epilogue serves three purposes: (1) I would like readers to utilize both the suffering as well as deep insights that have come to my family due to false complaints to understand the many discernments involved in the issue of false complaints, and to recognize that although students are vulnerable to their spiritual teachers, teachers are also very vulnerable to their students; (2) to clarify any lingering misconceptions that have resulted by the false complaints directed toward Marc; and (3) naturally, to bring harmony into the family and radiance and joy into our lives.

I am fully aware that it would be easy for people to dismiss my analysis of this situation because of my proximity to it, but I believe that the precise opposite is true: that my inquiry into and understanding of these issues for many years prior to my relationship with my partner is what allowed me to enter the situation with confidence (based on my thorough research of his circumstance prior to my relationship with Marc), and is what allows me to navigate the complex distinctions that arise throughout the journey. For those readers who do have a teacher, you might imagine that if false complaints were directed at him or her, you would feel a deep need to clarify the truth in order to ensure full access to his or her teachings and writings. As a seasoned student of the spiritual path, I hold a deep wish that students can benefit widely from the depth and beauty of Marc's teachings, for there is a real need for them.

Generally teachers are unequivocally assumed to be guilty when there is any complaint of financial, emotional, or sexual abuse. For many reasons we will come to understand throughout this epilogue, it is very difficult for people to clearly see the circumstances around harsh accusations, and it is also extremely difficult for a teacher to rise from the devastation of false complaints. People want the teacher to take full responsibility for accusations even when they are false—it makes everything easier.

Yet for a teacher to do this (aside from necessarily being accountable for his or her part in the situation) is a violation of the very
truth and integrity that they teach. Most teachers are destroyed
by false complaints. Occasionally a teacher survives. Even more
rarely a teacher re-emerges—both deepened and transformed by
the experience. Fortunately such is the story in this epilogue.

In spring of 2006, Marc's work was thriving in Israel and the
United States. As a spiritual teacher, public intellectual, and the
builder of spiritual and social movements, he had catalyzed a
movement in Israel called Bayit Hadash. It had an inner core of
several hundred people and ripple effects on tens of thousands.
He had hosted a national TV show on spirituality, and had just
completed writing his doctorate at Oxford. Marc had long been
known as a controversial teacher. This was partly because of the
unorthodox style of his presentations and their content, the large-
ness of the space he held, and the challenge that many people felt
in his presence, but it was also due to religious politics. His high
profile and style aroused the love and admiration of many—but
also, as they always do, seemed to provoke primal negative feelings
in some of the powerful rabbis in the world in which he lived.

When Marc was in his early twenties, a combination of his
strong qualities of intellectual rigor and passionate charisma,
alongside a youthful pugnacity, audaciousness, and bohemian
nature created conflict with two Orthodox Jewish teachers. These
two teachers would later be significant catalysts in the underlying dynamics that made possible the false accusations. Without a
discernment of these unseen dynamics, the superficial story seems
to be very different from what actually happened.

In *Listen Little Man,* Wilhelm Reich describes how certain
larger-than-life personalities incarnate a raw life-force that moves

others, who feel threatened or diminished by them, to try and "murder" that very life-force. People who are threatened, over-whelmed, and jealous are drawn together by a magnetic attraction in an attempt to remove the threatening presence. One of Marc's colleagues, spiritual teacher, former feminist leader, and writer Sally Kempton, said to me, "Marc was always primarily a pure lover and an artist of spirit. His brilliance in dharma stems not only from this mind but from his radically overflowing heart. He was never a conventional rabbi nor really a conventional anything else, and yet he lived in a conventional system that could not hold him, and which caused enormous suffering to him."

It was this kind of energy that animated a decade-long effort to discredit Marc, using his mistakes as the justification to "create" the discreditors' cause. Given that Marc had also researched and published on the subject of Eros, which pushed the boundaries in Jewish thought, the makings of a "sex scandal" were waiting to happen.

In May 2006, returning home to Israel late in the day to run a festival after a long and exhausting teaching trip, Marc got off the plane and turned on his cell phone. He called one of his staff members to check in and was met by the voice of a screaming woman whom he did not recognize saying, "You are over!" He was instructed to go to a certain lawyer's address, at midnight, where people would be waiting to tell him what was going on. And so the "horror story" began.

Marc had no idea what was happening or why, only that some-thing was terribly wrong. When Marc arrived at the designated lawyer's office, he was told that women in his inner circle had filed complaints of sexual harassment against him to the Israeli police. This made absolutely no sense to him, as there was no truth in the complaints. He felt as if he had stumbled into a scene from Kafka's novel *The Trial*,[1] in which the protagonist is accused of crimes that he has not committed, yet is caught in a system in which his guilt is assumed and in which no evidence to the contrary is accepted. Marc went into a kind of shock due to his utter confusion and the devastation caused by what was going on.

It occurred to him that he should be able to easily refute the complaints, for he had extensive e-mail correspondence not only from these women, but from all the women he had dated in the years he had been single. The e-mails would make it clear that these relationships—including those addressed by the complainants—had been fully appropriate and completely mutual. However, when Marc checked his computer, he realized that all of his e-mail correspondence had been erased, apparently intentionally, by one of the involved parties who had access to his computer. After seeking help from several sources, he called a friend who told him that in Israel sexual harassment is legally termed a criminal rather than a civil offense. Another prominent Israeli figure with close ties to the police told him that it was well documented that the Israeli police were often corrupt in these kinds of situations. Marc realized that without the evidence of the e-mail correspondence, he stood a chance of being wrongly incarcerated in the Israeli prison system. This prospect seemed horrifying, not only for himself but for his children and community.

His friends and advisors determined that it was both wise and legal for him to leave the country in order to recover the data from his computer and to determine what his next steps should be. The police had indicated that they had no interest in talking to him; they did not object to his leaving the country. Besides recovering his e-mail history in order to protect himself and his family against the false complaints, Marc knew that he needed to search his soul in order to understand his part in the contribution system that had brought this about, and to find a path through it that allowed optimal healing for all involved—the accusers included. From the beginning of this drama, Marc strove to avoid unnecessary hurt to others, and to find his way back through love and forgiveness for those who had betrayed him. This was made more complicated because once the false complaints were made, Israeli law prohibited Marc's having any kind of contact, including healing or clarifying conversation, with the complainants.

Safety for both sides is absolutely necessary for any real healing dialogue. For example, when false complaints are filed in a legal system, and the accused lacks evidence to combat them, he may have no choice but to act strategically in order to protect his essential safety. While in Marc's case the complaints were never pursued and never became charges, he was nonetheless advised in the first days to take all responsibility upon himself, and to promise to seek help in order to stop the hysteria and have time to recover the inner and objective resources (e-mail records) necessary to prove his innocence. Because his very safety was threatened, because he was in shock from the betrayal, because he nobly but wrongly believed he was obligated to take onto himself any sickness that appeared in the system he had created, and for a host of other reasons, he (mistakenly, I believe) signed a letter prepared for him by a scared board member taking all responsibility on himself.

It took about a year to fully reconstruct Marc's computer and to deploy other important methods of gathering information. The reconstruction yielded dozens of erased e-mails and instant messages to and from the complainants, as well as the other women Marc had dated during that period. Expert evaluation made it clear beyond any question that the complaints reported in the press were categorically false. The relationships had been loving, mutual, largely initiated by the women, and clearly without any implicit or explicit deception or coercion of any kind on Marc's part—and without any inappropriate deployment of authority.

In my opinion, one attribute of a teacher of integrity is the ability and willingness to step back and engage a deep and rigorous process of self-investigation and self-honesty when accused of any significant misstep or inappropriate action. I believe this process of self-inquiry should be engaged even when the teacher is innocent. In my experience over many years, there are those teachers who engage a rigorous process of self-investigation and interiority when faced with any challenging situation, and then there are those teachers who consistently remain unwilling to look for and take responsibility for any part they may have had in the contribution system, often articulating this defense in the armor of dharma or spiritual teachings, themselves.

In the two years following the filing of false complaints in Israel, Marc engaged an intensive process of self-reflection and therapeutic work to try to understand his part in creating the circumstances that gave rise to the complaints. He did an intensive life review. He looked into his own relationship history, recognized where his post-conventional tendencies had been at odds with his position as a rabbi, and did whatever was possible to make amends to anyone he felt he had hurt in his life. At the same time, Marc engaged in an intensive process of research on sexual and relational behavior. He read widely in feminist and post-feminist literature and studied the nature of masculine and feminine shadow. He examined the cultural, political, and communal conditions that can produce circumstances in which false complaints of sexual harassment are believed without investigation and checking the perspectives of both sides.

After two agonizing years of public silence, necessitated by the legal requirement to gather the information required to fully repudiate the complaints should that ever become necessary, Marc and his supporters posted a website containing a response to the false complaints. As part of his response, he explained publicly why he had written the original letter taking responsibility upon himself. Naturally his original adversaries spun this as further cover-up, rather than an honest explanation. Marc began to teach once again, now informed by the brokenheartedness and humility of one who has gone through trial by fire and emerged.

Marc's teaching has drawn many people to him once again, and he is again creating new leading-edge teaching. His evolutionary teachings on the Unique Self have opened hearts, even as they challenge and redefine the understanding and dharma of many teachers and students alike. And his teachings on World Spirituality are launching new waves of spirit that are moving the hearts and minds of many thousands of people once again. Through the power of grace and the depth of who he is as a teacher, Marc has somehow avoided bitterness and emerged more loving and open than before.

Yet he, like all teachers who have been falsely accused, still suffers intensely in numerous ways. His detractors continually try to sabotage his work in the public arena, refuse to participate in mediated meetings initiated by him aimed at truth and healing, and are unwilling to review the extensive evidence that would refute their rationale for trying to keep Marc's work and teachings from fully flourishing once again. Marc decided not to return to Israel because of the almost certain damage that would come to many in his former circle if the issue turned into a public drama there. He has decided to focus his teaching in the United States and the international arena. In addition to Marc's own losses, what happened both represents a significant loss for Marc's former students in Israel and the United States and prevents a very rare and precious teaching on Judaism to be given to a widespread audience that is deeply in need of, and craves, this teaching.

This story offers us a lens through which we can view the phenomenon of false complaints, as well as the dynamics surrounding the corrupt students and the corrupt colleagues of a spiritual teacher who has experienced false accusations. This is the reverse face of the shadow of spiritual authority.

The Need for Discernment in Understanding False Complaints

The most challenging aspect of the false-complaint syndrome is simply that there exist both true and false complaints, as well as varying degrees of truth in complaints. The discernment to be made here is that just because real complaints do exist—a significant number of them are accurate—it does not make all, or even most, complaints true. To honor our commitment to conscious disciple-ship to the teacher and to life, we must learn to discern what we are encountering when hearing, relating to, and in some cases propa-gating the circumstance of spiritual scandal and publicly defaming a teacher. There are times when it is appropriate to speak out against an experience of injustice and violation, but sometimes the teacher, as well as the student, is the subject of injustice and violation. We need to understand not only the complex dynamics involved, but the mutual complicity that creates any given circumstance.

Often, when there is a complaint of sexual abuse—whether against a professor, an employer, or a teacher—there is a collective assumption that it must be true. Yet this is oftentimes not accurate. There are many reasons why individuals and groups of individuals make false complaints. In addition, there are just as many rea-sons—many of them political or having to do with professional, competitive envy—why individuals and groups of people from behind the scenes encourage women or men to make these false or distorted complaints, and then support them once they are made. This is done under the veneer of protecting the ostensibly abused student.

Many of us have had a false complaint leveled against us at least
once in our lives, even if on a much smaller scale than Marc. In
my own experience, I was once falsely accused of racism by one
of my African-American students at the university. She did not
like my style of teaching writing, and wrote a final paper com-
paring my university class to genocide in Rwanda. I remember
burning with feelings of injustice, fear, and voicelessness against
such an accusation. If we magnify this experience exponentially,
we understand what someone like Marc and other teachers have
experienced due to false complaints.

In Marc's particular case, the harm included: loss—for a time—
of his ability to make a living, as many doors were closed that
could have otherwise been open; the loss of being able to see his
children regularly and to provide for their needs in the way he
had previously been able to do; loss of a community of students;
loss of being able to teach in the Jewish community; and the loss
of a network of friends, colleagues, and financial backers, as well
as much more. Marc lost the entire world that he had spent his
whole life creating and serving. The analogy that best expresses
this loss is that of a parent whose child is murdered, and the parent
is then falsely accused of the murder. That Marc, after several
years of intense suffering, has been able to reclaim much of this
through a new wave of creativity and love makes him very much
the exception and not the rule. A parallel toll of loss may arise for
anyone who is falsely accused, particularly of sexual harassment.

As Harvard professor Alan Dershowitz and a group of feminist
writers point out,[2] the initiators of false complaints are often a
group that coalesces through a mixture of ulterior motives, who
in turn wins to its cause a legion of well-meaning supporters
of the so-called victim. A narrative is developed, aided by the
easy and quick communication provided by the Internet, and
the surface appearance of a righteous campaign to protect the

victim—in this case, the "hurt woman"—is put into place. Since everyone feels sorry for hurt women, it is not hard for the story to be set in place without anyone noticing that hidden motives involving competition, envy, and personal resentment are driving the core energy of the story.

The false narrative becomes a dogma that cannot be challenged without one's being accused of heresy, since as in the church of old, there are many hidden agendas of power that require the perpetuation of the false dogma. In Marc's story, as in the case of the Duke lacrosse players and many other false-complaint scenarios, the facts are vastly distorted and exaggerated in order to realize the conscious and unconscious drives and motivations of the accusers.[3]

Masculine Shadow, Feminine Shadow, and Victim Feminism

Many of us are aware of the masculine shadow—a need to compete, dominate, and destroy anyone who gets in the way of the individual's identity and "territory." But fewer are cognizant of the feminine shadow—the desperate need for relationship, intimacy, and communion, which when threatened triggers shadow responses. It is to this truism that Shakespeare referred to when he said, "Hell hath no fury like a woman scorned." But both masculine and feminine shadow are equally real, and similarly destructive. The masculine shadow lies, paradoxically, behind many expressions of the feminine shadow. The teacher-student abuse narrative becomes an easy veneer behind which malice can hide.

This fact does not excuse feminine shadow, which will, of course, loudly deny and protest any suggestion that it has been manipulated. What it does inject is the element of masculine shadow, which stands behind this and so many other similar stories. As has happened over the centuries, patriarchy uses the feminine for its own ends of power and status. The Trojan War was not, truly speaking, undertaken so that Menelaus could recover his straying wife, Helen. Helen was merely an excuse for an ambitious Greek king to invade a wealthy kingdom whose riches he coveted.

This example gives rise to a subtle point of spiritual discernment: the feminine tends to be viewed as good and nurturing, while the masculine is inevitably portrayed as aggressive, narcissistic, base, and depraved. In my brief survey of victim-feminist literature, I collected a number of casual comparisons between men and Nazis, implicitly analogizing in various ways the Nazis' oppression of Jews with the patriarchy's oppression of women. In virtually all of these accounts, women are depicted as "survivors," and words like *holocaust* and *concentration camps* are deployed liberally in descriptions of the masculine—terms that are exaggerated, misleading, and in many cases could be labeled outright abusive. In these distorted accounts, men not only have shadow, they *are* shadow. Women not only have light, they *are* light. The truth, of course, is that both men and women have great light and potentially great shadow. In each gender, shadow is triggered by a threat to that which each group sees as most essential to its identity.

Victim feminism derives from the premise that women are powerless victims and always innocent, while men are powerful aggressors and always guilty. This stands in contrast with power feminism—the great reclamation of authentic feminine power and values. It requires a great effort at discernment and profound willingness to break the silence to dare to speak the truth about these matters. But we must do so, for to remain silent while our teachers—who are none other than our brothers and sons—are attacked is a tragic abandonment of the integrity and honor of the feminine.

There is no question that women have suffered for centuries from the patriarchy's commitment to protecting its own at the expense of the feminine. Forty years ago, a female student who challenged and accused a male teacher of sexual harassment, for example, was often disbelieved. The power in that situation resided largely with the teacher, and the student had little recourse. All of that changed for the better with the advent of the sexual-harassment law that made it an actionable offense to sexually harass a student. This shift, which began with sexual-harassment legislation in the seventies and crystallized in a series of court cases in the eighties, was a critical and important claiming of power for the feminine. It redressed a historical power imbalance that desperately required addressing. The shift, however, moved almost all of the power to the feminine.

In Marc's case, the complaining women were not students in any formal sense, but rather women who were part of his informal inner circle. It is clear that Marc made mistakes in discernment in the decisions that left him and his teaching unknowingly vulnerable to this kind of dynamic, and that undoubtedly turned out to be hurtful to the women. There is, however, a vast gulf between having a part in a contribution system and people attempting to destroy your life. The degree of distortion, and therefore destruction, that can arise in spiritual scandals where an element of victim feminism is present, supported by masculine shadow, is essential to understanding these situations.

Let's look at the modern power dynamic in relations between teacher and student. Today, a woman or group of women who know each other or who are otherwise linked can easily file complaints of sexual harassment. In many circumstances, the complaints by themselves, even if they later turn out to be false, are enough to set dynamics into play that can destroy or cause significant damage to a male teacher. The potential to inflict damage merely through the complaint, with virtually no risk to the complainant—and in fact potential social and psychological gain—gives the feminine (and her masculine backers) enormous power and makes even the innocent masculine dangerously vulnerable to the abuse of this power. Whenever there is power, there is the potential for corruption. This is true for the feminine no less than for the masculine. None of these dynamics let the teacher off the hook—we must all be held accountable to be responsible and discerning in our choices.

One must also be aware of the fear factor that drives many people to support false complaints without full discernment. We tend to fear association with someone accused of sexual misconduct, even when we know the accusations are untrue. Associates fear liability, loss of status, or being perceived as not protecting the women. Tellingly, Alan Dershowitz points out that it is often the case that men who do not stand up against false complaints are guilty of sexual misdeeds, afraid themselves of being falsely accused, or fearful of the loss of status they may incur by supporting the attacked teacher.[3] They are, therefore, either silent or supportive of what they know to be at least in part false complaints, their support driven by a mixture of fear, cowardice, and self-protection. Understanding victim feminism helps us to overcome the myth that women and groups of women do not lie and distort the truth. They do, just as men do.

Not surprisingly, some of the very same rabbis and spiritual teachers who condemned Marc, and who have acted against him behind the scenes, have themselves engaged in unconventional sexual behavior and made similar mistakes. It would appear that when what one writer called "sexual hysteria" takes over, self-protective fear in many forms overcomes decency, fairness, and friendship. All this contributes to an atmosphere that Alan Dershowitz correctly labeled "sexual McCarthyism."

The Fig Leaf of Hurt

All hurt needs to be honored and attended to. However, we need to distinguish between degrees of hurt: the very real and natural hurt that springs from the challenges and misunderstandings that arise in love relationships, for example, in contrast to the hurt intentionally caused by the malicious and conscious attempt to publically destroy a teacher by deploying or supporting false complaints. We particularly need to discern cases in which the hurt of the alleged victim is deployed as a fig leaf to cover up malice or a host of other conscious and unconscious agendas. This is mentioned because with respect to false complaints of sexual harassment, one of the most common things one hears from individuals who have not examined the story is "The women got hurt" or "We need to protect the women."

Of course I want to protect women. I was once a young woman who needed protecting, as earlier chapters of this book reveal, and yet I was determined to learn from my own mistakes—and it is exactly these lessons that became the basis for all of my books, including this one. We might really ask, who is truly hurt in a story like that of Hozi, my drunk Mexican shaman, in which I colluded with his antics, consciously and unconsciously, because I wanted to get something from him and the situation? I did hurt, but I hurt myself, and I grew well from it over time. Not all levels of hurt are the same. Sometimes we are hurt because we don't get what we want, or because the specific hurt triggers our ancient pain in a particular arena in our lives, often one in which we keep repeating that hurt. Sometimes we are hurt by malice and deception, but no less often our hurt is simply carried over from the past and is part of our karma to meet, understand, and unravel.

Here is a point of refinement in our discernment in relationship to false complaints: do those who have been hurt or feel angry with respect to a spiritual teacher have the right to voice these complaints? The answer, of course, is yes, *in the appropriate context*. But what is that context? For on both practical and karmic levels, we must be responsible for the effects of our actions. Do we want to send a young boy to prison for stealing from a store? Or in Marc's case, do we want to attempt to ruin the life of a teacher and his family because we were hurt in a sexual or romantic relationship that was fully mutual and freely engaged in on both sides?

Rationalizations for False Complaints

There are two additional dynamics that often take place in situations of false complaints. Both are an expression of the movement to demonize the teacher that almost always accompanies false complaints. The first might be called the "Narcissist" move, and the second is the "Lifelong Pattern" move.

The "Narcissist" move is very simple. Complaints of a very particular and condemning nature are made against a spiritual teacher. Over time, it becomes gradually clear to at least some significant number of people that the complaints may have been false. The false complaints are neither withdrawn, rectified, nor apologized for. Rather, the false complainants and their supporters seek to shift the focus of attention from the falsity of the complaints to various forms of character assassination against the teacher. For example, they might say, "Our real issue with him was not sexual [or financial, or whatever the false complaints were about]—really he is a bad guy." They might analyze the teacher as "narcissistic," "self-serving," "manipulative," or "having a lifelong pattern" of whatever the criticism might be. If the teacher happens to be an obviously loving and caring person, then they might say, "All of his or her love and care was really self-serving."

If the teacher was strategically wise, they say, "He or she is really just manipulative."

The "Narcissist" move is virtually always distorted to some significant degree. Moreover, it is usually insidious on at least three distinct levels. All three are easy to miss and therefore need to be pointed out to facilitate appropriate discernment. First, attacks on character or motivation are *subjective* claims, which are notoriously difficult either to prove or to refute. Second, such attacks almost always ignore all the values, goodness, and loving to which the teacher may well have dedicated his or her life. They furthermore dismiss or degrade that body of work by claiming that it was all based on agendas of ambition and power, when it is truer that motives are always complex, mixed, and fluid. It is often the case that a spiritual teacher is able to clarify and purify his or her motives with the fullness of years, practice, and experience. Moreover, motives and character are only truly known in the interior of a person, and even there self-deception is always possible.

The third level at which this dynamic of "demonization" plays out in an insidious way is via the individuals who make false complaints, support them, or who are silent in the face of them needing a rationalization to support their position. If they were to truly face the implications of their actions—whether overt or silent—it could destroy their whole self-perception of their character (as spiritual, wise, ethical, and so on), and thus the stakes are very high in maintaining their position.

A stunning example of rationalized silence can be seen in the powerful example of the genocide in Rwanda in which eight hundred thousand Tutsi were brutally butchered with machetes by Hutu tribe members. Samantha Power, in her book *A Problem from Hell,* describes the silence of the United States, which was fully aware of the genocide yet stood by and did nothing.[4] One of the key reasons given for not acting was a series of ostensible moral blemishes on the part of the Tutsi tribe. It was said in State Department memos that a few decades earlier, the Tutsi had massacred the Hutus. Since the parents of the present-day Tutsi were now deemed culpable, this justified silence in the face of the most recent genocide of the Tutsi. Finding fault with the victim is the most common way of rationalizing silence and cowardice.

This is precisely the dynamic that took place in Marc's story. The false complaints were insidiously linked by the complainants to reports that had been circulated in the Jewish press and on disreputable Internet sites claiming that Marc, twenty-five and thirty years prior, had sexual relations with two underage women. This is not true. These allegations as reported on the Internet distorted both the nature of those relationships and the substance of the engagements. An internationally respected expert in polygraph testing administered three polygraph tests to Marc, supporting the assertion that these two claims are untrue in the manner that they were reported on the Internet and in the press.

It is important here to understand the lack of discernment and outright lack of any form of integrity in these kinds of reports. The way they are related in the blogosphere, it seems very clear that, as one site says, "It is well known that Rabbi Gafni confessed to sexual relations with a fourteen-year-old girl." The level of the distortion that exists as a matter of course in the more malicious tabloid sites in the blogosphere has been addressed in a number of recent books, including Daniel Solove's excellent *The Future of Reputation*. The tragedy of the Web is its shadow side, which as Ken Wilber, Jorgen Haabermas, and others have pointed out is all too often a tabloid-like cesspool of disinformation, outright lies, and distortion. For someone unfamiliar with this phenomenon, it is almost beyond imagination.

In this case, for example, the reports that suggest that Rabbi Gafni, age forty-five, was involved with a fourteen-year-old girl in fact reference a story in which Marc himself was only nineteen and just out of high school, and the woman was in the first year of high school. The relationship involved no more than mutual petting between teenagers, both of whom experienced this as a deeply loving relationship. The limited nature and quality of this relationship as described here has been supported by polygraph. The key point, however, is that the atmosphere created by circulated distortions of old stories is then used as an excuse to justify the fear- or agenda-driven silence regarding the support of false complaints.

The "Lifelong Pattern" argument is another form of rationalization. Potent teachers generally arouse strong reactions that are both negative and positive. This will generally be true throughout the course of their lives. A teacher may be supported by a vast majority of the public, and disapproved of by a small group of people. Link together the naysayers and a small number of distorted incidents, while ignoring all the positive, and a very sullied overall picture results.

While most people who know and love the teacher will reject this negative picture, the supporters of the teacher are almost always the rational, stable, but silent majority. It's the most vocally aggressive figures who usually launch and support false complaints, and who populate the nastier neighborhoods in the blogosphere. The result is that the false accusers become those who gather and disseminate the discourse of the disaffected. All of this is in no way to deny that a teacher may need to work on his or her shadow.

Are Dual Relationships Possible?

This is a complex question, with no single, clear, morally correct answer. We can, however, deeply consider the question. To begin with, two discernments need to be made: (1) the distinction between a formal student-teacher relationship and a more informal, loosely knit situation; and (2) within the context of the teacher-student relationship, what is the nature of the relationship? Is it based on formal commitments and obedience, or is it a relationship that explicitly and implicitly affirms the mutuality of the relationship and the autonomy of both sides? I would like to be clear that there are circumstances in which dual relationships almost categorically do not work, such as a formal psychotherapeutic relationship, but most situations are not that clear-cut.

Dual relationships are what happens anyway: people befriend the teacher, or their children play with the teacher's children, or the individual is in a secretarial or managerial function, with only peripheral involvement as a student. There are no clear-cut rights and wrongs, and, as stated throughout this book, there will always be exceptions. With respect to the question of dual relationships, people occupy different places along the spectrum of this issue, yet oftentimes we understand our particular perspective to be *the* correct moral perspective on the issue.

For many years, well before I knew Marc, when speaking on this subject I would often ask the group, "If a teacher is 100 percent committed to his or her students, and wishes to have a relationship, and is surrounded by like-minded people, is he or she expected to go to a bar far from his or her community in order to find a relationship?" It simply did not make sense to me, as the teacher is much more likely to find himself or herself attracted to someone whose deep spiritual orientation is resonant with his or her own.

The next question that emerges is, "Is the teacher entitled to a private life, or must his or her entire life be transparent to the community?" Often, as in Marc's case, the legitimate request for privacy in a relationship or encounter is distorted as "swearing the woman to silence." My personal response to this question is that the teacher is entitled to a private life. My teacher, Lee Lozowick, was an exception to most teachers in that he claimed no privacy for his personal life. There were no private telephone lines in the community, including his own. His family lived in the ashram with his students. He chose an unconventional lifestyle, but it was fully visible for the world to see, and no one found it out of integrity.

Yet most people will not, nor should they be expected to, live with that level of self-disclosure. Whereas it is hypocritical to teach against homosexuality while carrying on a homosexual affair or relationship, it is not out of integrity to engage and face the challenges of dating and relationships, just because one is a teacher. This is especially the case with Marc's story, where there was no formal policy on this issue, and the organization was loosely knit and slightly bohemian in style and tone.

Due to the nature of my work, I happen to know a tremendous amount about the personal lives of many leading teachers—their love affairs, relationship breakdowns, depressions, and medications. They do not disclose many of these things to their students, nor is there a need to, as long as they are working through their life lessons with diligence. I do not judge any of this from an ethical standpoint, unless there is outright abuse. I simply try to understand what is effective and what is ineffective in terms of the teacher's reliability as a guide. Again, like most issues in the student-teacher relationship, there are no clear-cut rights and wrongs, only the need for ongoing discernment.

I do not believe it is fair to ask a teacher to share the details of his or her romantic life, particularly if he or she is single, or even if he or she is in a marriage, which will inevitably have some years that are more challenging, with the mistakes that human beings make along the way. It is the teacher's responsibility to stay in integrity with respect to his or her teaching function and to his or her students, but the student should not feel betrayed when there has not been a full personal disclosure. The teacher must be allowed his or her own process as well, as long as he or she is responsible and accountable for his or her actions, and non-defensive when given feedback.

Reemergence

Healing is always possible. As is reemergence. Even in a case like that of Yogi Amrit Desai—a well-known Indian guru, who in the seventies was rightfully called to task for having sexual relationships with multiple students while claiming celibacy—he could still atone, make amends, and recover. Even when complaints are real, it is still possible to forgive and move on. *Everybody* deserves another chance.

Once when I was organizing a large event with dozens of renowned teachers from across the country, somebody called to complain that one of the individuals should not be included, as he had had an affair during his marriage. When I recounted this suggestion to my co-organizer, she said, "If we had to eliminate everyone from this event who had had an affair, there would be almost nobody left." Again, I am not endorsing this behavior, but it remains critical to make distinctions with respect to these complex issues.

The individual who has been turned against and accused by those whom he or she considered the closest of friends and allies must struggle mightily not to become bitter at the destruction of his or her work and the distortion of his or her personality. He or she must find a way to experience the trauma from a transformational perspective, and to reap the fruits of its life lessons, even if they have left him or her broken. "There is nothing as whole as a broken heart," says the old Hebrew mystical maxim.

When complaints are made, it is critical to create forums for mediation and potential reconciliation between accuser(s) and accused. When false complaints are motivated by power-hunger and anger over past grievances, oftentimes the individuals who have asserted the complaints are unwilling to provide this, and thus they are inadvertently responsible for propagating false complaints. When the political or religious leaders of a community move to block a teacher's reemergence, yet remain unwilling to meet with the teacher either publicly and privately—even mediated by a colleague respected by both parties if necessary—they are themselves engaged in the abuse of spiritual power. When they use ostensibly sexual issues as a fig leaf to hide their true motivations, which are often animated by many of the compulsions of shadow and ego that all too often animate spiritual politics, then they are engaged in a form of sexual abuse. They are abusing sexuality and sexual principles to accomplish their own corrupt egoic ends.

Four Simple Litmus Tests for Spiritual Scandals

There are a number of simple litmus tests of discernment that reveal whether the critique of a teacher in an apparent scandal is primarily motivated by a desire to protect the innocent or is just a convenient veneer that hides the malice, fear, jealousy, or power motivations of those who initiate the scandal and who may even benefit from it. The first litmus test is: have the spiritual leaders and others involved spoken carefully to all parties involved in the issue *before* taking action? Second: has a fact-checking mechanism been set up to check, and cross-check, all available evidence regarding the claims of both sides *before* taking action? Third: is there a protocol for healing and forgiveness that is effective and safe for both sides? And fourth: is the accused party treated with dignity, or is he or she dehumanized, demonized, and treated with cruelty?

No easy formulas apply across the board for any given circumstance. However, if someone with a discerning heart applies these four litmus tests, he or she can generally discover the truth about what is actually driving a scandal's events from behind the scenes. All too often, dubious complaints are encouraged or supported because they serve the interests of various parties with agendas of malice, greed, power, and envy. When political agendas are at play, there will be a reluctance to investigate both sides, and even to systematically check the facts.

Various strategies of denial and justification can be deployed by those who may not instigate or directly support false complaints, but who also refrain from speaking out to object to the complaints even when they intuitively or actually know them not to be true. How does one explain not speaking out on behalf of a friend or colleague? Most people prefer to think of themselves as loyal friends who live in integrity and not in fear. Their unconscious strategies of denial and justification allow them to excuse their silence with statements like, "Even if the complaints are not true, he or she had it coming to him or her anyway for this or that reason, and therefore it's OK for me not to speak out on his or her behalf." At this level, the individual will rationalize his or her own inaction by saying that the person being brought down "deserved it" because he or she was arrogant, self-involved, narcissistic, hard to work with, overly ambitious, or whatever rationalization they choose to tell themselves.

Even if people's self-justifying estimations of the accused individual's personal faults were to have some grain of truth, said faults do not in any way warrant the cruel treatment, life destruction, and social shunning that occurs in so many of these instances. The failure to set up proper investigative or healing mechanisms is nearly always an indication that there is an Iago factor lurking in the situation, or that the goal of the accusers is not justice, but instead malice or retaliation.

To fully reemerge, the teacher who has been falsely accused will need to learn to allow the breakdown that has occurred to break him or her open to deeper love, compassion, and understanding. The teacher is invited, and even required, to turn the fate of the injustice into the destiny of internal liberation, both for his or her own sake, as well as for that of all the people who have been and will be touched by him or her. When Saint Francis was asked by a disciple what, for him, would be the most perfect joy, he replied that it would be to seek shelter in a house, be rejected and thrown out, and then left to lie in the mud with the dogs. Although most of us would consider this a fairly extreme position, it is nonetheless true that depth and humility arise when suffering is accepted and used as a way to open one's own heart. In his journal, Marc wrote, "To be firm in your knowing of love even when you are desperate, and to be strong in your heart of forgiveness even when you are betrayed, is what it means to be holy."

At some point, however, the teacher may need to share the truth of what has happened, and the complex motivations of the people involved, both to clear the public record for him- or herself and his or her family, and, for the sake of truth and integrity, to expose the byzantine spiritual politics and power dynamics that led to the situation. If there is some reason that the whole story cannot be told, the teacher should let his or her public know that full disclosure is not possible because it would harm relatively innocent people and their lives.

In some cases, circumstances can make it difficult to make full amends and to resolve the complexities that gave rise to the false complaints. Sometimes people do not want to resolve the situation because they are gaining position, power, or some other advantage by the individual's being ousted from his or her function. So the question is, who decides whether a given teacher has made full amends, and according to what criteria is that decision made? Clearly those who make this decision cannot be the very people who made the false complaints. Do they not need to be, at a minimum, part of the overall accountability to which everyone in the system needs to be held?

As we considered in chapter 8, in attempting to evaluate any teacher's capacity and authenticity, there is no single set of clear cut, moral criteria, but rather countless criteria, all circumstantially dependent. We can only use pointers. For example, one might ask, "Who are the people close to this individual? How do they act, and what depth of integrity and genuineness do you perceive in them? How do you feel when you are in this person's presence, and does your intuitive response to him or her feel like a deep perception that is trustworthy? Does this human being seem like someone who is not defensive, and who can be trusted to be accountable to his or her actions? These are qualities that we perceive and feel, and this capacity to perceive with discernment can be learned.

I was a young and critical seeker when I asked Robert McDermott, three decades my senior on the path, what he thought about people who had made mistakes on the spiritual path, or even caused harm. He surprised me when he said, "I'm not even interested in hearing about a scandal that is more than five years old. If I cannot allow people to make mistakes and to learn from them, I am not the spiritual practitioner I believe myself to be." For myself, I would not study, much less live, with a person in whom I did not perceive an extraordinary degree of integrity and authenticity, including an awareness of his or her own weaknesses and gifts. From two decades of research in this arena, I have learned to trust my own discernment in these areas, and am grateful that others have trusted me to guide them in this respect.

One thing we come to understand through maturing in the student-teacher relationship is that any teacher can be both highly developed in a number of areas, and at the same time inevitably human. My experience of knowing the inside story of many renowned teacher's lives reveals this to be true in most, if not all, cases. Of course, it is complex and challenging to learn how to fully trust a teacher when we accept that he or she is also human. But to expect our teachers, or any human being, to be infallible is to simply not understand what it is to be human. To be human is to engage an endless process of learning from our mistakes, to err often and hopefully in the right direction, and to live in dignity and integrity. We cannot expect ourselves, or our teachers, to be perfect, only for each of us to strive to be deeply conscious, responsible, loving, and forgiving.

APPENDIX
Interviews with
Teachers and Scholars

INTRODUCTION TO
THE APPENDIX

L ife is ephemeral, precious, and fleeting. The following interviews were conducted for research on the first edition of this book, mostly throughout the year 2000, as I traveled the globe in search of the most knowledgeable individuals on these subjects. Since that time, two of the individuals interviewed in this appendix have left the world: Vimala Thakar (April 15, 1923–March 11, 2009) and George Leonard (August 9, 1923–January 6, 2010). My own teacher, Lee Lozowick (November 18, 1943–November 16, 2010), who I wrote about throughout this book, has also passed. These interviews are precious archives, capturing a poignant moment in human history and the great East-West encounter, as the question of the guru became a relevant and real possibility throughout the Western world. May we honor the wisdom of these individuals, continue to live the questions and possibilities that their lives and teachings brought forth into the world, and take our part to evolve and carry forth their wisdom!

Vimala Thakar

THE COMPASSION OF THE COSMIC INTELLIGENCE

Vimala Thakar (1923–2009) was an extraordinary meditation
teacher and close companion of the late J. Krishnamurti. After
she served as a renowned activist in the rural land-reform
movement in India, Krishnamurti asked her to begin to teach
and set the world "on fire." She taught meditation internationally
for several decades and wrote more than a dozen books,
including *On an Eternal Voyage* and *Being and Becoming*.

How did you meet Krishnamurti?

I was traveling with the land movement. I had no idea who
Krishnamurti was. Life brought us together. All this is due to the
compassion of the cosmic intelligence.

**How does one magnetize that cosmic intelligence
to oneself in order to attract the teacher?**

Through your inquiry, which itself becomes understanding. The
guru doesn't give anything but *love* and the light of his or her own
life. When your inquiry is genuine, as opposed to empty intellectual theory, then life is love and life brings you to the person who
can be of help to you.

**It is my understanding that Krishnamurti abnegated the need
for the teacher, though he still taught. Could you explain that?**

Krishnamurti communicated his own understanding. He shared
it because that was his role. It helped *many,* but *he* did not

consciously help. He communicated. He responded to questions. He had some healing powers. Krishnamurti lived his life, and thousands came to be helped through his communication and the presence of his person.

You have taught in both the East and West. Do you think the student-teacher relationship has a place in Western culture?

Western culture is changing. Eastern culture is changing. All cultures are a melting pot. When this form comes to the West, it can be very difficult to cultivate the correct inner attitude and approach in the one who claims to be a guru, and the one who tries to be a disciple. The student and teacher must meet as friends. They must share—the student shares inquiry, and the teacher shares understanding.

Why is it difficult to cultivate the correct inner attitude?

In the West you see more of a teacher-student relationship rather than a guru-disciple relationship. A disciple, in the traditional sense, lives with the guru under the same roof and learns by observing the guru's every action. The guru-disciple relationship is something very sacred. Unless a person is willing to devote himself fully to the guru, the relationship cannot happen. Such intimacy is a *fire*. For those who take the path of devotion, the melting of the ego takes place. The Hindu songs say, "I'm related to *It*. Let me remember that in my daily relationships."

Can you be more specific about the challenges for the Western individual who seriously engages the student-teacher relationship?

In the West, students have to go beyond the mental. They understand the words—they get the concept—but understanding the concept is not touching the understanding beyond the concept.

When it comes to uncovering the mystery of reality, the sophisticated brain has no relevance. Spirituality is quite different from philosophy, theories, concepts. If a Westerner would like to get to the secret of *bhakti* yoga [the path of devotion], he must go beyond logic.

In spirituality, the guru-disciple relationship has no limits. In a traditional guru-disciple relationship, if the guru observes that you are overwhelmed by your ego, the guru will point it out in a simple, straightforward way. Will the disciple in the West—who is primarily an intellectual animal—be able to hear it?

How, as a single woman in India with all odds against you, did you manage to sustain your search for truth?

My love of life and the urge to discover the truth firsthand sustained me. I had read so much, but I could not be satisfied in borrowing anyone's version of truth. I would probe and probe until the light dawned on me.

Living here in India, a woman unmarried—it was not a path of roses. There were many difficulties and handicaps. But a revolutionary cannot have the luxury of defeat—pessimism, negativity. Never. Difficulties can be converted into opportunities, challenges into the call for more creativity. Everything in life has two aspects: if you know how to use it, it becomes an advantage; and if you don't know how to use it, it becomes a disadvantage. That's what I have done, my dear. For every challenge I received, I would say, "This is a love letter from the Divine, and I must find an answer from within."

Ram Dass

THE PREDICAMENT OF RAM DASS

Ram Dass, also known as Richard Alpert, is the renowned Harvard professor turned spiritual icon. In the late sixties, he traveled to India and met Neem Karoli Baba—the famous Indian saint— who gave his blessing for Ram Dass to write *Be Here Now,* a book that was unprecedented in bringing knowledge of Eastern spirituality and the guru to the Western world. Ram Dass has endeared himself to the public by being candid about his own spiritual unfolding. A documentary in celebration of his life, *Fierce Grace,* was made after his transformational stroke in 1997.

You are a great advocate of the guru-disciple relationship. Were you receptive to the idea from the beginning?

When I first visited India in the sixties, my attitudes were still very Western. I met Neem Karoli Baba and saw people touching his feet, but I decided I wasn't going to get sucked into bowing down like that. After all, I was a Harvard professor. But he worked on me—the whole cultural scene of India worked on me—and I came back committed to the relationship with my guru. But here in the West, there was no opportunity to talk about it.

Even though people wanted to hear you speak, they didn't want to hear about your guru?

They wanted to hear about him as a spiritual figure, but they didn't want to understand anything about guru yoga. The West is so antagonistic toward gurus. I am careful when I talk about my relationship to my guru because of the way it will be interpreted by this culture. People will always listen through their own cultural ideas and will therefore always misunderstand the guru. Every time they hear the word *guru,* they freak out, thinking it will be another Jim Jones. And so they put up a wall. It doesn't bother me now as much as it affects the way I communicate with others. This is perhaps the most difficult problem I have: how to share my spirit. My sadhana is guru yoga, and there is no room for it in this culture.

But there is room for *you* in this culture. If what you are representing is your guru, even if others don't quite understand it, won't people still get the guru through you?

People need to look within and discover what they want from the guru: Do they want the guru as a good daddy? Do they want to have decisions made for them? Do they want a guru for sadhana? Do they want a spiritual scene? If people in this culture want a guru, they are forced to deal with their own truth.

But they see *you* as a guru, even though I've never heard you refer to yourself that way.

People don't understand the guru, and if they don't understand the guru, they can't understand what my function is in relationship to Neem Karoli Baba. I am not what he is. He is the most important being in my universe. I feel so lucky to have him. But he's dead now, so I can't offer him to people in a tangible way, only subtly through my books and stories. So now people look to me to be that lineage. They say to me, "You're my guru. I know you're a real one." But I'm not a real one. I can't give people that. It just doesn't work. A guru is somebody who is a doorway to the infinite.

Are people insistent upon putting you in that role in spite of what you tell them?

Yes. I'll give you an example. I was at a conference last week, and afterward there was a party. I was sitting stationary in my wheelchair, and various people came up to visit with me. A woman came in who was very argumentative, and since I wear these dark sunglasses to protect my eyes, people don't know exactly what I'm up to. I decided to be silent instead of engaging her trip. A man who was in the room watching me came up afterward and said, "How do you stand the vibration you get when you meditate that way?" He thought I was meditating when I was really trying to avoid the woman. But he projected meditation onto me so that's what he got.

Did he only get his projection, or did he get something else?

Well, he *was* getting something. But what? What is *it* compared to the saints?

But since he wasn't *doing it* onto a saint, and instead doing it onto *you,* could he still receive the benefit of the transmission—even if you are not functioning at the same level as your guru?

People will get my teacher, Neem Karoli Baba, through me, even though it is colored by my psychology and my hang-ups. I can tell you that these people are driving me—that's for sure. Driving me not to drink, but to spirit.

What do you mean?

They are wanting something I can't give them, or that I can only partially give. But their wanting drives me to look inside for what the truth is.

If people are unable or unwilling to understand the guru-principle through you—the infamous Ram Dass who is perhaps accepted more widely than any other Western spiritual leader—how are they going to get it?

I'm such a phony! What are they getting? People think of the guru as a role. The guru is not a role. The guru is an internal message. It's heart-to-heart resuscitation. The role is a power position in this society. For me to take on the role of wise man, or the guru, is very corrupting. Yet I don't mind being wise and spiritual, and therefore I want to help others to become wisdom and become spirit. In this culture, people see me for the roles I play and have played: I was at Harvard, I was featured in *People* magazine. It is very important to people that I am famous. But it's horrible. Of all possible motivations, being near to somebody famous is not the reason to have a guru.

If people's primary interest in you is their desire to associate with your fame, how do you deal with the temptation of it?

I deal with a lot of false motivations within myself. Fame is one of them. People come to me because I'm famous. I remember a time when I was giving a talk and women were running up to me and pulling buttons off my jacket as souvenirs.

You are painting a pretty devastating picture here.

It's too devastating!

Does it make you suspicious?

It sure does, and it should. It means there is something to look at.

You've gotten yourself into an interesting situation: you have the capacity to reach the masses with your guru's

teaching, and at the same time you are offered every possibility to fulfill ego's dream.

This is the sadhana I have come to embrace. I have to be truthful with myself, because things like my power needs, my sexual needs, and my psychological needs to feel wanted or needed are all potential traps. When somebody says to me, "I want you as my guru," I laugh because of the massive discrepancy between my guru's realization and my own. He sees over the mountain; I only see him. But I tell myself, "He set me up to do this. He must assume I can handle it."

So you're in a situation in which you can run any number of power trips and get distracted from your sadhana, and nobody will stop you but yourself because you're Ram Dass and everybody wants something from you. For most of us, the universe just won't mirror our egos and give us what we want, but in your case, particularly because your teacher is not alive, you have to catch yourself. What an admirable and precarious position you find yourself in.

That's how it is. Yes. You understand it. Oh lucky, lucky me [laughing]. Fortunately, my guru is with me inside all the time, and having him with me keeps me straight.

Perhaps people really can get something from you they aren't willing to get from one of the hard-core, traditional gurus.

Here's the picture. There are many gurus who come from guru-loving cultures like Tibet and India, and within their own cultures they function impeccably. But they start falling like flies once they come to the West because they can't deal with this culture—the sexual promiscuity, the materialism. People get disillusioned by these gurus and then come to a psychologist like me saying, "I can't get what I'm looking for from these cultures like Tibet, but I can get it from you because you are sensitive to my situation."

In Western culture, we have four recognized modes of spiritual guidance: rabbi, priest, therapist, or teacher. Most people want me to play one of those traditional roles. In order to give them what I want to give them, I find myself playing into one of these roles. So I therapize to them, but only to get into them, to get my foothold.

When people come to you for what you really have to offer, what do they get?

I love the Beloved so much, and that's what makes me the guru in moments. But the guru is never a role. The roles attract people to me, but when they get close, what they get in their heart is my love for my Guru, which is my love for God, my love for spirit. We have to transcend the roles that we meet in, and then we're heart to heart. We meet, and their spiritual heart is mirrored by my own. They can get close to me through the roles, but when we get close enough they see reflected in me their own spiritual heart—that's the function of the guru.

What would you like people to understand about the guru?

In your book, portray that the guru is real. Let people know there is something there. But let them know that the guru-disciple relationship is ultimately an inner mood. It is not one of roles. It's not social. It's not a relationship. It's an inner sharing. You have an *atman* (self) and I have an atman and it's the same atman. The guru represents that atman to your heart. When my guru died, some people were sobbing. But I knew that he and I were related internally, and death didn't have anything to do with that level.

Has your relationship with your guru changed since he died?

The only thing that has changed is that before he died, I was always thinking, "He's in India. I've got to get to India." Now I know he's right here.

Llewellyn Vaughan-Lee

THE BOND WITH THE BELOVED

Llewellyn Vaughan-Lee is a Sufi sheik in the Naqshbandi lineage and the successor to the Sufi master Irina Tweedie. He is the founder of the Golden Sufi Center in Inverness, California, and the author of more than a dozen books, including *The Bond with the Beloved, The Circle of Love,* and *The Face Before I Was Born.*

The topic I am addressing in this book is a deep consideration of the issue of spiritual authority and discipleship.

You will be totally misunderstood.

I want help to elucidate this topic from a variety of perspectives in order to increase the likelihood of conveying some understanding on the matter.

I'm sure you do! So are you proposing a six-volume book? You see, in the West it's become very complicated because spiritual authority is understood on the wrong levels. The difficulty for me in talking about this is that it has never been a problem for me personally. I met Mrs. Tweedie when I was nineteen years old. When you encounter a real spiritual authority, something in you just bows down. I was always a rebel in school and never accepted any authority, and got into a lot of trouble because of that, so it was a bit strange to suddenly to find myself in the presence of somebody for whom I would unconditionally do anything she said. But something in me just bowed down and accepted her authority.

Yet people are afraid to agree to such a relationship because they fear they will be taken advantage of in some way.

A real master is totally free and wants to give you freedom, and therefore has no interest in imposing his or her will on you. He or she doesn't even have any will because their will is the Will of God.

What is not understood is that a real teacher will never threaten the free will of a human being because they know that it is a gift from God. A real teacher will never force somebody to do something against their will, because they respect the freedom of the human being. Before the master tests a human being, he or she has to give permission to be tested. He or she has to say, "Yes." Because certain things can't be done to a human being, spiritually, without the human being saying, "Yes, do with me as thou wilt."

What can't be done without permission?

The human being has to be turned inside out, has to be burnt to ashes, and a master can't do that to a human being unless they say, "Yes." They don't have the right to. Because everybody is free. The disciple, at each place along the way, is given a choice: do you want to continue, do you *not* want to continue? The teacher is there to open your heart, to tear you apart and feed you to the lions of love. But not everybody wants that. They would prefer to argue about authority dynamics. It's so petty and so irrelevant.

There are some souls that come into this world already surrendered to God. There is a desire to be with God that overrules any human desire. But those people are rare. Most people say they want, but they don't want. This is the whole struggle of the spiritual path—do they want to surrender, or do they not want to surrender? Do they want the world? Do they want a love affair?

Do they want all the illusions that come up? The teacher has to respect their free will in regard to each of these issues.

The free will you speak about seems very different from a teacher's freedom. Is it really free or just some mechanical function?

You have the choice to say yes to God or to say yes to your ego. And it's a very definite choice. I have seen people choose—not necessarily knowing that they have chosen—but I've seen it. They rapidly drift away from the path, and suddenly they are back in the world. Maybe they get something they always thought they wanted like a new career, or a new lover in their life, and they don't know that they have said no, but they have said no. They were given a choice.

Even if they don't know they were given a choice?

They know somewhere within. It depends how strong the longing is in the human being, and how much pushes them from within. It is said that even until the last initiation, the teacher does not know what choice the disciple will make. The disciple can say yes, or the disciple can say no. It *has* to be like that.

What is the function of the teacher?

People make the mistake of thinking that spiritual power is about telling somebody what to do. Spiritual power is about being able to take a human soul and turn it back to God, to be given the authority to work with the soul of a human being, to work in the secret places of the heart that belong only to God. That is *real authority*. And that requires tremendous humanity.

In the West, individuality is so important, and we project that into this relationship with the teacher and make a mess of it. We stir it up and get confused, and fight imaginary demons, but the teacher wants nothing from the disciple, because the teacher is free. How can the teacher want anything from a disciple? If they do, they're not a teacher because they're not free. But the disciple projects into this empty space of the teacher all of their psychological dramas. They find something that the teacher said that they disagree with, and then they fight about it and go off and say, "The teacher said this and this and this." Maybe the teacher did and maybe the teacher didn't. It really doesn't matter. The disciple is·given the opportunity to play out all of their dramas, all of their psychological problems, and some people get stuck in the psychology of it all. And I've seen that happen. They walk away angry and resentful. And that's fine, too, because human beings are free.

Those who don't walk away—who begin to see that there is something else underneath—start to find what is there. They get a little bit closer to themselves, to their own true nature. They walk another few steps on the path and the teacher just watches.

How do you handle people's psychological projections onto you?

I did discover people like to play power games against me, but I also discovered that "it takes two to tango." If I don't involve myself in it, then there is no game and the person is left chasing his or her own shadow. I have other things to do with my time. You see, the relationship of the teacher to the disciple is just love. The love is present there at the beginning, and the love is present there at the end. As a teacher, you see the disciple's potential to realize. You have no interest in playing authority games.

Occasionally you have to be a bit rude—to wake something up in them. Sometimes they take it right and sometimes they don't, but that's up to them. If they don't want to remain a student, they are welcome to go. Sometimes they come back after a few months or a few years. Sometimes they don't, and that's fine, too.

Tell me about your teacher.

I went from upper-middle-class English boarding school to sitting at the feet of a woman intoxicated with God. And I stayed there. It was my only reality. My wife and I lived and stayed in the same house with Mrs. Tweedie for ten years, and she was always under orders from her teacher. So we lived in a house with somebody who was under orders. And there was never a question. We couldn't have lived there if we didn't jump when we were told to jump. What I'm trying to say is that with *real authority,* you can't question it.

How should a student work?

It's different for each of us and a mystery, as well. The moment you try to crystallize it, it's like a dream, like a butterfly. The moment you try to hold it, it's gone. Spiritual life is alive! One day it's like this, the next day it's like that. The Sufis say it has more to do with inner attitude. There is no rigidity. This is why it is so difficult for people in the West. They want to be told what to do. They want to remain like children, so they project the father or the mother onto the teacher. Then there is an inevitable authority conflict and all sorts of exciting dynamics.

But spiritual life is *not* about that. It is about catching this golden thread of your own destiny and looking for the signs of God everywhere. Those hidden signs in yourself, in the outer world, listening to your dreams, your intuitions, what books come your way, what your teacher says and what your teacher doesn't say.

The moment you try to crystallize a spiritual path in the rules of this world, you've lost it. Because the whole purpose of the spiritual path is you attune to something which isn't quite in this world, which is faster than the vibrations of this world, which isn't caught in crystallized patterns.

Given the ambiguity of it all, how should a student proceed?

You will attract the experiences you need. You will learn what you need to learn. If you need to learn to be deceived by a charlatan, a charlatan will deceive you. You will learn something and you will go on. And the next time, if your karma allows, you will find a real teacher. It is so simple. It is your attitude that matters. The light of the higher self will guide you where you need to go. If your attitude is correct, then you will see what you need to see. You will get the experiences you need to get. And that's the way it is. It is the attitude of the disciple that matters.

Can you do it without a teacher?

You can't do it on your own. You need a certain energy—what Sufis call the *grace of the guru*—to reach reality. It is given into the heart, given to the higher organs of consciousness. That's what the teacher does. The teacher makes sure that you are living in a way that doesn't interfere with this inner process so that you can develop, get in touch with, and awaken to your higher consciousness. That's all.

Those who want to find the way to God will find the way to God, because God wants them to find the way. He will guide them and He will show them the way. Even if it's not apparent. Even if it's not visible at the beginning. He will give them hints. He will give them signs. He will talk to their hearts. That is how it happens, and that's how it always has happened since the beginning of time.

And you can't convince anybody else about it, because you either have experienced it and you know it's real, or not. It is like trying to explain the effect of being drunk to somebody who has never tasted wine. You can't. You can write books about it, but being drunk is something else. When you have sat at the feet of a true spiritual teacher—it doesn't even have to be *your* teacher—you know. Something inside you knows. And you can't explain how or what. The mind can argue with it and the personality can defend itself against it, but it's *real* and you know that it's real.

What do you do until that clarity arises?

You know, once you have really meditated, it is so fulfilling. That's why all of these power dynamics seem so odd to me. Why would anybody want to engage [in] messy power dynamics when they could go into meditation and be with their Beloved? Why?

John Welwood

EAST MEETS WEST:
THE PSYCHOLOGY OF THE
STUDENT-TEACHER RELATIONSHIP

John Welwood, PhD, is a clinical psychologist and long-term student of the Tibetan master Chögyam Trungpa Rinpoche. His numerous books include *Perfect Love, Imperfect Relationships: Healing the Wound of the Heart* and *Toward a Psychology of Awakening*.

I was pleasantly surprised to see how you treated the student-teacher relationship in your new book, *Toward a Psychology of Awakening*. Not that many people are supportive of the spiritual possibilities of the student-teacher relationship. It's not a popular viewpoint.

Yes. I know. It is a really complex topic.

Let's get the shovels and start digging.

To begin with, there is cultural karma that we all participate in. We are Westerners, not Indians or Tibetans. It's not easy for us to relate to authority. It's not in our bones. It's not in our cells. It's not in our genes. It's something really foreign to us.

So the fact that we are poorly trained as students should come as no surprise.

It is easy to criticize Western students, but the fact is that we don't have a guru tradition in our culture. It's not that we're screwed up because we don't know how to relate to gurus. That's a cheap shot. In the traditional cultures of Asia, it was much easier to relate to a spiritual teacher. Guru devotion was more congruent with the structure of their culture and family systems. So it fit right into their ego structure. The term for that in Western psychology is *ego syntonic:* "compatible with the ego." In a culture that regards individual interests as subservient to family and group needs, it is compatible with the ego to obey authority, to do what one is told.

Almost in a mechanical way . . .

Exactly. In fact, some Tibetan teachers I know really appreciate their Western students because we don't just go along automatically. If they wanted submissive students, they could have just stayed in Asia where they could find lots of people to follow them devotedly. I've heard several of them point out the problem in that. In Asia, many people listen to the teachings without chewing them over and really taking them in. They go along with the outer form—the prostrations, the honoring of authority—but they do not personally engage with the teachings in a way that goes in deeply.

It is as if Easterners' easy acceptance of authority can be as mechanical as . . .

. . . the Westerners' rejection of it. Yes. I think we are going through a shift where the old guru-disciple relationship has to change somewhat in coming to the West. It's not that we have to do everything democratically—I certainly would not suggest that—but there is something very interesting happening now, and there is more to it than meets the eye. When people dismiss Western students with the attitude of, "They don't know how to be students because they just want to be individualistic," it's a little too facile. My current Tibetan teacher actually says he finds

Americans quite interesting because they are all so different from one another.

Are you suggesting that by bringing the Western strengths to the guru–disciple relationship, you could conceivably come up with a stronger breed of disciple?

Yes.

A kind of conscious discipleship.

Yes. There's a potential to move to a new level. In the Asian system, the notion of discipleship is built in, and it may have gone as far as it can go there. Making a shift to the West requires a different kind of conscious discipleship. There needs to be a dialogue between the traditional Eastern model of liberation and surrender and the Western model of individuation, where individuality is seen to have important value. Conscious discipleship in the West might include the recognition that individuality is not just some flaw or obstacle or resistance to the teachings, but rather that it can be a vehicle for embodying the teachings more fully. If individual development is valued as part of the spiritual path, then it can be transformed and brought to a higher octave. That, to me, is where we are going. That is actually how the *mandala* principle operates: all the different elements of reality and all the different personality types and their unique contributions are brought together and included in the sacred world that constellates around a realized master. Trungpa Rinpoche called that "enlightened society."

So conceivably, our individual nature would allow us to consider our discipleship more consciously and not just fall into blind discipleship?

Yes, exactly. We can't just take the Asian model and say, "OK. That is what they did in Asia, and since these great teachers we are studying with are Asian, we should do it the way they did; and anything in our Western culture that doesn't fit that model, we'll just throw overboard." I don't think that works. It actually sets people up for a lot of problems. What happens is that the parts of yourself that don't fit the model you're trying to adopt get denied and come back in unforeseen ways. I've seen that a lot in spiritual communities.

For example?

In certain spiritual groups, it is hard to have personal conversations. The members are trying so hard to live up to a certain spiritual ideal of how they should be, trying to be "good disciples," that they do not consider their personal experience valid or important. So when personal conflicts arise in the community, people have a hard time dealing with them and talking it out together because they've given up the capacity to think for themselves and [to] trust their own experience. I've also known many people who married someone else in the community because that person was a good disciple. They would think, "You're devoted, and we share the same teacher, so we'll have a great marriage . . ." Then the marriage would often turn out to be a horror show because all of their unworked personal material would start to come up. But they didn't have a way of working with it because they are supposed to be surrendering, hoping that the process of surrender and practice would take care of all their neurosis somehow. Personal relationships are where all the denied parts of us come back with a vengeance, because that is where all our interpersonal wounding shows up.

In this modern world, I find that psychological work is an important adjunct to the spiritual path in terms of working through material that is otherwise acted out unconsciously, becoming an obstacle to integrating any spiritual realization that you may have.

I think it is clear that some things have to change in this transition from East to West, but there are also things that appear to be necessary to the path no matter what culture they are placed in, like the principle of surrender or the realization of nonduality.

OK, but just to make it interesting, let's consider the issue of surrender further. Let's face it: it is going to be a lot easier for some people to be devoted and surrender to a guru than it is for other people. But it would be naive to say, "Those who find it easy to be devoted are more advanced spiritually than those who find it hard." You wouldn't say that, would you?

Of course not.

In other words, it is ego syntonic for certain individuals to surrender. It fits their personality type. In some cases, it may even serve a covert psychological agenda. For example, a person with a dependent personality structure gets ego gratification from serving someone else. Yet for others, surrender is much harder. It forces them to consider deeply what it involves and to work through all their resistances. So the ones who really have to work harder at it might turn out to be the greater students. One thing Trungpa Rinpoche said about devotion was, "Even your struggle with the guru is devotion. Your resistance and your anger can be a sign of your devotion." That helped me a lot.

Given that, what do you see as the function and/or the value of surrender?

One of the ways I have been able to understand devotion and surrender to the guru is that it is a way of habituating and preparing the psyche for absolute surrender, which goes beyond the teacher–student relationship. The teacher–student relationship helps us learn to put something greater above us (which goes against the democratic spirit). Since the function of gurus is to represent the Absolute principle in human form, serving the guru helps us find our rightful relationship to what is greater than us. It is like lining up the forces inside us so that they are moving in that direction. It's a kind of play, a kind of practice.

Is it entirely necessary?

Yes, absolutely. The ego has to be able to surrender to the ultimate nature of reality. The separate self has to be able to let go if we are to receive the greatest blessings of life. This is a difficult path. Even though it is more ego syntonic for Asians to do that, it is probably hard for them, too, to really do that.

How do we prepare the Westernized ego for this kind of surrender?

It is hard for someone with a weak ego structure to genuinely surrender to a guru. For many people in Western culture, it is all they can do just to have a modicum of self-worth or self-esteem. That kind of person cannot surrender to a guru in a pure way because they want to get something back in return—approval, acceptance, rewards—that will validate them and make them feel good about themselves. But we shouldn't bash Western disciples and say, "Just because they have a hard time surrendering, they don't know what true spirituality is all about." Instead we could be more generous and say, "Okay. People are struggling with their issues, and they are doing the best they can in some way." And if they have low self-esteem, maybe some psychological work could help them with that.

Yes. I think that once you start getting involved in the student-teacher relationship, you see that you have to be incredibly strong psychologically to make any use of it.

There is another term in Western psychology called *borrowed functioning*. Students who surrender to prop up their self-esteem see the guru as big and powerful, and get a reflected sense of self from that. The strength of the leader or the group gives them greater capacity to be able to function in their lives. They are getting ego strength from the group and from the guru.

I agree, but it is tricky again, because there is a higher principle in there, as well: to borrow the strength of the guru or community in order to go deeper than you would ordinarily.

The whole issue is very tricky, because all the low-level dynamics that we can criticize are an imitation of genuine principles that exist on a higher octave.

Yes, very useful principles that you don't want to discount. I think that to project your highest self onto someone— especially someone worthy of that—is a pretty good thing. It shows that we are trying to grow into it.

Yes, even trying to get the guru to love you is OK, because it is a stepping-stone to opening to the deep love that is our very nature. So we begin to see that on the one hand, it is good to have ideals and aspirations, but the danger is that we put these ideals on ourselves in a way that makes them hard to live up to. Compassion, for example, is obviously a crucial part of the path. But we all have parts of us that are not compassionate. Maybe we strive to be compassionate, but that ideal in itself doesn't make us compassionate. So then the question arises, do we grow in compassion by lording an ideal of compassion over ourselves? No—that is regressive. In other words, taking an ideal of where you are not, and putting that on where you are, telling yourself you should be like your ideal, is not very compassionate!

Yes. That is our self-hating culture.

Exactly. It feeds right into the self-hatred that is rampant in the culture and in spiritual communities. That is why so many people in spiritual communities have dour looks on their faces. They are actually using spiritual ideals to keep themselves oppressed and make themselves feel worse.

The spiritual superego will manipulate anything.

But again, one of the good things about Western culture is that we are able to question these things. We can ask questions freshly and arrive at a more nuanced understanding about what these different things really mean. We need to inquire freshly and ask, "How is this particular aspect of the practice going to work for people here? What is it that students in this culture need at this time? And how can the teachings be more oriented toward individuals' different stages of development rather than some ideal state?" It's a big task we are talking about—which will probably take hundreds of years—and we are the guinea pigs.

And if we don't do it, who will?

Yes, who else is going to do it? My work has been about trying to see how these psychological understandings could be used in the service of spiritual development—so that people could work on their obstacles and resistances and use them as part of the path, rather than just rejecting them as hindrances they shouldn't be having.

So somehow we need to work this notion of the individual into the process of opening to a more Absolute perspective?

Yes. Spiritual teachings always talk about the Absolute—the mystery of the Absolute, the mystery of the Divine. But equally mysterious is the individual person. Since we have this tradition of the individual in the West, maybe we can contribute to the development of a new integration between absolute being and relative personhood.

Do you really think something new is possible?

Sri Aurobindo was one of the few Indian teachers who spoke about East and West coming together and what this meant as a new possibility for humanity. His path was not about the human just becoming divine, but rather [about] bringing the Absolute back down through the human vehicle. From this perspective, the spiritual view, or higher octave, of the principle of individuation would involve the individual becoming a vehicle for the ultimate, beyond just being a self-actualizing person.

How do you see that coming about?

Now we have psychological tools, which the ancients didn't have, to work on the personal dimensions of our being. They had methods to take you to the Absolute, but not to work on your personal stuff. Now both sets of tools are available to us. This makes it possible to explore individuation in the context of spiritual development, so that the person can become transparent to the Absolute without leaving shadow elements uncooked. In this model, you are not just pursuing some divine principle on high, but actually bringing yourself along at every level.

George Leonard

Spiritual Authority Is a Bad Idea

George Leonard (1923–2010) was a pioneer in the human
potential movement and author of twelve books, including
*The Way of Aikido: Life Lessons from an American Sensei, Education
and Ecstasy* and *Mastery.* He was cofounder with Michael
Murphy of Esalen Institute and Integral Transformative Practice
(ITP). Leonard held a fifth-degree black belt in Aikido.

**How do you view the student-teacher relationship in
spiritual life?**

I teach people to listen to all teachers, because from all teachers
you can get something, *but* to keep their own center. A good
student has to uphold two ideals simultaneously: (1) respect and
acknowledge your teacher, and (2) in the final analysis, keep your
own judgment. One of the things that we as teachers should
model is being a student.

In the book *The Life We Are Given,* which Michael Murphy and
I wrote, we suggest multiple mentors rather than a single, all-powerful guru type. The single, all-powerful guru rarely gets feedback,
and it's really a question of feedback rather than a question of power.

**Why do you say it is a question of feedback rather
than authority?**

It's not a question of whether you *have* authority. It's not that the
teacher should lack authority but that he or she should be able

to hear and work with and deal with relevant feedback. That's where it often goes wrong. The test is whether the teacher can hear feedback—or are they beginning to think that they have *all* the answers? I do believe in certain authority, certain leadership. That has to be. To do away with leadership often leads to tyranny, which is the same thing we're trying to get away from. Here in the United States, we've got a pretty good model of checks and balances. There has got to be some way to check a guru who is going to lead the people to drink Kool-Aid laced with arsenic, and the Eastern model of an all-powerful teacher doesn't allow for it. I just don't think [spiritual authority] is such a good idea.

In the West, or for everybody?

For everybody. Period. I'm going to be radical here. I look around the world and I see the adherents of some very fine teachers—Mohammed, Jesus, Confucius—and I see them killing and slaughtering other people primarily because they are on the other side. So I'm not sure it's the greatest model we can have.

But is the weakness in the teacher or in the adherents?

It's within the system, which includes both. That's what I'm saying. It may go against your thesis, but this is what I believe.

That's okay. Readers should hear this side of the issue, as well.

The greatest outrages of history have been committed in the name of the greatest religious teachers, not secular teachers. We have to look at that when we look at spiritual authority. This is not to say that authority is wrong. There should be authority. I have authority in my Aikido workshops. I speak clearly to students from my center and I want them to speak, too, but I also want their feedback. I don't want to lead people down a blind alley.

What is the value of them relating to you as an authority in that domain?

It shows a respect for the art and a respect for themselves. Why do we bow? Why do we bow to Morihei Ueshiba, O Sensei, our founder's picture? A lot of people think that's a heathen thing to do. We bow to O Sensei's [Great Teacher's] picture because he was a wonderful teacher. We are bowing for respect for him, for the art, for the community that has developed, for our *dojo,* and most of all for respect for ourselves. But this doesn't mean we're going to say Judo is bad and we have to go terrorize Judo people or Karate people. We bow as an act of respect for ourselves, ultimately. I don't think it is necessary to make yourself an exalted being. God is in every one of us. The whole idea that God is in one person, I don't like that. In my way of looking at it, God is in everything in the universe. I know that I could easily put myself in the role of guru—let my white hair grow a little longer and get a white beard. I could make my voice a little more resonant and louder in order to get the crowd to cheer and say "Hallelujah" and all that kind of stuff, but I do not choose that path.

I imagine there are people who try to put you there.

Yes!

How do you work with them?

I just laugh about it. I say, "Come on. You've got to be kidding. I'm just a flawed being." The thing we've got to understand is, "I'm the center of the universe and so are you. I have God within me and so do you and so does the next person." We've got to realize God is in everybody. We don't need to have anybody as a representative of God. We're all representatives.

Robert Frager

How Do You Find Your Way through the Desert When There Is No Road?

Robert Frager, PhD, is a Sufi sheik, psychologist, and Aikido master. He is the cofounder of the Institute of Transpersonal Psychology in Palo Alto, California, and the author of *Heart, Self, and Soul* and *Essential Sufism*.

A primary function of the spiritual teacher is to confront the student's ego. Why is that difficult for people?

There is an old Arab saying: "The enemy of my enemy is my friend." The enemy of any spiritual seeker is the ego, and one of the teacher's roles is to be an enemy of that ego. The problem is, we don't see the ego as our enemy—we see it as who we are. So when the spiritual teacher says, "Stop that. Change that," the disciple thinks the teacher is *their* enemy instead of the enemy of their ego.

Being a teacher is a terrible job. When I work seriously with somebody, sometimes they get it, but much of the time they think I'm attacking them. But if I let them go, I'm failing them. How long do you let someone make the same mistakes?

Why would a spiritual seeker turn to a teacher?

If you have a cut, you can bandage yourself, but you can't take out your own appendix. For major transformational change, you can't do it yourself. When you go in for surgery, you have to have tremendous faith in your doctor, and you must have the same kind of faith in your teacher. Check your surgeon's capabilities, but then say, "I'm going to trust the surgeon to know enough." It's the same way with your teacher.

There are problems in the student-teacher relationship, but to say that we should cease giving authority to teachers is like saying surgeons shouldn't be given scalpels because they could hurt people with them. Doctors are human, and so are teachers. To be expected to be perfect is a terrible burden for any teacher. For every one case against a teacher who has hurt a student, thousands of people have been helped. Do you fire a doctor if one operation goes wrong?

Why do we give authority to the surgeon but not the teacher?

We have a culture that teaches us trust for our medical profession, but we don't have a culture that teaches us to trust the spiritual teacher. Our culture doesn't teach us to support our spiritual quest. Still, there are advantages and disadvantages for Western students of spirituality. The famous Indian saint Yogananda said, "Give me a Western businessman. Their skills in time management are the skills of a great yogi!"

Westerners who are critical of the authority of the teacher often don't know what they are talking about because they've never had a relationship with a real teacher. Meeting a teacher and interviewing them is not the same as understanding how the relationship works, especially if you come at it from a Western perspective. Ram Dass used to say when a Western New Age seeker sees a saint, all they see is their New Age eyes. The very term *guru* has become so pejorative that it really means "bad spiritual teacher."

Is there a distinction between self-proclaimed teachers and those who belong to a lineage?

In my own experience, what is important is that the teacher is the representative of a lineage. The teacher is a link in a chain. My metaphor is that the lineage is a pipeline, and what flows through that pipeline is the blessing and energy of a tradition that connects us all the way back to the Divine. The important thing is that it is connected well to the section before it and that it doesn't leak. If a teacher is firmly connected to *their* teacher—and doesn't leak—they become a transmitter for something larger.

In the Sufi tradition, the teacher is a representative. To the extent one remembers this, it moderates this absolute submission to the teacher. To submit to the Divine is the goal. Ideally, whatever devotion is given to the teacher is given right to the Divine.

Doesn't that get distorted?

Yes, it does. You'll get teachers who say, "Submit to me." Instead the teacher needs to say, "I am only the agent for something higher. Submit *through* me."

What is the role of discipleship in your tradition?

It is said that a teacher is just a function, whereas to be a disciple requires one's whole being.

How do you learn to be a disciple?

By watching other disciples. I learned so much from the old Turkish dervishes I saw. The senior dervishes were the most humble. They were more aware of those around them. If someone ran out of water or needed a piece of bread, they would demonstrate the capacity to serve. There was an old dervish named Raji—one of the personal assistants to my teacher. Raji was one of the only dervishes our teacher would ever holler at because Raji was the only one who could handle it. "Where's my tea?! Where are my cigarettes?!" my teacher would scream. And Raji would just smile, as if he was thinking, "Oh, I have a chance to serve my teacher." He was delighted to be of service, while the rest of us were clear that if we were talked to like that, we would leave. It was a beautiful game they played to show us how a dervish should be. For most of us, just a little snap in [our teacher's] voice would knock us over. I learned most by watching real dervishes serve tea to each other: one of them was completely grateful to be serving, and the other was completely grateful to be served. The senior didn't say to the junior, "I've been at this twenty years longer, so *you* pour *my* tea."

But how do you *learn* to be the kind of student who serves like that?

You have to come into the relationship to the teacher with an empty cup. If you enter with all your preconceptions, how can you learn anything? Nothing is going to get in. One of the interesting things in Japan is that the Japanese don't look at people in terms of their skills—assessing whether they would be a great artist or a great football player. They ask, "Is this student teachable? Do they have the ability to take something in, and take it in well?" They do not say, "Are they gifted?"

I want to know if potential students can empty their cup. Can they say, "This teacher is not my father. This is not my highschool teacher or principal. This is my *teacher,*" and see with fresh eyes the person in front of them?

What is the most helpful thing you received from your teacher?

My master's unconditional acceptance of me is what helped me more than anything else did. The critics of spiritual authority cannot know what this relationship is like. The authority I gave my teacher was out of love, certainly not out of his demand for it. One of our traditions is that you kiss your teacher's hand as a mark of respect. My teacher would say to people, "Please don't try to kiss my hand too much, because when you kiss my hand, I inwardly kiss your feet." When someone models so beautifully the ideals of the path, how can you help but love them, follow them, serve them?

His love is what made him so powerful as a teacher, not by sitting on a throne. In our center in Istanbul, he would often sit on the floor and have everyone else sit on couches that were higher than he was. Of course, there will always be trappings, but the more the teacher cares about the trappings, the less they are a teacher.

What about personality flaws in the teacher?

If a teacher lies about their flaw, that's a problem; but the problem is the lie, not the flaw. Teachers can have flaws. One of my Sufi teachers said, "When I talk to you about all of these egoic things, I'm talking about myself first. I may have been struggling longer, or at a more subtle level, but I'm still struggling."

Is it possible to know the Truth without the teacher?

When somebody asked Rumi that, he said that it was possible, only that the journey that would take two days with the teacher would take two hundred years without. How do you find your way through the desert when there is no road?

Lama Palden Drolma

COMING TO TERMS WITH OURSELVES

Lama Palden Drolma is a teacher of Tibetan Vajrayana Buddhism. In addition to her primary teacher, Kalu Rinpoche, she studied with many of the great Tibetan masters, including His Holiness the Dalai Lama, His Holiness the sixteenth Gyalwa Karmapa, and His Holiness Dudjom Rinpoche. Since her teenage years, she has practiced in the Sufi, Christian, Native American, and Hindu traditions. She is also a licensed psychotherapist. She currently practices and teaches in Northern California.

What is it like for you to serve in the public function of a spiritual teacher?

For me, I had to make a choice between being in a public position and taking on an incredible amount of responsibility and work, and living a more private life of retreat and practice. I never entered the spiritual path with an aim to teach. Even when I was little, the only thing I felt I really received nourishment or meaning from was spiritual practice.

Being a teacher is not a glamorous job at all. The only part of us that could enjoy things like other people's devotion and projections onto us is the ego, and if the ego survives while you are being a spiritual teacher, you've got problems. If your ego isn't tamed by the time you're a visible spiritual teacher with the responsibility for students, you've gotten yourself in a difficult position.

What I really enjoy is sharing the dharma with people and practicing together. I also enjoy the satisfaction that comes through facilitating other people's spiritual unfoldment. The rest of it I find awkward.

What are the main difficulties of your position?

It is a lot of responsibility to guide someone's spiritual path. Our spiritual life affects everything—our whole experience of being a human being—so it's a precious responsibility. There is also an incredible amount of transference—the object relations of Mommy and Daddy being projected on the teacher. It's not fun, and it takes skill and energy to separate oneself from all of that and not buy into the projections—the positive as well as the negative ones.

When students are more mature it's easier for a teacher because they have done more of their own inner work. Then there is the joy of the shared relationship—learning together and unfolding together in our realization.

I also try to never get involved in a codependent loop with students. Some teachers, who lack skillful means and wisdom in certain areas, fall into a codependent loop in which they *need* to be the teacher and they *need* to have students who think of them in a certain way. I don't feel like I personally need my students. It's not that I don't have needs, but I meet them in other ways— through having close friends, having my own spiritual teachers, having my own full life.

What is your function in relationship to students?

In general, the way I teach is acknowledging that I'm *not* realized. I don't tell people I'm realized. I feel that I am a vehicle for the teachings. I am willing to be that. I have devoted my adult life to spiritual training and spiritual practice, so I'm sharing both what I have learned and understood intellectually, as well as the realization and understanding I have discovered through my own practice. Even the Dalai Lama doesn't say he's realized, and he's a lot farther along the path than most of us.

What are the particular challenges facing Western students of spirituality?

People in Western culture are wounded. During a three-year retreat in the eighties, I realized that in our culture we tend to think there is something fundamentally wrong with us—a sense that we are bad that traces back collectively to the idea of original sin. We believe that there was an original flaw and that as a result of it, we became flawed. I think no matter how you were raised, this permeates Western culture: original sin and the belief that there is something wrong with us.

Several people began to understand this at the same time. When it was explained to the Dalai Lama, he later said publicly that he was so mind-blown by the fact that many people in the West hate themselves that it took him two years of thinking about this to understand it. Then he said that he finally comprehended many things about Western culture he had never understood before.

Most Western students feel there is something wrong with them, and this belief system either has to be dealt with before a student enters the path or the teachings need to be reworked in order to tend to that as the students proceed along the path.

It seems like that dynamic would apply even more strongly to women. What are the greatest challenges for female students?

I think because of the male/female gender issues, it's been very challenging for many women to surrender to a male teacher if they have had negative experiences of men previous to finding a spiritual teacher. Also, many male teachers have abused their position, adding further to the problem by re-traumatizing women who were already wounded as children. But I don't think in an awakened being it actually makes a difference whether one is male or female.

Why do you think there aren't more women teachers in the Western world?

I think one reason is that women haven't felt supported as teachers. Due to patriarchy and history, I think there is an unconscious fear of being attacked if a woman steps out into a more worldly position as spiritual teacher or healer. I know for myself, even though I was completely supported by my teachers and my family, I was still very reluctant to assume the role of spiritual teacher.

When I asked Kalu Rinpoche why there weren't more women teachers historically, he said that there were a lot of women with deep realization who didn't *want* to teach. Most of them couldn't be bothered. They were having too much of a good time just being yoginis—enjoying being up in the Himalayas and meditating and being with their comrades and colleagues in their communities or nunneries.

How would you describe yourself, given the various roles and functions you serve?

Since I came to the dharma, I often experienced myself as two distinct, separate streams of being. One as this Tibetan yogini, and one as this Western, American woman.

You keep them separate?

No—they *felt* separate, up until a few years ago. The last few years they have come much more into integration. I don't think that process is totally complete, but much more so than before. I see myself as a Marin County woman, as well as being a Tibetan Lama, a yogini, and a psychotherapist. I have ordinary American friends, and we share what we're going through very honestly and deeply. I'm not their teacher. I'm just one of them. One of my own particular manifestations as a woman is that I like beauty. I like the feminine. I like things like clothes and jewelry. I even wear silk shirts with my Tibetan robes. I've just always been like that all my life. So to me that's just part of the manifestation of who I am. I'm not trying to be something different from what I am.

Charles Tart

ALLOWING FOR HUMAN IMPERFECTION

Charles T. Tart, PhD, is internationally known for his investigations
into the nature of consciousness, as one of the founders of
the field of transpersonal psychology, and for his research in
scientific parapsychology. His many books include the classics
Altered States of Consciousness and *Transpersonal Psychologies.*

**From my previous discussion with you for *Halfway Up the
Mountain*, I feel that you have a solid grasp of the role of
psychological projections in the student-teacher relationship.
I would like to focus some of our discussion on that.**

We had an incident in class [at the Institute of Transpersonal
Psychology] the other day. I was leading people in a Gurdjieffian-
type experience that involved the students touching each other
while they did some internal body sensing. There were an odd
number of students, so one of them partnered with me. Afterward
he mentioned that he felt this great energy coming out of me
and that it must be because I am an advanced Buddhist meditator. It made me groan. The truth is that I'm a lousy meditator.
So we had to have a talk about the concept of transference with
the whole class. It was very amusing. One of my students sum-
marized the discussion as, "OK. I believe it! You're not God. All
right, good."

How did you explain it to them?

I talked about the whole problem of projections and transference onto the teacher. When you have a positive transference relationship with somebody, they are *wonderful*. They understand you, they love you, but the relationship is still built on an unrealistic basis. At any moment, something can happen that will switch that transference from positive to negative, and all of a sudden, of the very same person you will think, "That bastard was exploiting me my whole life! He/she never taught me anything! He/she just used me!"

Can transference be useful in order to build trust?

You have to give a certain amount of trust and authority to a teacher if you want to learn from them. If you go to a teacher with the attitude of "I am going to question every single thing this person says because most spiritual teachers are out to get you," then you won't take anything seriously. With that kind of emotional paranoia, you will remain suspicious and you won't try anything the teacher suggests. That means you won't get any results, and *that* will prove you were right in the first place—that they don't know anything! So you have to give a certain amount of trust, with an attitude of "OK, I don't fully understand what this teacher is suggesting, but I assume this person knows something I need to know, so I'll put some energy into doing the suggested practice." You engage it on an "It works if I work" basis.

The obvious question is, when to experiment with that trust and when not to?

This is one of the murkiest areas of spiritual authority, because you have to experiment with trust while using discrimination. The obvious problem is that whenever your ego gets challenged, what is experienced at that moment as "discrimination" and "self-reflection" is probably going to be based upon egoic resistance.

The prevalent attitude in the contemporary spiritual scene is to discount the value of spiritual mastery in favor of the inner guide, yet I continually question whether people have enough inner wisdom to know what the inner guide is.

Yes, and how do you know that your inner guide is all that evolved? I have certainly made choices in my life that I believed were coming from some deep inner source within. Later, I realized they were coming from a neurotic defense mechanism.

Is it a common tendency to call our neurotic choices and judgments our "deep intuition?"

It is, and sometimes we may need to take our "deep intuitions" lightly. We should cultivate the attitude of "OK. I feel strongly that things are like this, but *maybe* it is not the ultimate truth forever and ever. Maybe I'll need to check back once in awhile." On the other hand, you *do* have to put some trust in the process.

It seems like we can err on either side.

Yes, that's the other part of it. I might have lunch with the most evolved, enlightened being on the planet and think they are a very ordinary person because I'm simply too blind to notice their important qualities. Nevertheless, I have to constantly make decisions about what I will do next and how I will respond based upon what I know.

Given your appreciation for uncertainty, how do you proceed?

I know that some people have a direct connection to God and know *the* truth. Some of these people are interesting, wonderful, powerful people, and some of them are mad fanatics. For me—and I assume some other people are like me—maturity involves having to accept a world of uncertainty. I know that I want the truth, yet if I try to *grab* the truth and make it mine and hold on to it, that very attitude is going to shut me off from the actual flow of reality.

In terms of relating to a spiritual teacher, I have to watch how I open myself. Am I really paying attention and opening myself, or am I holding back too much? If I am vulnerable and listening, am I willing to try to practice some of the suggestions and see what actually happens in my life? Am I just enjoying the idea and believing I've got the idea—thinking that I've somehow *got* the actual accomplishment just because I have understood? For me, it is a constant self-examination about what I am doing—with long lapses, of course, where I forget about examining myself altogether—but then coming back again and trying to stay open to reality.

What you seem to be saying is that in spite of *all* these weaknesses and possible places to fall short, there is still value in spiritual authority. Is that correct?

I'd like to believe that I am so mature and intelligent and motivated that I will accomplish everything necessary on my own, but I'm too honest to believe that crap. I need someone to inspire me from time to time at the least, and occasionally I need somebody to give me a kick in the ass. Fortunately, my wife is quite a good teacher for kicking me in the ass when I need it sometimes.

I will also say that there have been other times in my life when I've needed teachers to say, "Do this whether you like it or not, because you are resisting this block." And incidentally, a teacher might not always be right about their recommendations. Again, if we project onto a spiritual teacher the idea that they must *always* be right, we are setting ourselves up to deepen our transference. Then we will have to rationalize what are their obvious mistakes, to make them seem right after all. We are also putting the teacher in danger because if we project that [they have] to be right *all the time,* that is a powerful archetype that may overtake them, giving them inflated ideas of what they can do. Then, in order to defend that, they will cover over their mistakes. And that is a very dangerous situation.

The trust involves sometimes letting a spiritual teacher push you to do things that you are resisting. And with the trust, you say to yourself, "This is a wise person, with good intentions, who thinks this will be good for me, but there are no guarantees."

Most people cannot accept the idea of spiritual teachers making mistakes, even if they can justify it intellectually.

To me it doesn't seem like such a big deal. I make mistakes all the time, and yet I'm considered reasonably competent as a teacher on the ordinary level. My humanity fits—why can't I allow other spiritual teachers that humanity?

Why do most people discount the value of the teacher the first time they get their ass kicked?

It takes us back to transference. The Magic Mommy couldn't *not* know. If she kissed our hurt finger and said that this would make it "better" and it didn't get "better," it is because we are "bad," not because Magic Mommy isn't who we believe her to be. That sounds quite silly when I say it, and to consciousness it is silly, but that is the style of primitive thinking that goes on at unconscious levels.

It seems like you are proposing a modicum of moderation in our approach to spiritual teachers.

I suppose I am, but I don't want to leave it at that either, because part of me worries about that. I am giving what I consider to be very sensible advice based on my own experience, but it can also serve as a rationalization for not trying. I think there are times in life when you need to trust much more deeply than you would ordinarily think [you need] to. Sometimes you have to get a little crazy; sometimes you have to get a lot crazy. There are circumstances in life when you have to take more of a chance, and if you take my advice too strongly and never take a *deep* chance, you may miss an important opportunity.

The whole focus of our conversation is this: we are learning how to become mature and discriminating students who will draw the best out of teachers who are human beings. It is not easy. We are fumbling. We are experimenting. The big question is, how can we learn from it? If only it were simpler.

Jai Uttal

THE MASTER'S GRACE

Jai Uttal is a pioneer in the world-music community.
For more than thirty years he has been a disciple of Neem
Karoli Baba—"Maharaji"—and an apprentice to the musical
genius of Ustad Ali Akbar Khan. His musical releases include
Journey, Beggars and Saints, Shiva Station, and *Mondo Rama.*

**I would like to know the story of how you came to meet
your guru, Neem Karoli Baba.**

I usually don't talk about my relationship with him—either in
interviews or during kirtan [chanting of God's name] evenings or
on my CDs. I feel the relationship with the guru is so private, so
personal, so hard to put into words that it will be misunderstood.
But for this interview, I will.

I met Maharaji [Neem Karoli Baba] in 1971. I was nineteen.
I had gone to India on a pilgrimage to see another guru. But
when I got there, I found that the guru I was going to see was
in prison. He was being held for murdering thirty of his monks.
I was shocked. I had projected the whole teenage, guru/disciple
thing on this man (whom I had never met) only to find out he
was a mass murderer. Yet the miracle was that rather than feeling disillusioned and harmed, I felt free. Somehow I knew that I
had been projecting an artificial devotion to him, and suddenly
it was lifted.

So how did you end up meeting Neem Karoli Baba if you weren't looking for a guru?

I went into a bookstore in New Delhi, and they told me Ram Dass [Richard Alpert] was at a hotel nearby. I had known him, so I went to see him. When I got to the hotel, they told me he had left for Brindavan to see his guru, Neem Karoli Baba, and so I went, too. At this time, though, the last thing I wanted was a guru, since I felt I had entered into the previous situation with so much naiveté.

Still, you went to Brindavan?

Yes. We went to visit Maharaji in the temple, and it was like entering a magical world. Everything was glistening. The sound reverberated from the kirtan singers, and Maharaji was glowing—his colors were radiant in the sun. He sat on his *tucket*—a little table—and started throwing fruits around and laughing and asking questions of the new people who were there. He said to my girlfriend, "Who is your guru?" And she told him the name of our intended guru, who was now in jail. "Oh, you Americans are so easily deceived!" and he was laughing and laughing. The whole scene was hypnotic, captivating, majestic.

We had many, many more days like that, but I still didn't want a guru. I wasn't critiquing him as a guru, nor auditioning him as a guru. I was just captivated. When you're with someone like that, the inner fire really gets turned up. It's like being in love, though I never would have described it that way at the time. Gradually, through dreams, I began to get an incredible sense of the connection between Maharaji and me—that timeless, ancient connection.

The story you describe took place thirty years ago. What happened to that relationship over time?

My perception of the relationship I have with my guru really doesn't have very much to do with the relationship itself. Sometimes my awareness of the relationship is so strong that I just cry from the grace, and then two days later I am shocked to discover that I've forgotten that grace. But the grace doesn't go away; it's just my perception of it that goes, colored by my mood. My relationship with Maharaji is so conditional, but when I think about Maharaji's relationship with me, I feel it as an unconditional relationship. My perception sees the relationship as constantly changing and evolving, but my sense is that the relationship is an eternal relationship, and the change has more to do with how clear or unclear I am. I suspect that, from moment to moment, I go from total projection to total receiving of Maharaji's grace, and don't necessarily even know the difference!

What do you mean by "grace"?

Grace is Maharaji's, or God's, blessings. It has nothing to do with what I think or feel. I'm not a great yogi by any means, nor a great devotee, nor a great practitioner. I do my practices. Grace comes regardless of the practices, but I continue to do my practices as an offering.

Did you ever go through cycles of doubt, distrust, and distance in relationship to your teacher?

I did, and still do, but it is less a doubting of who he is and more doubting his love for me. And I've gone through periods of being angry with him. I've gone through periods of feeling deserted by him. But strangely enough, I keep doing my practices. I never really doubted the practices. I didn't doubt God's name; I didn't doubt the prayer; I didn't doubt the kirtan.

Is there a connection between your practice of public kirtan, in which you engage the Western public in ecstatic chanting, and your relationship with Maharaji?

The practice of singing does a lot for me on many levels. The chanting is my prayer that my connection with Maharaji be made stronger and stronger in my own day-to-day reality. My efforts can make me feel more tuned in, and when I am tuned in, it changes things I think and do. I don't know what "spiritual" means, but the chanting opens me. I can breathe better, I can eat better, I can sleep better, and I can go to the bathroom better!

Someone may wonder, "How can he possibly have a relationship with a guru who has been dead for almost thirty years?"

I can't answer that. I don't know. I just do. It doesn't make any sense. Many things in the spirit world don't make sense, even what I choose to do with my life. For example, I ask myself, "Why should I expect people to come and sing kirtan with me to gods they have never heard of and probably don't believe in anyway?"

Why do you think they do?

Because singing in the spirit world creates transformation. It offers an incredible opening in the heart-world, in the non-intellectual world. People come to my performances to chant, we sing for a few hours, and then, regardless of whatever the individuals' belief systems are, the experience happens and we leave completely different.

In considering the topic of projections onto the teacher, I imagine that now that you are an acclaimed singer, you are in the position of knowing what it is like to be the object of those projections.

What has been a revelation to me is how much I could fall prey to those projections while thinking that I'm *not* falling for them. In terms of the really intense projections people have about me, although they can be heavy and a little scary and sometimes make me uncomfortable, I don't take them too seriously. I think I've suffered and caused suffering for others by believing that adulation even a little bit.

In no way do I believe I'm a guru, and in all the things I do I try to minimize the role of teacher. So I disavow that projection as much as I can, but still I have realized how much my ego has grabbed onto subtle adulation without my even knowing it. I thought I was free of it, and yet I was eating the energy of people's projections up because of some of my ego needs.

How did you come to terms with that?

I think I got to a point where I had to look at those projections as projections and had to feel the effects. Once you see it, it's less risky, but it is such a dangerous thing when you don't realize it is happening. Because then you are acting in so many unconscious ways, fulfilling so many different unconscious needs. You feel good when you believe in people's projections, but it is only ego that feels better. You feel like a highly adorned peacock.

When you are clear about yourself, then you don't get caught. Or you watch yourself getting caught, but the caught part doesn't stay. There are so many levels of denial and self-blindness. You can't blame it on anyone else. You can't blame anything on anyone else . . . except your guru!

Arnaud Desjardins

MASTER AS DISCIPLE

Arnaud Desjardins is one of the most widely respected spiritual
teachers in the French-speaking world today. Renowned as
a filmmaker for French National Television, Desjardins, at the
suggestion of his teacher (Swami Prajnanpad; 1891–1974), left his
television career to open his first ashram in 1973. Today he lives
and teaches at his Hauteville ashram, in southern France. He is
the author of more than a dozen books, including two English
translations: *The Jump Into Life* and *Toward the Fullness of Life*.

**How can someone distinguish authentic authority in
a teacher?**

The *disciple* gives the authority (regarding who is a real master
and who is not) when they are convinced that a given teacher is
authentic. When I first met Ma Anandamayi and Swami Ramdas,
I was sure that they were authentic—their being was fully convincing. But the fact is that many admired people have sooner or
later proven to be fake gurus.

My feeling on the matter is simple: if I want to learn to play
piano, I will accept the authority of the teacher. If I want to
become a classical singer, I will accept the authority of the teacher
who says, "Use breath like this" or "Make the voice vibrate in this
part of the face." And if I go to the doctor, I accept his authority.

**Many people will accept the doctor or the music teacher
but not the spiritual master.**

I would say that that is *their* problem! For thousands of years, the authority of the spiritual master has been accepted. Yet to accept a specific teacher, we must feel: "He knows. I don't know. He has the experience that I do not have, and I *need* his help." Many years ago, my teacher, Swami Prajnanpad, wrote to his group of students in France: "You must be asked the fundamental question once again, 'What do you want?'"

We were to ask ourselves if we truly *felt* that he could be of help to us. From that point on, it became clear to me that if I wanted to proceed further in my work with him, I needed to do what he asked of me. I needed to follow his advice and not take what I liked but refuse what I didn't like. It took some time for me to be ready to surrender to the guru in that way.

A lot of people want to surrender to the teacher like that but have great difficulty in doing so.

Complete surrender will only come little by little. One day, I started telling Swami Prajnanpad, "Swamiji is Hindu, but has French disciples . . ." He interrupted me and said, "Swamiji has no disciples. Swamiji has only candidates to discipleship!" That was a grand lesson for me. I understood that to be a disciple is much more than being an ordinary student or devotee of a master.

So my aim from that day on was to become a disciple—to have complete trust and confidence in the guru. It does not mean that the guru cannot be wrong or that he or she knows all and everything, but when he or she gives an instruction, we have complete trust in them. But this comes little by little.

In the West, obedience and surrender are considered weaknesses.

The question is not one of obedience. The question is, "How can I expect to be helped by someone to see what I don't see, to understand what I don't understand, to awaken when I am asleep, if I don't follow his or her advice completely?"

Many people come to the guru with great sincerity and want to follow what is asked in order to receive help, but they are acting from a childish position of looking for approval and salvation.

There is no sin—there is only childishness. All sins are manifestations of our childishness. Be childlike but not childish. It is a very important distinction. A sage is an enlightened child—simple, but never childish. The great temptation is to go to the master with the attitude of "Father, Mother, love me!" thinking that if we remain a child, a good child and a nice child, that this true adult will take care of us. But that's not the business of the guru.

It's not a question of remaining a child—putting my small hand in the big hand of a perfect father or a perfect mother. It has nothing to do with childishness or dependence. We go to the master because we intuit that the master is not other than ourselves. If he is a genuine guru, he is my Self. It is said that if the guru and disciple are together in the same room, there is not two in that room. There is only one: the disciple. The guru is not other than the disciple. He or she is the disciple already enlightened. *We* are the proof that the guru is one with us.

Does the individual who is serious about the spiritual path *need* a teacher?

You cannot progress on the way without recognizing the authority of a master and following his instructions. That is my 100 percent conviction. Of course, there are some geniuses—very, very few—who become fully enlightened without a long and deep relationship with the master. But it's not the rule.

What is the distinction between a guru and teacher?

In your first book, *Halfway Up the Mountain,* it was clear that there are two kinds of teachers: those who have studied with a master or masters and those who have not. They may have a personal gift and be a person of very high human quality: noble, generous, and deserving of respect. But they are on their own. They do not have a teacher, a lineage, a tradition to follow. Of their heart, I would ask, "To whom do you pranam [bow to] from within?" They say, "Oh, I have great respect for all the sages. I fully agree with what the Buddha said." But it's not the same.

How about those people who would like to have a teacher but haven't found one?

First comes the inner urge to change—to go beyond the limitations of ego. One must cultivate Being. One must feel, "I want to have this experience and I am ready to pay the price for it." Even if he or she is weak, lost, and far from the goal, one who seeks has a chance to be found. The guru will come if the disciple is convinced that some sort of realization is possible.

After finding the teacher, how does a student then progress?

Those who are inspired by the highest goal will be in a far better position to go through the first stage of fears, desire, neurosis, contradictions—the whole domain of psychotherapy. First we have to face what psychologists call the shadow: not knowledge of the ultimate Self, but knowledge of oneself—one's contradictions and unconsciousness. We cannot avoid that, but we will go through that with much more success if our aim is not only to feel better but also to find God.

Whereas I once believed all I wanted was God, my experience through years of practice is that there is more

than one strong desire in me—one is to find God, but there are many other desires for personal fulfillment.

You have this strong desire, and you have to pay the price. What is the price? To take into account all the sides of yourself. All the *vasanas* and *samskaras*. How do you reach the other shore? By crossing the ocean of life, of experience. That is very important for most of us—not only the monastery, the prayer, the meditation, but to express consciously within limits. Until we can really say, "I've done what I have to do. I've got what I have to get. I have given what I have to give," we will not be really free. You can accelerate the process, but you cannot jump.

So we move into the expression of desire as a way to become free from the attachment to it?

There is great freedom in "knowing that I know." You may wish to believe, "Money will not bring me happiness." So get some money; see if it brings you happiness. Or you try to convince yourself, "Ooh, success and fame will not give me happiness." Get some success. Get some fame. [Do they] give you lasting happiness?

It is a rather dangerous way because it is true that desire increases desire, yet we have to experience life as consciously as possible, not repressing anything. Then we can be free to fulfill our spiritual destiny. When we have done this, we are ripe, fit for the ultimate sadhana, because we have lived.

Did you go through this process yourself?

Swamiji was always tempting me to see if I was *really* ready. When I complained to Swami Prajnanpad that I was still so interested in pleasure, and becoming a famous film director, and doing so many things, he told me, "Be faithful to yourself as you are situated here and now."

"But that has nothing to do with *atma darshan,*" I told Swamiji.

"Leave atma darshan for the time being. Be what you are. Do it with awareness and with open eyes. See and accept all. You want pleasure? Go ahead and find pleasure. With pleasure and happiness will come other things. Take both."

So it was my good fortune to meet very rich people and famous French movie stars and performers, and to experience that pleasurable lifestyle. At one point, I fell in love with a very famous singer in France—a woman with thousands of admirers and a woman of depth and sincerity, different from the others. And she was in love with me. It felt so wonderful. And yet I saw that my five-year-old son could not understand what was happening. The atmosphere at home was not the same. His mother was weeping. I could not have one side without the other. This is how Swami Prajnanpad led me, by teaching me through experience.

Still, sometimes the temptations were so strong. I would be in a French restaurant, beautifully dressed, with a lovely, famous film star, leading the high life. Somebody would come up and say, "You are Arnaud Desjardins. I saw your program yesterday on television," and I would swell with pride. And then I would remember the great saints I had known—Ramdas, Ma Anandamayi, the great Tibetan masters—and I would have to ask myself, "What do I want?"

Until we know what we want, do we remain candidates for discipleship?

A candidate to discipleship feels, "I want God—that's for sure—but I also want great love, sex, fame. I want to meet bright, fascinating people, to travel, to enjoy the seashore." A disciple is no longer interested in these things. The thought and accompanying attraction for various things may arise, but there is no inclination to follow it. To be a disciple means that the goal is One. Freedom,

God, and compassion are one's only interest. Once you are a disciple, and God is most important, the way will go fast. This is my experience for myself, and also for many people I have known.

Daniel Moran

LIVING IN THE SHADOW
OF THE MASTER

Daniel Moran is a senior teacher at Arnaud Desjardins' Hauteville
ashram, in southern France. He is known for his piercing clarity
and his uncompromising approach toward self-knowledge. He
has been a disciple of Desjardins for more than thirty years.

What is the function of the spiritual master?

The master is not someone who gives. The master cannot give
anything. He or she can only be transparent. The master is not
something that contains, but is only a channel. He receives
from his own master, keeping nothing. He transmits, but he
does not give.

**You are a highly respected teacher within your tradition.
Many people say, "Daniel could leave and still have many
disciples." Yet you stay here and live and work closely with
your master.**

I stay because this experience with my teacher is still getting
better and better; it is still moving. I am always seeking to be
in alignment with the master behind me, while focusing on the
person in front of me.

I have heard that you once said, "The greatest disciple lives in the shadow of the master, not the spotlight." What do you mean by that?

One meaning of "living in the shadow" is to respect the lineage. It is not for the son to wish to put down the father. It is logical that the master remains the master, because he or she is the disciple's link to God. If my ego desires to outshine the master or to show him how great I am, I lose my link with God. So one meaning of "living in the shadow of the master" is that we serve the master without trying to take his or her place.

You can be in the spotlight and still be very humble, or you can wash the dishes with false humility. The worst kind of pride is to be falsely humble. It's not very easy to find the balance between false humility and true humility.

That's a good point. So what does it mean to be invisible?

It means not to interfere in the space of the master—not to be a parasite on the energetic charge that he emits. It is to serve the master and not use the master to serve oneself.

Again, that is a helpful distinction, because the common egoic strategies are either to become a big, important student or a humble, submissive disciple, but both are self-serving.

Those strategies are widespread. From the moment one considers oneself as an ego, or separate entity, the other, in turn, is also a separate entity. In the relationship between master and disciple, when we look from the point of view of the master, the relationship is already perfect, but the same relationship as seen from the view of the disciple is troublesome. It comes back to the dance between the Divine and the human. From the point of view of the Divine, there is no difference between the Divine and the human; but from a human point of view in that same relationship with the Divine, there is a difference.

What is the most important quality of a good disciple?

Obedience. He or she has to take the *risk* of being obedient. But we don't want to obey because we fear that the master won't nourish us on a spiritual level, just as our parents were unable to nourish us on an emotional level. We are afraid, because we see this "other" as holding power over us, and we feel imprisoned, confined. We fear obedience will keep us in a prison, so we decide not to obey. We think that if we obey we will lose our freedom, but in fact the opposite is true. The more you obey the master, the more you have your own life. Because in fact, the master is not an "other." The master is none other than our own self.

What is the difference between blind obedience and conscious following?

If we take the words of the master as being the truth—"The master said it, and therefore it is"—it is pure blindness that leads nowhere. So to follow the master is to listen to what he says, but we need to really work to make it our own understanding. For it to become our own experience, we need to have a turn of mind in which we become quite critical and look for the weakness. If we look for the fault but can't find it, only then can whatever is being communicated become our experience. There is only one thing that can make us at ease and free—our *own* experience, not the teacher's experience.

In other words, we cannot live from the food we have simply swallowed. We can only live from the food that we have digested. At the moment of digesting the master's words, they become alive in us. They become part of ourselves. What is being asked of us is to take what he or she says and make it our own. It must be incorporated into the body—the head is in agreement, but the feet must express it. If we simply repeat the words of the master, it will be an exact copy in terms of the words, but completely false in terms of the actions. Only at that moment, when we have made the master's words our own, do our actions become useful for the general good.

Many students feel it is a natural progression to "graduate" from the master and move on, presumably to a circumstance in which they themselves become the master.

If we forget the master, we will lose something, because the master is the link. We arrive at this foolishness when we pretend to reach a state with no conditions, and at the same time say that the condition of the master is a barrier. The master is the bond and the link to that light. He represents "what is." Each time I say no to "what is," I deny the master—the link that connects me with the light.

So you are not talking about a submissive stance, but something more "lawful" perhaps?

Wanting to be in the spotlight means wanting to be in the place of the master, and that is disrespectful toward the Divine Order. It is not in alignment with God's order. We pretend that we are God, and then we tell God to go to hell!

Swami Prajnanpad, the head of your lineage, said, "You can follow Swamiji, but you cannot imitate him." Would you discuss that statement in terms of learning to be a mature student?

My teacher, Arnaud, asks us to always be ourselves. The way that my teacher expresses himself and the way that I express myself are completely different. I can never become him, and I dare say he cannot be me. But that doesn't prevent the sense of our expressions from being exactly the same in essence.

In our desire to be one with the teacher, we often mistakenly imitate the *personality* of the teacher. Students will demonstrate the same expressions as the master, the same commentaries, and the same affectations. I noticed within myself that even after many, many years of discipleship, without even realizing what I was doing, I was wearing the same kind of clothes my teacher wears. I even had the same tics and the same gestures! I think we want so much to be like them—who they *really* are—that we unconsciously do anything we can to try to be in communion with them. We even imitate true practice.

Georg Feuerstein

UNDERSTANDING THE GURU-PRINCIPLE

Georg Feuerstein, PhD, is founder-director of the Yoga Research
Center, in Northern California. He is the author of more than
thirty books, including *Holy Madness, The Shambhala Encyclopedia
of Yoga, Tantra: The Path of Ecstasy,* and *The Yoga Tradition.*

**How can one tell if the guru's work with the disciple is
effective or not?**

It takes a long time for the changes made on the subtle level to
actually show up in self-expression on this level. But you *would*
see certain changes. If someone who has been part of the scum
of the earth engages a guru who is acting compassionately, it is
not possible for that person to remain the same. But how much
of the person's behavior will change in the course of one lifetime?
It's really dependent entirely on how hard that person works on
himself or herself. The guru can only put the light in them. That
is why teachers always say, "I cannot make you enlightened." If
they could, they would have done so with everybody. Instead it
depends upon the individual's free will. The guru can put enough
energy into the system to say, "OK, now run with it." But if you
don't run with it, the energy has to come again the next lifetime.
You start all over again.

You seem to be saying that even if a person doesn't work as hard as they conceivably can, even if they relate to the master over time and do at least some work, something will change.

You never just "hang out" with a teacher like that. You always have to overcome yourself to be in the presence of a great adept. Even if you don't do the meditation as he tells you to, and you don't do this and that, just being in the presence of a person like that will always challenge your ego. It will inevitably make profound inner changes even if those changes are not completely obvious in all aspects of your personality now.

But once you are only the subtle system, you will shine. You will be different. We must assume that anybody who is in the company of a great master like that was very likely with that master before. Because what gives a person the capacity to hang in with such a person? Each destiny is so unique. You may only see the master once in your lifetime. You may see him or her at a distance. But already the change begins.

What does it mean to be a good disciple? How does someone new to the path learn to be a good disciple?

The first thing is the student's qualification, which in Sanskrit is called *adhikara*. And this is where I think Western students are very ignorant because they don't understand that traditionally it wasn't just the disciple checking out the guru, but the guru *really* checking out the disciple. When the guru takes on the disciple as a *disciple,* not just a student, it is a major commitment that goes beyond this lifetime.

So traditionally, a guru will test a student. The potential disciple says, "Please teach me!" And the guru will perhaps ignore him for the first year, or make him do all the donkey-work on the ashram and never give him the time of day otherwise. Then the potential student may start complaining and walking away. The guru knew he didn't have the stuff necessary to stick it out for the rest of his lifetime. Disciples had to bring a certain determination, and they had to have the stamina to be constantly tested. But also, traditionally, part of the game is that the guru completely accepted that he would be tested, too. The disciple was expected to look at a teacher and ask: "What is this guy made of? Where is this authority coming from? Is it just scriptural learning, or is there realization, too?"

Could a student have more than one guru?

Guru-hopping and being sent by your own teacher to another Lama to receive teachings are, of course, totally different things. The serious Tibetan Buddhist student is already established in relationship with his or her root guru—which means there is already a relationship of a devotional nature to the guru—before going to study with other teachers. The tradition prescribes that the guru be looked at by the disciple as a Buddha—even if he is not enlightened. You have to look at your teacher as a Buddha, as a fully awakened being. Because if you don't, you already have lost the game. But in the West, we don't have that capacity. We are intent on our own greatness.

Once you have accepted a teacher as your guru, after testing that person carefully for however long you need to for your satisfaction, you have to stick with that guru. If you don't, that's when everything becomes turmoil inside. The moment we accept a teacher as our guru and that movement is reciprocated (which the guru, if he's clever, won't do lightly), a point is made at the most subtle level of our existence. If we casually throw that away, we can do great damage to our spiritual practice. And people don't usually understand that.

What is the cost of discipleship?

Being a disciple has nothing to do with social life. It's the end of social life. It's the end of your own personal ideologies. It's the end of your own dreams. After that, there is only the dream of waking up.

The guru–disciple relationship seems to be a particular construct, which some people choose to engage while others don't.

Yes. It's an artificial situation.

Why do people take it on?

It helps us grow. We can't understand the mechanism of the ego in a vacuum. The ego can only be reflected back to itself when it looks in the mirror. We are blind, and so the guru puts up all these mirrors around us. And wherever we look, we see our own chaos, which of course has to do also with the chaos of society, the arbitrariness of the arrangement. We realize that the ego is a just a product of all of this craziness of mind. When we really, really see that it's a convention, a device that was reinvented in order to make meaning out of nothing, we can step beyond it. So the guru constantly undermines meaning. And then you let go. And then there's freedom. Genuine freedom, not just a vacuum within the chaos.

Why can't we do it alone?

The process requires a being who stands outside the stream of *samsara* and activates a different function, which we call the *guru function,* in order for you to see the craziness of your own bondage. You can analyze your mind till kingdom come, but unless somebody stands outside and obliges you to continue to look deeper and deeper and deeper, you don't see all the links that you make in your mind to explain away your confusion.

So you engage in this artificial construct because there's an element of that construct that's not bound?

Yes.

And in order to do that you need an element that is outside of your control?

Yes, and that element is the guru.

Yet you have to choose to fully believe in the construct and go through it in order to *really* be taught to see that it is a construct?

Yes. That's the paradox. The guru goes around your artificial world and cuts all the bonds slowly. It's a very skillful dance, because if it goes too fast, you go crazy. You literally go nuts. If things are taken away before their time, you don't know who you are anymore. The guru is a very skillful physician. The teacher, *if* he or she is skillful, knows the limits of your construct and what you're able to let go of.

How does the earnest disciple deal with apparent imperfections in the teacher?

It's a simple answer, truly. If a teacher's behavior causes you more conflict than you are capable of practicing with, it's better to leave. *It's better to leave.* There has to be a fit between a teacher's behavior and your capacity to handle and negotiate that behavior while still seeing it as a transformative tool.

How do we recognize the true teacher?

This is really the challenge for disciples. Real teachers are chameleons. They can be anything. They are in all forms. Why not activate all possible forms of the human being? For a disciple, it's really more a matter of determining whether you can trust. And if there is no trust in the ultimate goodness of the teacher, you had better not even start. There may be moments of doubt, but if you sit back, apart from the situation that has arisen, and you still conclude, "No, I trust the teacher," then go ahead. If we can engage the process by saying, "Yes," then we have won! It's a game. The teacher can tell you, "I'm enlightened," and you say, "Oh, great! I want to study with you!" And then it turns out he's a rogue. But you could benefit tremendously, even from a rogue, if you trust him or her.

Do all disciples come to the guru with the same potential?

The scriptures are very clear that there are three types of disciples. The first are the really lowly ones that are constantly obnoxious, arguing, refusing. Gurus have them because they are compassionate and they recognize that people have to start somewhere. The second category, which includes most disciples, are people who are generally committed to the teacher and have a basic interest in the teaching. There is change in them over time, but there is not a lot of capacity. But then there's the third type that comes with a burning impulse to liberation that is not neurotic.

In most cases, when people come to the teacher and say, "Oh, I want to be enlightened in this lifetime," it's just an illusion. An illusion! It has nothing to do with what is possible for them in this lifetime. That's the first illusion to drop away when you are with the guru. You realize that it's a lot harder than you thought it was. But there are disciples belonging to the third category who are genuinely manifesting this deep, deep impulse to be liberated. We need to make peace with our present capacities as disciples, assuming that there's grace at work. If we hang in there long enough, making whatever effort we can, we will change and our capacity will increase. But we have to be patient.

It's a frightening time in our culture now, and easy to be impatient.

It's a great time! Truly. No better time to practice! Wartime and this kind of social, cultural, [and] environmental chaos create a great opportunity. We see the world all possibly disappearing in front of our eyes, so what is it we are hanging on to? It motivates us to practice if we look clearly enough. You ask yourself, "What is it all about? Why am I hanging on to this and that? Where will I go with it all?" It makes for great spiritual practice.

Father Bruno Barnhart

BECOMING GOD

Father Bruno Barnhart is a Camaldolese monk living in
Big Sur, California. He is the author of *Second Simplicity:
The Inner Shape of Christianity* and *The Good Wine: Reading
John from the Center*. His work has focused upon the
Christian wisdom tradition and its rebirth in our time.

**I'm interested in learning about spiritual authority and
discipleship from a Christian perspective.**

In Christianity, ideally, the mediation of the teacher is temporary.
Ultimately, the only thing the teacher can do is acquaint you with
who you are. The fullness is given to you in your initiation at your
baptism. The teacher plays a secondary role.

In the early centuries of monasticism, at the time of the Desert
Fathers, a monk had what was called a spiritual father—the close,
one-on-one relationship of disciple and master. The spiritual
father was in touch with every aspect of the disciple's life. But in
the West, monasticism became institutionalized. The abbot exists
today as a symbol of Christ, but the relationship has become
largely externalized and somewhat impersonal.

Have you ever had a close relationship with a spiritual teacher?

When I was a young monk, I was looking for a spiritual father—a
senior monk who could really adopt me, guide me, and lead me

along the path. But I didn't find one. There was one monk whom I looked upon as a spiritual father, yet the intimate communion and deep, interior spiritual guidance weren't there. It is rare to find that. Most of that has disappeared, at least in the Western Church. Around the time of the Reformation, there were tremendous abuses of power in the Church. Now the individual living in the West will no longer accept permanent and absolute authority of another human being over him.

Yet if you had found your spiritual father, wouldn't his function precisely be to help you to discover your own authority?

It would, and then he'd say, "Go. You don't need me anymore. I'll just be in the way." Even Jesus did that. He had his disciples around him for three years, and they all felt that they couldn't live without him. Then he disappeared. He gave them the Holy Spirit, as we say in Christianity, which means that what was in Jesus was discovered in them.

It sounds like the principle of transmission.

Yes, it's the transmission principle, but Christianity translates it to mean your immediate relationship to God or Christ.

Why, if spiritual authority is outdated in Christianity, is there such a strong model of Jesus and his disciples?

Let's look at Jesus. Jesus is divine and human at the same time. The point of this, which is very often missed by Christians, is that we are meant to be what Jesus is. The fathers of the Church would say that God became a human being in Jesus, so that human beings might become God. That's pretty strong, but it is at the core of Christian theology. Do you see the nondual aspect of it? It's not nondual consciousness like the Eastern traditions, where everything is seen as one, but more of a channeled nonduality. It becomes like a river, an organic thing. The nonduality is contained within a *body*.

If I'm not mistaken, that sounds very much like the traditional teachings of the guru-principle. The student and master are not separate, and the point of the relationship is to realize that you are that—that you are Jesus in terms of our discussion.

Then Jesus goes away so that the disciple can awaken as Jesus. Now that's not the common Christian teaching, but it's the heart of the Christian truth. In John's Gospel, Jesus can be seen as having a nondual relationship with God when he says, "I am." He assumes that Divine identity and then gives that same identity to us so that those words are also true of us. When we look at it that way, it's very similar to the Buddhist and Hindu traditions. The essence of the initiation of baptism is to drown in God and be reborn as that which Jesus *is*. And if you are what Jesus is, you have a nondual relationship with God. All the teacher can do is help you to descend into that nondual relationship with God and Christ.

But many are baptized and very few seem to abide in that nondual relationship with God.

That's true. But I think there is a nondual relationship that consists of living and acting in God no matter where one's consciousness is at. That is what faith is about. In faith, Jewish and Christian people relate to God as embodied beings, with limited consciousness. Yet this life of faith begins to be a nondual participation in God. Christianity then takes a further step by making Jesus human and Divine at the same moment, so that one's faith puts them *in* Jesus in a unitive way, even when one is not conscious of it. I think there are a lot of simple people of great faith who live that way. They never have a great enlightenment experience. Yet their life of faith, paradoxically, is a life of nonduality.

If that's the case, why are there still teachers? Weren't you the Prior at your monastery for eighteen years?

The teacher–student relationship is still very important. The role of the teacher is to help a novice through obstacles. A teacher guides them and shows them the pitfalls and helps them to discern their own inner movements. When the monastic life is a solitary life, there is a real danger [that you] start to see solitude as absolute. If ego identifies with that absolute, you can be in real trouble.

How so?

Think of living by yourself in a hermit's cell, listening *only* to God, attempting to live a purely interior life without any human interaction or feedback. There is something about it that really appeals to both the individualist and to the introvert, and it can lead someone into a spiritual cul-de-sac. Spiritual experiences, in that kind of lifestyle, may easily lead to ego inflation.

Is that why you need the Prior?

Yes. You need an authority to pull students back down to earth. In the old days, the Desert Fathers said, "If you see a young man climbing up to heaven by himself, grab him by the leg and pull him down." Christian tradition emphasizes the spiritual *descent*, but it's very hard for the male ego to make a descent. It needs to collide with something. The rule of Saint Benedict is built entirely upon obedience to the authority figure as a means to deal with the ego.

That leads me to the question of obedience in your tradition. What do you think the limitation of obedience is, and what do you think its value is?

At its worst, obedience can be a perfect suppressing of the emergence of the person. Certain people pick an external thing to obey and to conform to as a substitute for a real response of the heart. Those are generally people who are submissive. They never dialogue about something they are asked to do, instead remaining as a child because they haven't allowed the conflict to become conscious.

What is that conflict?

There is a tension between my ego—my own ideas and preferences—on the one hand, and the external voice of authority (and ultimately of reality, or the will of God) on the other. Ideally, there should be a dialogue going on between those two poles within us, and if I suppress my ego to the extent that I don't permit that, I won't grow. Somehow ego has to be able to engage with the contrary reality, like Jacob wrestling with his mysterious opponent rather than immediately surrendering and going limp.

Is there another side?

Of course. I think the value of obedience is that it can relate you directly to God through the mediation of somebody else. It also enables you to transcend your own will because the only thing that can reach into you and *really* get you is another human being. It is the only thing that will really find your ego and kill it. You can outwit almost anything else, since anything else can become a servant and tool of ego, but obedience to another human being can get in there and find it. A willing and conscious obedience can expose your ego perfectly to the transforming power of the

Spirit, opening you to a will that is intelligent and flexible enough to find you. Then you can become a perfectly pliable instrument in the hands of the Spirit.

What are the important lessons you have learned over your decades in the monastic tradition?

Over the years, the "peak experience" of transmission or enlightenment disappears into the ordinary. I have become aware of a solid but unspectacular kind of spiritual growth in which the person becomes more and more able to do what he or she has to do. Divinization becomes manifest, paradoxically, as the person becomes genuinely human. Everything luminous and remarkable is disappearing, simply, into *what is*. Just as the honeymoon phase of a splendid love gives way to a day-to-day existence, the original charismatic experience disappears into the ordinariness of life. The Spirit incarnates itself in our bodily existence, becoming simply human. You can see a manifestation of the divine compassion, the divine "humanity" here. Spirit pours down into humanity, which devours it. Spirit does exactly what it must do: it permeates the ground like rain, disappears into the body of humanity.

BIBLIOGRAPHY AND
RECOMMENDED READING

Anthony, Dick, Bruce Ecker, and Ken Wilber. *Spiritual Choices: The Problems of Recognizing Authentic Paths to Inner Transformation.* NY: Paragon House, 1987.

Aryashura. *Fifty Stanzas on the Spiritual Teacher.* 2nd ed. Dharamsala: Library of Tibetan Works and Archives, 1991.

Aurobindo, Ghose. *Integral Yoga.* Twin Lakes, WI: Lotus Press, 1998.

Avabhasa, Da. *Divine Distraction: A Guide to the Guru-Devotee Relationship.* Clearlake, CA: The Dawn Horse Press, 1991.

Bache, Chris. *Dark Night, Early Dawn.* Albany: State University of New York Press, 2000.

Barnhart, Bruno. *Second Simplicity: The Inner Shape of Christianity.* Mahwah, NJ: Paulist Press, 1999.

Barrett, William E. *The Lady of the Lotus: The Untold Story of the Buddha and His Wife.* Los Angeles: Jeremy P. Tarcher, 1989.

Berzin, Alexander. *Relating to a Spiritual Teacher.* Ithaca, NY: Snow Lion Publications, 2000.

Bogart, Greg. *The Nine Stages of Spiritual Apprenticeship.* Berkeley, CA: Dawn Mountain Press, 1997.

Caplan, Mariana. "Adventures of a New Age Traveler." In *Radical Spirit: Spiritual Writings from the Voices of Tomorrow,* edited by Stephen Dinan, 187–200. Novato, CA: New World Library, 2002.

———. *Do You Need a Guru?: Understanding the Student-Teacher Relationship in an Era of False Prophets.* London: Thorsons, 2002.

———. *Eyes Wide Open: Cultivating Discernment on the Spiritual Path.* Boulder, CO: Sounds True, 2009.

————. *Halfway Up the Mountain: The Error of Premature Claims to Enlightenment.* Prescott, AZ: Hohm Press, 1999.

————. *To Touch Is to Live.* Prescott, AZ: Hohm Press, 2002.

————. *The Way of Failure: Winning Through Losing.* Prescott, AZ: Hohm Press, 2001.

————. *When Sons and Daughters Choose Alternative Lifestyles.* Prescott, AZ: Hohm Press, 1996.

Chadwick, David. *Crooked Cucumber: The Life and Zen Teaching of Shunryu Suzuki.* New York: Broadway Books, 1990.

Charlton, Hilda. *Saints Alive.* Woodstock, NY: Golden Quest, 1989.

Cohen, Leonard. *Book of Mercy.* Toronto: McClelland & Stewart, 1986.

Crane, George. *Bones of the Master.* New York: Bantam, 2000.

Crook, John and James Low. *The Yogins of Ladakh: A Pilgrimage Among the Hermits of the Buddhist Himalayas.* New Delhi: Motilal Banarsidass, 1997.

De Boulay, Shirley. *Beyond the Darkness: A Biography of Bede Griffiths.* New York: Doubleday, 1998.

Deida, David. *Wild Nights.* Austin, TX: Plexus, 2000.

De Mello, Anthony. *Awareness: A De Mello Conference in His Own Words.* New York: Image Books, 1990.

Desikachar, T. K.V. *The Heart of Yoga: Developing a Personal Practice.* Rochester, VT: Inner Traditions International, 1995.

Desjardins, Arnaud. *Jump into Life.* Prescott, AZ: Hohm Press, 1994.

————. *L'Ami Spirituel.* Paris: Les Editions de La Table Ronde, 1996.

Dorje, Rig'dzin. *Dangerous Friend.* Boston: Shambhala, 2001.

Dowman, Keith. *Buddhist Masters of Enchantment.* Rochester, VT: Inner Traditions International, 1998.

————. *Sky Dancer: The Secret Life and Songs of the Lady Yeshe Tsogyel.* Ithaca, NY: Snow Lion Publications, 1996.

Eliade, Micea. *Yoga: Immortality and Freedom.* Princeton: Princeton University Press, 1970.

Evans-Wentz, Walter. *Tibet's Great Yogi Milarepa.* 2nd ed. London: Oxford University Press, 1969.

Farcet, Gilles, ed. *Radical Awakening: Cutting Through the Conditioned Mind: Dialogues with Stephen Jourdain.* Carlsbad, CA: Inner Directions, 2001.

Fedorschak, V. J. *The Shadow on the Path: Clearing Psychological Blocks to Spiritual Development.* Prescott, AZ: Hohm Press, 1999.

Ferrer, Jorge. *Revisioning Transpersonal Theory.* Albany: State University of New York Press, 2002.

Feuerstein, Georg. *Holy Madness: The Shock Tactics and Radical Teachings of Crazy-Wise Adepts, Holy Fools, and Rascal Gurus.* New York: Penguin, 1992.

———. *The Philosophy of Classical Yoga.* Rochester, VT: Inner Traditions International, 1996.

———. *Tantra: The Path of Ecstasy.* Boston: Shambhala, 1998.

———. *The Yoga Tradition.* Prescott, AZ: Hohm Press, 1998.

Frager, Robert. *Heart, Self and Soul.* Wheaton, IL: Quest Books, 1997.

Gold, E. J. *The Human Biological Machine as a Transformational Apparatus.* Nevada City, CA: Gateways, 1985.

Harvey, Andrew. *The Direct Path.* New York: Broadway Books, 2001.

Iyengar, B. K. S. *Light on the Yoga Sutras of Patañjali.* New Delhi: HarperCollins Publishers India, 2005.

Jodorowsky, Alejandro. *The Spiritual Journey of Alejandro Jodorowsky.* Rochester, VT: Park Street Press, 2008.

Keen, Sam. *Hymns to an Unknown God.* New York: Bantam, 1995.

Khytense, Dzongsar Jamyang. *What Makes You Not a Buddhist?* Boston: Shambhala, 2007.

Kinsley, David. *Tantric Visions of the Divine Feminine.* Berkeley: University of California Press, 1997.

Kramer, Joel, and Diana Alstad. *The Guru Papers.* Berkeley, CA: Frog Ltd., 1993.

Krishnamurti, J. *The First & Last Freedom.* New York: Harper & Row, 1975.

Leonard, George, and Michael Murphy. *The Life We Are Given.* New York: Jeremy P. Tarcher/Putnam, 1995.

Lewis, Rick. *The Perfection of Nothing.* Prescott, AZ: Hohm Press, 2000.

Lozowick, Lee. *The Alchemy of Transformation.* Prescott, AZ: Hohm Press, 1996.

———. *The Only Grace Is Loving God.* Prescott, AZ: Hohm Press, 1982.

Martin, Valerie. *Salvation: Scenes from the Life of St. Francis.* New York: Alfred A. Knopf, 2001.

McBrien, Richard. *Lives of Saints.* San Francisco: Harper San Francisco, 2001.

Merrell-Wolf, Franklin. *Experience and Philosophy: A Personal Record of Transformation and a Discussion of Transcendental Consciousness.* Albany: State University of New York Press, 1994.

Merton, Thomas. *Contemplation in a World of Action.* Notre Dame, IN: University of Notre Dame Press, 1998.

Nalanda Translation Committee. *The Life of Marpa the Translator.* Boston: Shambhala, 1995.

Nizami. *Layla and Majnun.* London: Blake Publishing, 1970.

Nyanaonika, Thera, and Hellmuth Hecker. *Great Disciples of the Buddha: Their Lives, Their Works, Their Legacy.* Boston: Wisdom Publications, 1997.

Patterson, William Patrick. *Eating the "I."* Fairfax, CA: Arete Communications, 1992.

———. *Struggle of the Magicians: Exploring the Teacher-Student Relationship.* Fairfax, CA: Arete Communications, 1996.

Prendergast, John and Kenneth Bradford, eds. *Listening from the Heart of Silence.* St. Paul, MN: Paragon House, 2007.

Prendergast, John, Peter Fenner, and Sheila Kristal, eds. *The Sacred Mirror.* New York: Omega Books, 2003.

Rabten, Geshe. *The Life of a Tibetan Monk.* Le Mont-Pelerin, Switzerland: Edition Rabten, 2000.

Ram Dass. *Be Here Now.* New York: Crown Publications, 1971.

———. *Still Here.* New York: Riverhead Books, 2001.

Ray, Reginald. *Indestructible Truth.* Boston: Shambhala, 2000.

———. *Secret of the Vajra World.* Boston: Shambhala, 2001.

Redington, James. *Vallabhacharya on the Love Games of Krishna.* 2nd ed. New Delhi: Motilal Banarsidass, 1989.

Reich, Wilhelm. *Listen Little Man.* New York: Farrar, Straus and Giroux, 1974.

Ryan, Regina Sara. *The Woman Awake: Feminine Wisdom for Spiritual Life.* Prescott, AZ: Hohm Press, 1999.

Saint John of the Cross. *Dark Night of the Soul.* Translated by Allison Peers. 3rd ed. New York: Image Books, 1959.

———. *Dark Night of the Soul.* Introduction by Mirabai Starr. New York: Riverhead Books, 2002.

Saint Teresa of Avila. *The Interior Castle.* New York: Riverhead Books, 2003.

Seager, Richard Hughs. *Buddhism in America.* New York: Columbia University Press, 1999.

Shaw, Miranda. *Passionate Enlightenment.* Princeton: Princeton University Press, 1994.

Simmer-Brown, Judith. *Dakini's Warm Breath: The Feminine Principle in Tibetan Buddhism.* Boston: Shambhala, 2002.

Smith, Huston. *The World's Religions: Our Great Wisdom Traditions.* San Francisco: HarperSanFrancisco, 1991.

———. *Why Religion Matters: The Fate of Human Spirit in an Age of Disbelief.* San Francisco: HarperSanFrancisco, 2001.

Smith, Ingram. *Truth Is a Pathless Land: A Journey with Krishnamurti.* Wheaton, IL: The Theosophical Publishing House, 1989.

Solove, Daniel. *The Future of Reputation: Gossip, Rumor, and Privacy on the Internet.* New Haven: Yale University Press, 2008.

Steiner, Rudolf. *Rosicrucian Wisdom.* London: Rudolf Steiner Press, 2000.

Svoboda, Robert. *Aghora: At the Left Hand of God.* Albuquerque: Brotherhood of Life Inc., 1993.

———. *Aghora II: Kundalini.* Albuquerque: Brotherhood of Life Inc., 1993.

———. *Aghora III: The Law of Karma.* Albuquerque: Brotherhood of Life Inc., 1997.

Swami Prahavananda and Christopher Isherwood, trans. *The Song God: Bhagavad-Gita.* New York: Penguin Books, 1972.

Swami Vivekananda. *Raja-Yoga*. Rev. ed. New York: Ramakrishna-Vivekananda Center, 1955.

Tart, Charles. *Mind Science: Meditation Training for Practical People*. Novato, CA: Wisdom Edition, 2000.

Thakar, Vimala. *On an Eternal Voyage*. Ahmedabad, India: Vimal Prakashan Trust, 1989.

Trungpa, Chögyam. *Crazy Wisdom*. Boston: Shambhala, 2001.

———. *Cutting Through Spiritual Materialism*. Boston: Shambhala, 1973.

———. *Shambhala: Sacred Path of the Warrior*. Boston: Shambhala, 1988.

Tweedie, Irina. *Chasm of Fire*. Inverness, CA: The Golden Sufi Center, 1986.

———. *Daughter of Fire*. Inverness, CA: The Golden Sufi Center, 1986.

Ullman, Robert, and Judyth Reichenberg-Ullman. *Mystics, Masters, Saints, and Sages*. Berkeley, CA: Conari Press, 2001.

Upton, Charles, trans. *Doorkeeper of the Heart: Versions of Rabi'a*. Putney, VT: Threshold Books, 1988.

Uspenskii, P. D. *In Search of the Miraculous*. New York: Harvest, 2001.

Vaughan-Lee, Llewellyn. *The Bond with the Beloved: The Mystical Relationship of the Lover and the Beloved*. Inverness, CA: The Golden Sufi Center, 1993.

———. *The Face Before I Was Born: A Spiritual Autobiography*. Inverness, CA: The Golden Sufi Center, 1997.

Welwood, John. *Toward a Psychology of Awakening*. Boston: Shambhala, 2000.

Wilber, Ken. *One Taste*. Boston: Shambhala, 1999.

———. *Integral Psychology*. Boston: Shambhala, 2000.

Willis, Janice D. *Enlightened Beings: Life Stories from the Ganden Oral Tradition*. Boston: Wisdom Publications, 1995.

Wilson, Colin. *Rogue Messiahs: Tales of Self-Proclaimed Saviors*. Charlottesville, VA: Hampton Roads Publishing Company, 2000.

Young, M. *As It Is*. Prescott, AZ: Hohm Press, 2000.

Chapter 1: Entering the Spiritual Supermarket

1. John Welwood, *Toward a Psychology of Awakening* (Boston: Shambhala, 2000), 273–6.
2. Ken Wilber, *One Taste* (Boston: Shambhala, 1999), 28–30.

Chapter 2: Types of Spiritual Authority

1. B. K. S. Iyengar, *Light on the Yoga Sutras of Patañjali* (New Delhi: HarperCollins, 1993).
2. Welwood, *Toward a Psychology,* 275–6.
3. Ken Wilber, *Integral Psychology* (Boston: Shambhala, 2000), 28–32.
4. *Karma* is a term readily thrown about but rarely understood in spiritual circles. As used here, it suggests that according to a law of cause and effect, there are circumstances and attachments we create in the journey of the soul in this lifetime or another that must come into balance. Excellent study on this subject can be found in Robert Svoboda's book *Aghora III: The Law of Karma* (Albuquerque, NM: Brotherhood of Life, 1997).
5. Jeanne de Salzman, "First Initiation," in *Gurdjieff: Essays and Reflections on the Man and His Teachings,* eds. Jacob Needleman and George Baker (New York: Continuum International Publishing, 2004), 5
6. Swami Muktananda, *Where Are You Going?* (South Fallsburg, NY: SYDA Foundation, 1981), 138.

Chapter 3: "Guru" as a Four-Letter Word: Criticism of Spiritual Teachers, and the Nature of Spiritual Scandals

1. Roger Walsh, "The Search for Synthesis: Transpersonal Psychology and the Meeting of East and West, Psychology and Religion, Personal and Transpersonal," *Journal of Humanistic Psychology* 32, no.1 (Winter 1992): 31.

2. A full account of Naranjo's story can be found in "The Sadhana of Disillusionment," chap. 21 in Mariana Caplan, *Halfway Up the Mountain: The Error of Premature Claims to Enlightenment* (Prescott, AZ: Hohm Press, 1999).

3. Wilber, *One Taste,* 43.

4. Ibid., 238.

5. John Welwood, "On Spiritual Authority," in *Spiritual Choices: The Problems of Recognizing Authentic Paths to Inner Transformation* (NY: Paragon House, 1987), 299–300.

Chapter 4: The Importance of a Spiritual Teacher

1. William Patrick Patterson, *Struggle of the Magicians: Exploring the Teacher-Student Relationship* (Fairfax, CA: Arete Communications, 1996), 269.

2. Rudolf Steiner, *Rosicrucian Wisdom* (London: Rudolf Steiner Press, 2000), 6–7.

3. Greg Bogart, *The Nine Stages of Spiritual Apprenticeship* (Berkeley, CA: Dawn Mountain Press, 1997), 36.

4. Guru Gita quote.

Chapter 6: Conscious Relationship to Power Dynamics

1. Further discussion on this topic can be found in "The Consequences of Assuming a Teaching Function Before One Is Prepared," chap. 14 in *Halfway Up the Mountain.*

Chapter 7: Mutual Trust and Surrender

1. An exemplary depiction of the intelligent use of psychoactive substances can be found in Chris Bache, *Dark Night, Early Dawn* (Albany: State University of New York Press, 2000).

2. Pema Chödrön, *When Things Fall Apart: Heartfelt Advice for Difficult Times* (Boston: Shambhala, 2000), 135.

3. Arnaud Desjardins in Lee Lozowick, *Death of a Dishonest Man: Poems and Prayers to Yogi Ramsuratkumar* (Prescott, AZ: Hohm Press 1998), 43.

Chapter 8: Meeting the Teacher: Defining Criteria for Teacher *and* Student

1. A full set of criteria for considering the master is found in "True Teacher—or False?" chap. 19 in *Halfway Up the Mountain*.

2. Georg Feuerstein, *Holy Madness: The Shock Tactics and Radical Teachings of Crazy-Wise Adepts, Holy Fools, and Rascal Gurus* (New York: Penguin, 1992), 143.

3. Frances Vaughan, "A Question of Balance: Health and Pathology in New Religious Movements" in Dick Anthony, Bruce Ecker, and Ken Wilber, *Spiritual Choices: The Problems of Recognizing Authentic Paths to Inner Transformation* (New York: Paragon House, 1987), 275.

4. Arnaud Desjardins, "Am I a Disciple?" in Lee Lozowick, *Death of a Dishonest Man* (Prescott, AZ: Hohm Press, 1998).

Chapter 9: Breaking the Rules

1. *Sunseed* directed by Frederick Cohn (1973, New Age Productions).

Chapter 10: Spiritual Monogamy versus "Sleeping Around"

1. William Patrick Patterson, *Struggle of the Magicians: Exploring the Teacher-Student Relationship* (Fairfax, CA: Arete Communications, 1996), 255.

Chapter 11: Guru Games and Crazy Wisdom

1. Walter Evans-Wentz, *Tibet's Great Yogi Milarepa,* 2nd ed. (London: Oxford University Press, 1969).

Chapter 12: Obedience

1. Swami Prahavananda and Christopher Isherwood, trans. *The Song of God: Bhagavad-Gita* (New York: Penguin Books, 1972), 37.

2. For further resources, see E. J. Gold, *The Tibetan Book of the Dead* (Nevada City, CA: Gateways, 1999) and Sogyal Rinpoche, *The Tibetan Book of Living and Dying* (San Francisco, CA: HarperSanFrancisco, 1993).

3. A further discussion on criteria for genuine spiritual teachers can be found in my earlier book, "True Teacher—or False?", chap. 19 in *Halfway Up the Mountain.*

Chapter 15: For the Glory of Love

1. James Redington, *Vallabhacharya on the Love Games of Krishna,* 2nd ed. (New Delhi: Motilal Banarsidass, 1989), p. 56–7, stanzas 5 and 6.

2. Arnaud Desjardins, Tawagoto 14, no. 2 (Spring 2001).

3. Regina Sara Ryan, *The Woman Awake: Feminine Wisdom for Spiritual Life* (Prescott, AZ: Hohm Press, 1999).

4. Nizami, *Layla and Majnun* (London: Blake Publishing, 1970), 36.

5. Irina Tweedie, *Daughter of Fire,* (Inverness, CA: Golden Sufi Center, 1986), 813; 819–820.

6. Sita Martin, *The Hunger of Love: Versions of the Ramayana* (Kanyakumari, India: Yogi Ramsuratkumar Trust, 1995), 14–15.

Chapter 16: Toward a Vision of World Spirituality

1. "Mission: The Center for World Spirituality," centerforworldspirituality.com/about

Epilogue: An Unexpected Twist: False Complaints Against Teachers

1. Kafka, Franz. *The Trial* (first edition in German, 1925). (New York: Alfred A. Knopf, 1937.)

2. Dershowitz, Alan. *The Abuse Excuse.* (New York: Little, Brown, and Co. 1994.)

3. In the 2006 Duke story, the players were falsely accused of rape. A number of diverse factors came together to create the tragedy. They included: a corrupt criminal prosecutor and police officials; hundreds of liberal faculty members who thought in victim-feminist terms and who therefore assumed the first wave of reports was true and publically excoriated the players; complex power dynamics at Duke University; an atmosphere in which challenging the original dogma was thought to be not protective of the powerless and always innocent feminine; and, supporting it all, a bloodthirsty press indoctrinated by victim-feminist dogma and looking for sensationalist stories. Had the players not come from wealthy families who had the means and the will to hire the best attorneys and investigators, there is little doubt that this innocent group of young men would now be in prison while the various perpetrators disguised as the victims, as well as their supporters and defenders, would be hailed as feminist heroes.

4. Samantha Power, *A Problem from Hell: America and the Age of Genocide* (New York: Harper Perennial, 2007).

INDEX

About the Author

Mariana Caplan, PhD, is a psychotherapist specializing in spiritual issues and somatic approaches to transformation. She is the author of seven books in the fields of psychology and spirituality, including the seminal book *Halfway Up the Mountain: The Error of Premature Claims to Enlightenment* and *Eyes Wide Open: Cultivating Discernment on the Spiritual Path,* which won five national book awards. She has degrees in cultural anthropology, counseling psychology, and contemporary spirituality, and she is a lifelong practitioner and teacher of yoga philosophy and asana.

She has spent the past two decades researching and practicing in the world's great mystical traditions, and has lived in villages in India, Central and South America, and Europe. Mariana resides in the San Francisco Bay Area, with her partner Marc Gafni and their son, Zion Lee. She has a private practice in psychotherapy in Marin County. She also teaches yoga philosophy and transpersonal psychology at the California Institute of Integral Studies and Naropa University. Her seminars, psychotherapy practice, and The Center for World Spirituality, can be found at: realspirituality. com and centerforworldspirituality.com

ABOUT SOUNDS TRUE

Sounds True is a multimedia publisher whose mission is to inspire and support personal transformation and spiritual awakening. Founded in 1985 and located in Boulder, Colorado, we work with many of the leading spiritual teachers, thinkers, healers, and visionary artists of our time. We strive with every title to preserve the essential "living wisdom" of the author or artist. It is our goal to create products that not only provide information to a reader or listener, but that also embody the quality of a wisdom transmission.

For those seeking genuine transformation, Sounds True is your trusted partner. At SoundsTrue.com you will find a wealth of free resources to support your journey, including exclusive weekly audio interviews, free downloads, interactive learning tools, and other special savings on all our titles.

For a free podcast interview with Mariana Caplan and Sounds True publisher Tami Simon, please visit SoundsTrue.com/bonus/Mariana_Caplan_Guru.

SOUNDS TRUE
many voices, one journey